Building Routes to Customers

Praise for *Building Routes to Customers*

"A key challenge in dynamic and fast changing markets is getting marketing and sales aligned. This book shows how to do this effectively and drive tactical execution better to achieve a dramatic increase in marketing and sales productivity."
—Ravi Venkatesan, Chairman of Microsoft Corporation (India)

"Routes-to-Market came as a breakthrough for IBM at a very challenging time in our industry. It had a big impact on our bottom line by enabling us to grow sales with a much more cost-effective mix of selling resources. Many companies need to solve that challenge today, before their competitors do. This book shows how to do it."
—Ned Lautenbach, Partner, Clayton, Dubilier & Rice, formerly Senior Vice President, Worldwide Sales & Services, IBM

"At Adobe we spent millions of dollars with consultants, both large and small. In most cases, a few months later, you couldn't remember the work they did. RTM was simple yet powerful and had lasting value to the company. It made it possible for each product manager to apply the correct resources and achieve an excellent ROI. Companies without this kind of methodology are flying blind."
—Kyle Mashima, VP of Strategic Development, Visible Measures Corp., formerly VP of Strategic Development, Adobe Systems Incorporated

"Technology innovation is not limited to the lab or the manufacturing process. Successfully marketing new technologies is about understanding change and helping customers adopt a new technology to create significant business value. RTM is a practical roadmap for maximizing revenue and profitability throughout the entire product life cycle. This book is a must read for anyone looking to drive technology adoption in today's evolving markets."
—Joan Jacobs, Executive Director of Itanium Solutions Alliance, formerly Global Alliance Director, Hewlett-Packard

"Routes-to-Market is a great tool for driving expansion into new markets and distribution channels. It also gets all of the management team on the same agenda. RTM has had a very positive impact at Plantronics."
—Ken Kannappan, President & CEO, Plantronics, Inc.

"Trying to go to market without a detailed route map is like driving cross-country with no directions - the motion feels good until you realize it's taking longer than you expected and the scenery looks familiar. This book distills the authors' methodology and best practices and clarifies how marketing and sales can pivot from abstract segmentation and go-to-market planning to pragmatic and tangible implementation steps. Big impact on marketing and sales productivity."

—Eugene Lee, CEO, Socialtext, Inc., formerly VP Worldwide Small/Medium Business Marketing, Cisco Systems, Inc.

"This book helps solve the marketer's dilemma: How do you reach your prospects in the fastest, most cost-effective way? Getting it right creates market leaders; getting it wrong relegates good products to the discount bin. IBM and Adobe have already found that Routes-to-Market is critical to their bottom lines; now the rest of us can join the party."

—Amy Bermar, President, Corporate Ink, The Wall Street Journal "Top Small Workplaces 2007" Winner

"Sound, practical advice on how to get marketing and sales aligned and performing at their peak."

—Buell Duncan, Vice President Marketing, IBM Software Group

"Using the Routes-to-Market methodology step by step enabled us to achieve record growth and dramatically turn around Baracoda's US operations."

—Alex Guillot, formerly VP Baracoda Americas

"What investments should I make across the channel segments and geos that I am responsible for, to ensure consistently high revenue growth and increasing profitability? The simple but powerful management system presented here can provide the answers to these critical questions, in the midst of dynamic market conditions and shifting strategies. This tool is a requirement for sustaining success in today's hyper-competitive business environment."

—Terry Haas, VP International Sales, WatchGuard Technologies, Inc., and formerly CEO of Solera Networks

"Too many marketing professionals rely upon untested gut instincts and last-of-breed programs when it comes to reaching new prospects. At the end of the day they really don't know if they're imitating success or failure. *Building Routes to Customers* demonstrates the power of fact-based marketing to take the art of marketing to new levels, especially for technology marketers in fast-changing markets."

—Gregory L. Ness, Vice President - Marketing, Blue Lane Technologies Inc.

"This book is an immensely valuable read. It outlines practical and executable strategies to accelerate and deepen market penetration and success. Our company is seeing powerful results as we begin to implement them. The authors bring their experience and analysis to communicate very tangible steps toward capturing the customer and creating a market win. I highly recommend it."

– Michael Forney, President, Rosetta Solutions, Inc.

"Most technology companies today seek the magic pill that engenders a productive partner ecosystem. As no such pill exists, leadership must draw a map to the customer through means that are not always obvious. *Building Routes to Customers* illuminates the fundamentals for doing this, based on years of success creating some of today's most effective partner programs."

—Lee Finck, formerly VP of Channels, F5 Networks, Inc.

"The greatest need in many companies today is finding a way to maximize their return on investments in products, people and services. In today's global marketplace of intense competition this has become increasingly difficult to accomplish. Routes-to-Market is a very smart way to make key decisions in marketing and sales – from packaging to demand generation to distribution – to maximize revenue and profitability throughout the product life cycle. Use of a consistent, effective process like Routes-to-Market is key to delivering the revenue and profitability all companies strive to achieve. At HaloSource, we used this process to rework our SeaKlear line of Water Treatment Solutions and have seen consistent, stronger than industry growth in revenue, margins and overall profitability for the past three years."

—Rick Lockett, Vice President, Water Treatment, HaloSource, Inc.

"We have conducted over 450 Routes-to-Market workshops over the last 10 years with companies of all sizes, from multinational giants to local technology solutions providers, application vendors and system integrators. RTM methodology and tools have been truly transformational for these companies and driven incremental revenues and profits for them. RTM has helped executives align their channels more effectively, interlock sales and marketing to recruit new customers productively, gain speed to market, and redirect their spending to the most qualified opportunities to generate sustainable growth. *Building Routes to Customers* explains how the RTM methodology works and translates into tactical actions that have driven measurable bottom line results."

—Dhun Zwirble & John Skinner, Co-Founders, Alliances & Channels, LLC

Peter Raulerson • Jean-Claude Malraison
Antoine Leboyer

Building Routes to Customers

Proven Strategies for Profitable Growth

 Springer

Peter Raulerson
PARA Marketing
227 Bellevue Way NE, Suite 605
Bellevue, WA 98004 USA
peter@paramarketing.com
www.paramarketing.com
www.RoutesToCustomers.com

Jean-Claude Malraison
56 rue Darwin
1050 Bruxelles
Belgium
jc.malraison@skynet.be
www.RoutesToCustomers.com

Antoine Leboyer
antoine.leboyer@gmail.com
www.RoutesToCustomers.com

ISBN: 978-0-387-79950-6   e-ISBN: 978-0-387-79951-3
DOI: 10.1007/978-0-387-79951-3

Library of Congress Control Number: 2008939891

Printed on acid-free paper

springer.com

Preface

The three authors of this book – Peter Raulerson, Jean-Claude Malraison, and Antoine Leboyer – trained and worked as engineers before taking sales, marketing, and executive roles in information technology companies.

Perhaps that's why we each saw the need for a practical tool that would be a big improvement over intuition in helping executives decide how much they should spend, and what they should spend it on, to drive profitable growth.

We met together for the first time in Jean-Claude's office at IBM's European headquarters in Paris in 1995. Jean-Claude and Antoine had developed a new methodology for determining objectively what to do in marketing, sales, and customer service, by product and market segment, to drive profitable growth. The methodology also helps to align everyone to a common plan and empower them to succeed.

Jean-Claude had named the new methodology "Routes-to-Market" (RTM) when he first envisioned it. The word "route" suggested a path or series of directions that, when followed, would enable people to reach their goals.

Antoine was the first RTM expert. Peter added sales and marketing analytics to the RTM methodology. We worked together to refine and roll out RTM across all of IBM's divisions and geographies. We saw how the RTM methodology enabled frontline IBMers to make good decisions quickly as a team, and then implement those decisions easily and effectively.

The results were spectacular. RTM transformed IBM's marketing and sales organizations, which had been the envy of the industry at one time, into a competitive force again.

RTM was designed for IBM, a company of significant complexity. Outside of IBM, we found that RTM delivered big benefits to small or mid-sized companies and ambitious start-ups as well as other large companies. RTM is flexible – it is valuable when used by a single group or at the divisional level, as well as when it is embraced as a corporate standard.

After leaving IBM, Jean-Claude brought RTM to Plantronics. Antoine brought it to Baracoda and, more recently, to GSX. Peter's consulting firm, The PARA Marketing Group, further refined RTM and introduced it to other technology companies, including Adobe, Canon, Cisco, F5 Networks, HaloSource, Hewlett-Packard, Hitachi, Knoa, Sharp, SumTotal Systems, and Sun Microsystems. Each one benefited from RTM.

Our purpose in writing this book is to share our experience and to enable you to use the RTM methodology in your company. Everything you need to start using RTM immediately is in this book and on the book's website, http://www. RoutesToCustomers.com. There you will find more information and tools that can help you get the most out of RTM, available at no charge. You can contact us there if you would like.

Acknowledgments

Thanks to Nick Philipson, Senior Editor, Business and Economics, Springer Science and Business Media, for his consistently cheerful and resourceful responses to our questions, and for giving us actionable feedback and truly helpful direction. Working with Nick has been a great experience.

Thanks to Amy Bermar, President of Corporate Ink, for her extra effort in providing a very thoughtful critique, and for inspiration to make the book much more readable.

Jean-Claude, Antoine, and Peter

Thanks to my colleagues around the world who contributed improvements to RTM to make it more and more efficient. Sorry for the frustrations we created when we pushed back. There were many suggestions that we did not implement in order to keep RTM easy to use. Thanks to my bosses for their support, in particular, Ned Lautenbach of IBM and Ken Kannappan of Plantronics. Their expectations forced us to always find a better way to do things. Thanks to my family and my wife Claire in particular for her patience and support.

Jean-Claude Malraison

RTM would never have happened without Jean-Claude's uniquely challenging "can-do attitude." On his team, Nick Coutts provided special support and insight. Many at the Harvard Business School, including Professor Kash Rangan, opened my eyes to the fact that industrial marketing is much more fun than anyone at Procter and Gamble would admit, and that business is such a deeply fulfilling and satisfying activity. My parents and my sister have been the best-seller writers in our family so far, so I am happy to follow in their footsteps. Above all, my thanks go to my family, my wife Margot, and our children Mathilde and Stephane for allowing me to spend time again and again on this manuscript on top of an already busy schedule.

Antoine Leboyer

Thanks to Jean-Claude and Antoine for inviting me to join the original project to refine and roll out RTM in 1995, and the project to write this book in 2007. Great discoveries and improvements invariably involve the cooperation of many minds. Thanks to my clients for the opportunity to contribute to their success, and to my colleagues for their help in fulfilling those commitments. Special thanks to my wife Cleo for the rarest combination of virtues – unfailing support and management expertise.

Peter Raulerson

Contents

Prologue

Bob Wilson joined National Software Corporation as a marketing manager 2 years ago to help launch its new business management software product. The launch was very successful, and sales grew steadily for the first year. However, Bob saw several troubling signs.

Bob's boss, the Vice President (VP) of Marketing, fought with his counterpart, the VP of Sales, over budgets and priorities. National's salespeople complained that the leads generated by marketing were worthless. Bob could see that the salespeople let the leads grow stale or did not follow up on them at all, and that was why sales did not get any value from the leads. Bob tried to work with the salespeople to adjust his demand-generation campaigns to fit their needs, but the lack of alignment at the top of their organizations blocked progress on this.

Another problem that Bob was concerned about was the fact that the VP of Sales had doubled the sales force during the first year of sales for the business management software product, forecasting that revenue would go up accordingly. But revenue had not doubled, and Bob calculated that sales costs were cutting the product's profit contribution in half.

Bob also saw signs that the market had shifted from being interested in the technical features of their product, to asking for information on how National's product fit their business needs. A few salespeople had told him that prospects had asked for information on how customers in their industries were using National's product. When Bob pressed his boss for funding to research the market to determine what customers really needed to know, and to write a case study or whitepaper to meet those needs, he got a flat "no."

Bob's boss told him to continue promoting the product's technology because their product was better than the competition, and they had to promote the product's strengths. He would not allocate any budget for research, new marketing collateral or any of the other initiatives that Bob proposed. Bob suggested using his current demand generation budget to do the research instead of continuing to generate leads that sales ignored, but his boss would not approve that either.

Sales peaked at the end of the first year and then fell for the next three quarters, even though the overall market was reported to be growing 10% per year. In the latest quarter, sales plummeted 25% from the same quarter a year ago, and National reported an unexpected loss.

Frustrated by the leadership vacuum at National, Bob quit. He immediately contacted his friends and acquaintances at other companies, looking for a new position. After a couple of weeks of networking, he got an introduction to Charlie Davis, the CEO of Skyline Software, one of National's direct competitors in the business management software market. Skyline had been growing rapidly. Sales and profits in the latest quarter were up by 18% from the prior year, almost the exact opposite of National's latest quarter.

Charlie scheduled time for Bob to meet with him the following week and asked for a copy of his resume. *Is Charlie going to interview me for a position at Skyline*, Bob thought, *or does he just want to find out what went wrong at National?*

When Bob arrived at Skyline for the meeting, Charlie had two other people in his office but he immediately invited Bob to join them. Charlie introduced Steve Campbell, Skyline's VP of Sales, and Maria Lopez, VP of Marketing. The four of them sat down at a round table in the corner of Charlie's office.

Charlie said, "Bob, I've heard some good things about you. Someone told me that you had lobbied the execs at National to fix alignment and productivity problems in their sales and marketing organizations. It looks like the execs must have focused on other things, based on last quarter's results. We pay a lot of attention to those things here. I wanted to get the four of us together to talk about what we're doing. We're growing fast and need more smart people. Tell us about your experience at National."

This is going to be an interesting meeting, Bob thought. Looking first at Charlie, then Steve and Maria, Bob said, "We, uh, National, that is, hasn't been doing very well lately. Up to nine months ago, we were pretty competitive with you. Our sales and profits were growing about as fast as yours. Our products had a good set of features. Our sales force was hitting their numbers. Then, nine months ago, sales started to slow. It was pretty clear that something in the market had changed. When I ran the numbers, I could see it was going to get worse if we didn't change what we were doing. But the executives couldn't agree on what to do, so they didn't take action. Last quarter, the bottom fell out. Sales fell twenty-five percent and the company lost money. I'd lost confidence in the leadership there, so I resigned."

Bob added, "Your sales jumped eighteen percent last quarter. In a market that's growing only ten percent a year, that's very impressive. Congratulations!"

Everyone smiled. Charlie said, "Thanks."

Maria explained, "A year ago, we realized that the market was going to transition from the technology-savvy early adopters that National and we had been selling to. We knew that the next set of buyers in the market would be mainstream business people who didn't care what kind of technology we had under the hood. They just want to know that the product works for other mainstream customers like themselves, in their own industry. And they need a complete solution – all of the products and services to make it work in their environment."

Bob thought to himself, *At National we were still selling to the tech crowd. Bits and bytes and speeds and feeds. That's what our salespeople were talking about. That's what I was told to put in the brochures and on the website. How did Skyline know a year ago that the market was going to transition to mainstream buyers?*

If I had spotted that at National, could I have gotten management to change what we were doing? Probably not.

Maria turned to Steve, who said, "The transition to the mainstream market is the main reason that we started signing up resellers a year ago. We chose the best resellers in the vertical markets that we decided to target. It took us about six months to recruit them, get their vertical-market expertise added to our product, and help them close a few sales. Our sales started to take off last quarter, just like we planned."

Bob remembered several conversations at National about setting up a reseller channel. He said, "I think that National is stuck with a direct sales mentality. A few resellers talked to me about opening up distribution, but our sales VP said 'Not interested.' The rest of the management team there was focused on adding more technology features, or giving our sales VP more budget to hire additional sales people."

Charlie picked up the conversation again. "Our sales growth is really just starting to accelerate. There are a lot more mainstream customers coming into the market now, than the early adopters that were buying a year ago. A few minutes ago, you said that the market was growing only ten percent a year. But that's a number from industry analysts who watch the whole market. We've got our own data for the market segments we're focused on, and their growth rate is going to be sixty percent this year."

Bob whistled when he heard 60%. He thought, *Penetrating fast-growing market segments before the competition arrives is a great way to grow.*

Charlie went on, "We think the early adopters are pretty much tapped out now – they have either bought already or they are not going to buy. Our goal is to be the number one supplier to the mainstream market. That's what we're focused on right now."

Bob thought, *National missed a big shift in the market and that's why sales fell off a cliff. I'm glad to be out of there. I really like the way these Skyline people think. And their results over the last year prove they can act. Skyline might be a great fit for me.*

Reflecting Charlie's last comment, Bob asked, "What are you doing to become the number one supplier to mainstream customers?"

Steve smiled and said, "That's a good question. One thing we're doing is expanding the number of complete solutions in our catalog by signing more resellers, especially those in market niches where we don't have a solution right now."

Bob thought, *That makes sense, but isn't the marketing VP normally the person responsible for the product catalog, not the sales VP?*

Maria must have been reading Bob's mind. She picked up the thread at this point. "The catalog that Steve is talking about is really a lot more than a catalog. It's our market segmentation – we put customers with exactly the same needs and the same buying behavior in one segment, and customers with different needs and different buying behavior in other segments. Then we design a specific route to each market segment."

Bob was not exactly sure what the word "route" meant. He looked at Maria and asked, "What's a route?"

She said, "A route is the combination of resources and activities that take the customer from the beginning to the end of the sales cycle. We're running three different routes right now in which direct marketing generates demand and telemarketing qualifies the leads that come in, which are then passed to resellers to close deals. They install our software along with other products, and then train and support the customer."

Maria continued, "For one of the three routes that we're running now, the direct marketing piece is an invitation to managers in small manufacturing companies to participate in a free seminar on the Internet, which we put on every week. Our telemarketing firm calls the attendees after the seminar to qualify them. They shoot the qualified leads to our five resellers in this segment, who jump on them immediately. This has been really successful for us. In four weeks since we started running this route, our resellers have closed six deals and added twenty more to the pipeline."

At this point, Bob thought, *That's amazing – getting six deals in four weeks, plus twenty more deals in the pipeline. This route stuff sounds like it puts together all of the things I thought we should do at National. And it sounds pretty productive. How come the marketing VP knows so much about the sales pipeline?*

Steve put up his hand at this point and said, "We started using an approach called 'Routes-to-Market' a year ago. That's what prompted us to figure out what phase of the life cycle we were in, and when the market would shift to the next phase. We knew that our technology was only going to be innovative for a short time. That's when the tech heads are interested in it – when it's really new and innovative. After that point, they move on to the next innovative thing, and our product moves on to mainstream customers, where all the profits are – if we do our job right."

Charlie added, "The thing that I like most about Routes-to-Market is that it helps us optimize and allocate spending on marketing, sales and customer service. It's like running a manufacturing plant. In manufacturing, you know how much raw material and components to order, and how to process them in order to produce finished goods at an acceptable cost. With Routes-to-Market, we can determine how much demand we need to generate, and how to connect with those prospects at every step of the sales cycle in order to achieve our goals–revenue, profitability market share, et cetera."

When Charlie paused, Bob said, "This sounds good to me. I never thought of running marketing and sales like a manufacturing plant. But it makes a lot of sense."

Bob paused, then went on, "Charlie, Maria and Steve, you keep finishing each other's sentences. I've never seen the CEO and the VPs in charge of marketing and sales aligned like you are."

They all smiled at Bob's comments. Maria said, "Our frontline people work in cross-functional teams to plan the routes and execute them. It takes them two to four hours a month to plan and monitor a route. Each team includes someone from product management, sales, marketing, customer service, channel marketing, and finance. If the route involves advertising, our ad agency puts someone on the team. Each person on the team is responsible for their organization's activity on the route.

Just being on the team aligns everyone pretty quickly. The team prioritizes where to put our limited resources to get the most bang for the buck in marketing, sales and customer service."

Steve jumped in, "And the teams get smarter every time they plan a new route because they use the results from the last route to fine-tune the new one. It's a virtuous circle."

Bob thought, *I think "virtuous circle" means a feedback loop that produces better and better results every time it runs. That sounds like the flywheel that builds up momentum and causes the breakthrough to greatness that Jim Collins wrote about in his book, "Good to Great." Being part of a company that makes the transition from good to great would be, well, it would be great.*

Bob asked, "So, what challenges do you have, if you've got Routes-to-Market working so well at this point?"

Charlie responded, "Actually, one of our challenges going forward is to shift from a single-tier distribution model to a two-tier distribution model. This means adding wholesale distributors to our channel mix. We have to do that in order to expand distribution fast enough to keep up with the growth of the market. And it's very profitable if we leverage the distributors to keep our costs down. Routes-to-Market helps with optimizing the costs, but we need to monitor the costs to make sure we get all of the savings we planned for. Those savings go straight to the bottom line. Any company that's spending twenty to thirty percent or more of revenue on sales and marketing can boost profit significantly by making that spending more productive, or by trimming the spending to cut out waste."

Charlie paused. He had one more point he wanted to make. "Bob," he said, "there is one more challenge. We've got some innovative products in development right now. They're really innovative, not just updates to what we're currently selling. The first customers to buy them will be technology-savvy early adopters, just like we used to sell to. When we start selling those products, we'll have to operate two different go-to-market models at the same time – one to sell our established product to mainstream customers through two-tier distribution, and the other go-to-market model will be to sell innovative technology directly to early adopters."

Charlie continued, "That's a really big challenge, operating two different marketing and sales models at the same time. And if we're going to become the eight hundred-pound gorilla that we want to be, we're going to need to operate many different go-to-market models at the same time because we're going to have products in each phase of the life cycle at the same time. Getting the right resources in place, spending the right amount on them to achieve our goals, optimizing across multiple go-to-market models, that's going to be our big challenge."

Charlie looked directly at Bob and said, "Is this a challenge you'd like to work on?"

Without hesitation, Bob said, "You bet! I'm really impressed with the depth of your thinking and the way you're running the business. When can I start?"

Charlie looked at Maria and Steve. They both nodded. Charlie said, "Maria, would you handle the rest of the interviewing process with Bob?"

Maria said, "Yes, I'd be happy to. Bob, let's go to my office and get started. There are a few more steps before you get to say 'You bet' again." Everyone laughed.

Bob joined Skyline the following week as a marketing manager reporting to Maria. He was given the marketing responsibility for one of the innovative products in development and joined the product's cross-functional Routes-to-Market (RTM) team. The team included the product manager for the product (who also reported to Maria), the software development project lead, and managers from sales, customer service, and finance.

The team used the RTM methodology to develop the go-to-market plan for the product. Bob became the team's leader over the next few months as he took them through the steps to research the market, prioritize market segments to target, select the most cost-effective marketing, sales and customer service resources to achieve their business objectives, and develop their tactical go-to-market plan. When they held the tactical kick-off meeting for the extended team, which included all of the people responsible for making their plan successful, the team was so energized by the way that everything had come together, that they stood up and cheered.

When their new product was launched, sales took off like a rocket. Bob's team became experts in using RTM to maximize the product's revenue and profitability. It quickly became Skyline's biggest profit producer. At the end of the product's first year of sales, Bob was promoted to VP and general manager of the business unit that was formed for that product line.

Chapter 1
What Is Routes-to-Market?

To see the big picture for Routes-to-Market (RTM), let us look at one of the biggest challenges faced by general managers: determining the total budget to set for marketing, sales, and customer service, and how that budget will be allocated across these departments. Without a method to determine objectively how much to spend in each area, management team meetings become debates between different factions trying to convince the general manager to adjust the budget in their favor.

- If revenue last quarter came in below expectations, the marketing and sales department heads may advocate spending more. Which of the two departments should get more funding, or should both departments' budgets be increased by the same percentage?
- Should money be pulled from the advertising budget to spend on direct marketing? Or should it be used to hire more sales people? Each department head may recommend redirecting spending from the other's department to his.
- Should the cash incentives for the distribution channel be increased, or should a new "buy 2, get 1 free" promotional campaign be targeted directly to customers? Many proposed initiatives may impact pricing or other components of the five Ps – product, positioning, price, promotion, and place.
- Is the problem the level of spending, or is it coordination between the departments? For example, marketing claims that it has generated hundreds of leads that sales has not followed up on, but sales complains that the leads are worthless. Meanwhile, no one has contacted the leads to determine which of them are qualified prospects.

It is not easy for general managers to select the best course to follow or to choose from all these suggestions. In theory, spending more on marketing, sales, and customer service will increase sales. But that will also impact profitability.

Is there a way to determine the optimal level of spending for each function in marketing, sales, and customer service, for each product or service, market segment, and competitive environment? Is there a way to get everyone in these functions aligned and working together to maximize results?

There is a way to do both. It is Routes-to-Market.

The RTM methodology enables cross-functional teams to develop tactical go-to-market plans that spell out what each function in marketing, sales, and customer

P. Raulerson et al., *Building Routes to Customers*, DOI: 10.1007/978-0-387-79951-3_1,   1
© 2009 Peter Raulerson, Jean-Claude Malraison and Antoine Leboyer

service is going to do, and how much will be spent to achieve the company's objectives for each product or service. The cross-functional teams include the following:

1. The executive responsible for the revenue and profit of the product or service.
2. The managers (or their representatives) responsible for the functional areas that are involved in marketing, selling, and supporting customers for this product or service. For example, if a tactical plan calls for direct marketing, then the manager of direct marketing (or her representative) must participate in the development and execution of that tactical plan. It is critical that the people representing these functions be able to make commitments for them, not just provide input during the team meetings.
3. The finance manager (or her representative) responsible for the financial data and calculations for this product or service

By doing the tactical planning in a cross-functional, team-oriented approach, RTM enables marketing, sales, and customer service to quickly align to a common objective. After the tactical plan is complete and approved, the cross-functional team holds a tactical kick-off meeting to get everyone who will be involved in executing the plan, committed to its success, and excited about working together with a common objective and plan. After the kick-off, team members use RTM to keep execution on track and to respond quickly to changing market conditions. RTM enables marketing, sales, and customer service to become more productive, cost-effective, and agile.

Companies that use RTM have achieved remarkable results. There are several case studies on them in this book. To highlight two:

- IBM had lost $16 billion on declining sales over 3 years, when Lou Gerstner came in as CEO in 1993. RTM contributed directly to IBM's turnaround by enabling marketing, sales and brand managers to use less-expensive resources to drive sales growth instead of relying on the more-costly direct salesforce. Revenue and profit hit new highs in the first 2 years after RTM was rolled out company-wide. IBM has continued using RTM, reporting in its annual report each year on the company's routes-to-market. Consultant Michael Hammer, author of *Re-engineering the Corporation*, said in 2005 that IBM's turnaround was "the single greatest turnaround in modern business history."
- After adopting RTM company-wide in 2001, Adobe Systems increased annual revenue 17% per year, and net profit 23% per year, over the next 6 years. These results propelled Adobe's stock price up by 179%, five times the growth of stock market indices and more than six times the total return of Adobe's primary competitor, Microsoft, from 2001 through 2007.

RTM is simple but versatile. Companies of any size can adopt it quickly and use it immediately in any market, for any product or service. RTM can be applied to a single product and market segment, or to a partnering initiative or alliance with another company. RTM can be spread in a progressive or incremental way throughout a company. A "big bang" changeover is not required for adoption.

Through June 2008, RTM has helped more than 400 companies of all shapes and sizes, located in almost every country around the world, significantly improve the performance of marketing, sales, and customer service.

Everything you need to know about RTM is in this book and on the book's Web site, www.RoutesToCustomers.com. You can see how it works and how to implement it within your company. You can start applying RTM next Monday if you are ready to lead the change.

This chapter provides an overview of the RTM methodology and a roadmap to the rest of the book. Chapter 2 brings together the key RTM concepts to show how RTM is used. It continues the story in the Prologue of Bob Wilson and other people at Skyline Software as they make key decisions on tactics and budgets to launch a new product.

The Route Concept

Purchase is just one step in the customer's buying process. (Throughout this book, "purchase" means acquire, buy, or rent.) The purchase step is preceded by others that have a huge impact on the purchase decision. It is followed by steps which impact the customer's satisfaction with the product or service, repeat purchases, and recommendations to others for their purchases.

In fact, the customer's purchase decision is impacted by his or her lifetime experience with the vendor's products and services, including perceptions of the vendor formed before the initial contact with the vendor and throughout the customer's exposure to the vendor's company and its partners and distribution channels. Aligning marketing, sales, and customer service resources to fit the customer's buying process is critical for maximizing the achievement of the vendor's business objectives.

Customers go through a sequence of five steps in their buying process or buying cycle. Vendors have a corresponding five-step process called the sales cycle, as shown in Fig. 1.1. A "route-to-market" (or simply, a "route") is the combination of resources selected by the vendor to communicate, provide, or support the product or service to the customer at any step of the sales cycle.

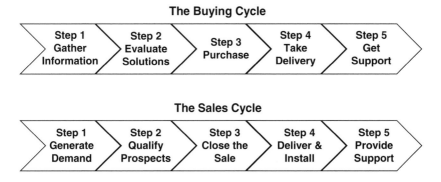

Fig. 1.1 The buying cycle and the sales cycle

As shown in Fig. 1.1, customers gather information about their needs and about potential solutions to those needs in step 1 of the buying cycle. In the corresponding step of the sales cycle, the vendor generates awareness and demand for its products or services as solutions to customer needs. Three of the many resources that vendors can use in step 1 are advertising, public relations, and direct marketing.

Customers transition from step 1 to step 2 of the buying cycle when they start to evaluate alternative solutions for purchase, based on their own criteria including how well the solution fits their needs. At step 2 of the sales cycle, the vendor qualifies prospects to determine which ones should get the most attention. Resources commonly used for this are call centers, direct salesforce, resellers, and dealers. Vendors need to focus their marketing and sales resources on their highest priority sales opportunities to maximize their results.

In step 3, customers make the final selection from the alternatives, and then purchase it. Of course, the goal for step 3 of the sales cycle is to be the vendor chosen by the customer, to close the sale, and obtain the purchase transaction. Call centers, e-commerce Web sites, and retailers are the kinds of resources used by vendors for step 3.

The next step for the customer is to take delivery of the product or service. This might be as simple as consuming the product right then and there (if it is ready-to-eat food, for example). Or it could be a complicated, multiyear project to deliver and install thousands of new computers. Resource examples for step 4 are logistics (shipping), wholesale distributors, and product installers.

Finally, in step 5, customers get ongoing support for using or maintaining the product or service. Potential resources include call centers, product support Web sites, and factory-authorized repair centers.

The buying and sales cycles do not really stop at step 5. Both cycles loop back to step 1 so that the customer can repeat purchases over time. There are very few products and services that a customer will only buy once and never need to buy again in the future. For many vendors, 80% or more of their profits come from ongoing or repeat customers.

We have found this simple structure with 5 steps to apply well to a wide variety of products, services, customers, and vendors. Alternative models were tested with more steps and different structures. They proved to be too complicated, too difficult to communicate, and too difficult to measure.

The next section compares the routes to market for three companies which sell nearly identical products through different routes.

Example Routes: Dell, Hewlett-Packard, and Lenovo

Dell sells PCs to small and mid-sized businesses (SMBs) in the USA through a direct route with no middlemen, which the company has branded as "Direct2Dell." Figure 1.2 shows how Dell's route compares to Hewlett-Packard's and Lenovo's routes, which rely on retailers and dealers.

Dell generates demand in the SMB market segment through a combination of public relations, advertising, direct marketing, and Dell's Web site. (Vendor Web sites can generate demand in several ways, including when a customer uses a search engine to find information about a product, and then clicks on a link in the search engine's results that goes directly to a page on the vendor's Web site.)

The "call to action" in Dell's advertising and direct marketing in step 1 of this route is for the customer to visit Dell's Web site to configure and order a PC or to get special deals, or to call Dell's call center. The customer can order from either Dell's sales Web site or call center. Delivery is made by Dell's logistics department through a shipping company, which transports the product to the customer. The customer is responsible for installing it himself. Finally, support is handled by Dell's support Web site and call center.

HP and Lenovo sell PCs to SMBs through retailers and dealers. Their routes to the SMB market are more costly than Dell's because their net revenue per sale is reduced by the discount they provide to their distribution channels. In 2006, HP profitably reclaimed its lead in PC sales over Dell by focusing demand generation, product packaging, new product development, and distribution on leveraging HP's independent retail store network, which is its primary differentiator versus Dell. HP capitalized on the fact that many SMBs and consumers buy notebook PCs in retail

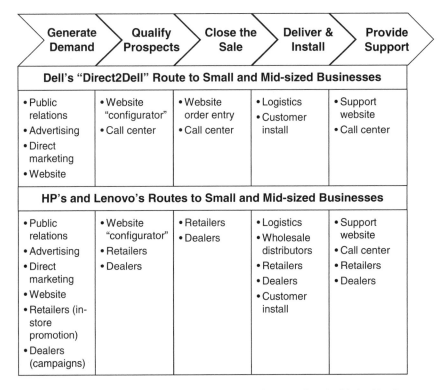

Generate Demand	Qualify Prospects	Close the Sale	Deliver & Install	Provide Support
Dell's "Direct2Dell" Route to Small and Mid-sized Businesses				
• Public relations • Advertising • Direct marketing • Website	• Website "configurator" • Call center	• Website order entry • Call center	• Logistics • Customer install	• Support website • Call center
HP's and Lenovo's Routes to Small and Mid-sized Businesses				
• Public relations • Advertising • Direct marketing • Website • Retailers (in-store promotion) • Dealers (campaigns)	• Website "configurator" • Retailers • Dealers	• Retailers • Dealers	• Logistics • Wholesale distributors • Retailers • Dealers • Customer install	• Support website • Call center • Retailers • Dealers

Fig. 1.2 Dell's, HP's, and Lenovo's routes for selling PCs to small and mid-sized businesses

stores, instead of via Web sites and call centers, because they can try them out "hands on" in the store before buying them. Selling through resources that best fit the target customer's buying behavior is one way that HP and Lenovo have competed successfully against Dell's lower-cost sales model.

Optimizing Route Costs

The RTM methodology includes tools to determine objectively how much to spend in marketing, sales, and customer service to achieve the company's business objectives. RTM enables the cost and performance of alternative resources to be considered before they are selected for a route. Every resource on a route has one or more assigned activities with quantified objectives and budgets. Performance and actual costs can be tracked and compared to the objectives and budgets. Historical cost and performance data can be used for future budgeting. Over time, this kind of feedback loop enables management to make smarter decisions on resource selection and budgeting, thereby optimizing the company's routes to market.

Let us look at an example of assigning resources, activities, and budgets for a route. Adobe Systems sells desktop and server software for graphic design, publishing, imaging, and other creative tasks. Adobe's first server software product, AlterCast, was announced in 2001. Before announcement, Adobe management set a revenue goal of $8.3 million for AlterCast, based on a market opportunity analysis. This was a relatively small amount of revenue for Adobe at the time, compared to Adobe's total revenue of $1.3 billion in the prior year. However, the target market for AlterCast was small but growing fast, and server software was a new type of product for Adobe to sell, so their goal was conservative.

Adobe used RTM to design a route to sell AlterCast to its target market. As they designed the route, they used RTM to evaluate alternative resources based on their capabilities, availability, performance, and cost. Figure 1.3 lists the resources they selected, and Table 1.1 shows the budget they set for the route.

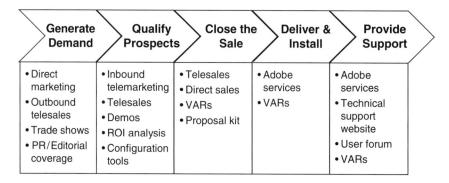

Generate Demand	Qualify Prospects	Close the Sale	Deliver & Install	Provide Support
• Direct marketing • Outbound telesales • Trade shows • PR/Editorial coverage	• Inbound telemarketing • Telesales • Demos • ROI analysis • Configuration tools	• Telesales • Direct sales • VARs • Proposal kit	• Adobe services • VARs	• Adobe services • Technical support website • User forum • VARs

Fig. 1.3 Adobe's AlterCast route

Table 1.1 Budget for Adobe's AlterCast Route

	Generate demand	Qualify prospects	Close the sale	Deliver and install	Provide support	Total budget
Program expenses	$709,763	$125,000	$5,000	$–	$135,000	$974,763
Head count expenses	$354,000	$879,527	$719,613	$242,100	$564,900	$2,760,140
Total	$1,063,763	$1,004,527	$724,613	$242,100	$699,900	$3,734,903
% of Total budget	28%	27%	19%	6%	19%	100%
% of product revenue	13%	12%	9%	3%	8%	45%

As shown in the bottom right cell in Table 1.1, the budget for the AlterCast route totaled 45% of AlterCast revenue. This figure – total route expenses divided by revenue from the route – is called the Expense-to-Revenue ratio, or E/R. The E/R ratio for the AlterCast route was 45%, much higher than the E/R ratio of 32% that Adobe averaged for its other products. Note that Adobe's marketing and sales expenses were 32% of revenue, on average, and Adobe's cost of revenue (cost of goods sold) averaged 11% of revenue, about the same as other software companies.

Adobe's use of the RTM methodology is discussed in detail in Chap. 8.

Changing the Routes as the Market Evolves

Up to this point, we have looked at routes in a static way, without considering how routes can be changed dynamically. The RTM methodology includes tools to antici-pate and respond to changing market conditions, especially changes in buyer behavior. This provides a significant advantage because quickly recognizing changes in market conditions enables management to make immediate adjustments to the route to maintain revenue and profitability.

One change in market conditions for almost every product or service is driven by people's reactions to innovation. A few people are enthusiastic about buying an innovative product or service as soon as it is available. Others want to wait until the product or service has been proven. The adoption of innovative products and serv-ices proceeds over time through a sequence of customer groups distinguished by their reactions to innovation. Everett Rogers conducted extensive research that laid the foundation for understanding how innovations spread through society in his book *Diffusion of Innovations,* first published in 1962 and most recently updated in 2003. Geoffrey Moore drew from Rogers' work to show that marketing strategies for technology products depend on the customers' attitudes about adopting the innovation in those products in his books, *Crossing the Chasm* (published in 1991), *Inside the Tornado* (1995), and *Dealing with Darwin* (2005).

In Rogers' and Moore's model, shown in Fig. 1.4, the first people to adopt an innovation are enthusiasts whose attitude about the innovation Moore summed up as "Just try it!" Innovations must first be adopted by enthusiasts before they can spread to the next group, visionaries, whose attitude about the innovation is "Get ahead of the herd!", that is, get the advantage provided by the innovation before anyone else. Visionaries look to enthusiasts to identify innovations that are worthy of their consideration and adoption. The same influence pattern applies to each successive group: from visionaries to pragmatists, then to conservatives, and finally to skeptics. People within a group also influence adoption by other members of their group.

As shown in Fig. 1.5, the transition from one group of like-minded adopters to the next group forces vendors to adjust their routes to market to fit the buying

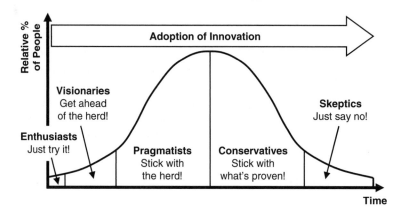

Fig. 1.4 Adoption of innovation over time

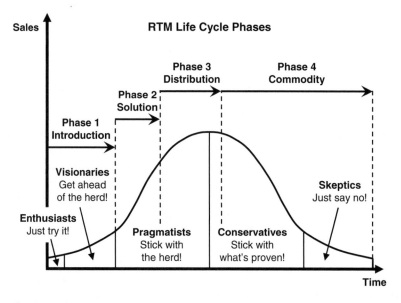

Fig. 1.5 RTM Life Cycle phases

behavior of each successive group, resulting in four distinct phases in the life cycle of a route: Introduction, Solution, Distribution, and Commodity.

To understand why the RTM Life Cycle is important, and how it can be used to anticipate and drive change, let us look next at an industry with short product life cycles: telephone headsets. For a thorough discussion of the RTM Life Cycle, see Chap. 5.

Routes for Mobile Phone Headsets

Plantronics, Inc., introduced the first Bluetooth wireless headset in 2001, designed to be used with the first Bluetooth-enabled generation of mobile phones from Nokia and other vendors. At the time, Bluetooth was a disruptive innovation because it changed the way that vendors and customers thought about connecting devices wirelessly. Before Bluetooth, it was a very error-prone process for both the vendor and the customer, because there were many conflicting ways to do it. When the Bluetooth standard was first introduced, competing standards (such as WiFi) were still being debated. The development teams at other headset vendors delayed their adoption of any wireless connectivity standard until one standard became the clear winner. Plantronics' management, however, decided to adopt Bluetooth immediately, gaining a significant time-to-market advantage over competitors.

Using RTM, Plantronics' management recognized in January 2001 that they could maximize sales of their Bluetooth headsets in the vital Christmas selling season if the adoption of Bluetooth technology had progressed to pragmatists and conservatives, who together outnumbered enthusiasts and visionaries by more than 4 to 1. They realized that they could accelerate adoption of Bluetooth technology by working to get enthusiasts on board as soon as possible, then speed up the transition from enthusiasts to visionaries and then to pragmatists.

To maximize sales of Plantronics' Bluetooth headset, the company dynamically adjusted its route-to-market three times from March 2001 through January 2002, as shown in Figs. 1.6 and 1.7.

Plantronics designed Route #1 to capture enthusiasts and visionaries in the Introduction phase of the RTM Life Cycle. Plantronics preannounced its Bluetooth headset at the CEBIT and CES trade shows in March, and publicly announced it shortly after that, with marketing messages tailored to enthusiasts and visionaries. Because Plantronics had the first and only Bluetooth headset at these trade shows, Plantronics got coverage in hundreds of publications worldwide in April and May, more than it had ever had before. Plantronics also recruited specialized consumer electronics resellers (which cater primarily to enthusiasts and visionaries) to sell limited volumes (fewer than 10,000 units).

Plantronics' goal was to get volume distributors to see the growing demand for the new Bluetooth headsets and order larger volumes (millions of units) in August for delivery in October for the Christmas season. If the volume distributors did not see the growing demand for the new headsets, they would not take the risk of carrying inventory.

In Route #2, Plantronics switched from specialized consumer electronics resellers to volume distributors and general consumer electronics retailers. Plantronics also started communicating marketing messages tailored for pragmatists, the group of customers who dominate the market in phases 2 and 3 of the RTM Life Cycle.

Plantronics transitioned to Route #3 just after the Christmas sales peak, to drive adoption by conservatives by discounting the headsets, increasing promotion, and expanding distribution to mass market retailers.

By evolving its route for selling Bluetooth headsets, Plantronics catapulted into the top echelon of the mobile headset market over the 12-month life cycle of its first Bluetooth headset.

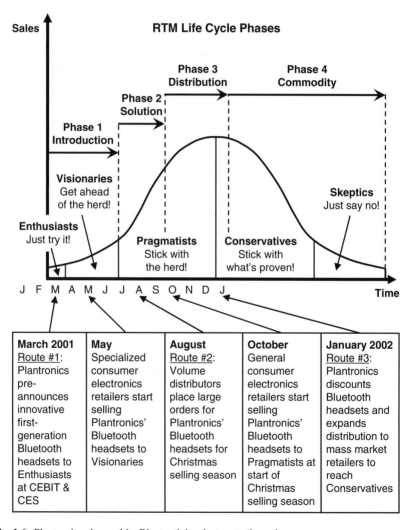

Fig. 1.6 Plantronics changed its Bluetooth headset route three times

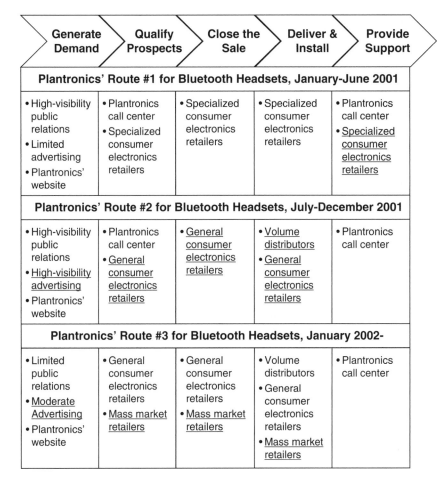

Generate Demand	Qualify Prospects	Close the Sale	Deliver & Install	Provide Support
Plantronics' Route #1 for Bluetooth Headsets, January-June 2001				
• High-visibility public relations • Limited advertising • Plantronics' website	• Plantronics call center • Specialized consumer electronics retailers	• Specialized consumer electronics retailers	• Specialized consumer electronics retailers	• Plantronics call center • Specialized consumer electronics retailers
Plantronics' Route #2 for Bluetooth Headsets, July-December 2001				
• High-visibility public relations • High-visibility advertising • Plantronics' website	• Plantronics call center • General consumer electronics retailers	• General consumer electronics retailers	• Volume distributors • General consumer electronics retailers	• Plantronics call center
Plantronics' Route #3 for Bluetooth Headsets, January 2002-				
• Limited public relations • Moderate Advertising • Plantronics' website	• General consumer electronics retailers • Mass market retailers	• General consumer electronics retailers • Mass market retailers	• Volume distributors • General consumer electronics retailers • Mass market retailers	• Plantronics call center

Fig. 1.7 Evolution of Plantronics' route for selling Bluetooth headsets (changes from one route to the next are underlined)

See Chap. 5 for a complete explanation of the RTM Life Cycle, including recommendations for resources for routes for each phase of the life cycle.

Adopting the Routes-to-Market Methodology

Most companies take a "pilot project" approach at the beginning with RTM by applying it to one product or service and one market segment. RTM was designed to be used in exactly this way. Figure 1.8 on the next page shows the four steps for a pilot RTM project.

1. RTM Workshop: Form a cross-functional team of the people who are responsible for the resources that will be involved in marketing, selling, and providing

support for a product or service, led by the person responsible for the revenue and profit for the product or service. The cross-functional team develops the Tactical Plan in an RTM Workshop, which normally takes 2–4 hours but can take a full day the first time. The Tactical Plan spells out what is going to be done, and how much will be spent, to achieve the company's objectives for the product or service. The RTM Workshop is the key decision-making event at the operational level for RTM. Preparation for the RTM Workshop can take several days depending on how much of the required data exists or needs to be generated.

2. Approve Tactical Plan: The Tactical Plan is approved and funded by management. In a pilot RTM project, this is an opportunity for management to learn how the cross-functional team used RTM.

3. Tactical Plan Kick-off: Assuming that the Tactical Plan is approved, the team holds a Tactical Kick-off meeting with everyone who will participate in executing the Tactical Plan, to get them aligned, energized, and committed to making it happen. The Tactical Plan is implemented at this point. Like the meeting with

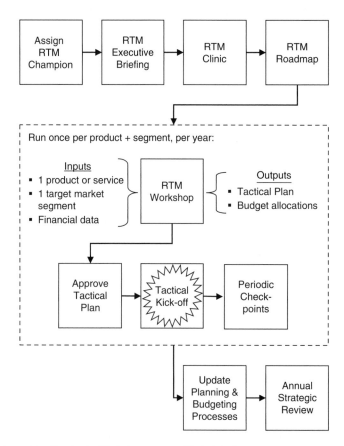

Fig. 1.8 Launching Routes-to-Market company-wide in ten steps

management to get the Tactical Plan approved, the Tactical Kick-off is an opportunity to explain how the team used RTM to develop the Tactical Plan.

4. Periodic Checkpoints: The cross-functional team runs Periodic Checkpoints to monitor performance and make mid-course corrections as necessary during execution. The last checkpoint would normally be after the end of the execution and should include an assessment of RTM itself and its usefulness to the company.

After a successful pilot, the next step in adopting RTM is to embrace it for more products or services, and more market segments, or for the entire business unit, division, or company. The steps to do this are explained in Chap. 9. Figure 1.8 shows the flowchart for launching RTM company-wide in ten steps. The center section of the flowchart, inside the rectangle bordered by a dashed line, shows the four steps for a pilot RTM project.

See Chap. 9 for detailed information on adopting RTM company-wide.

Roadmap for the Book

Prologue. A story about two competing software companies. One stumbled badly because of lack of alignment and poor decision-making in marketing and sales. The other succeeded by using RTM.

Chapter 1. What is Routes to Market? Provides an overview of the RTM methodology and a roadmap to the rest of the book.

Chapter 2. RTM Workshop. Brings together the key RTM concepts to show how RTM is used to design a route for the product that Bob Wilson is assigned to, in a continuation of the story in the Prologue.

Chapter 3. Market Segmentation. Discusses issues in developing an effective market segmentation.

Chapter 4. Define Whole Solutions. Clarifies the customer ecosystem and explains how to define whole solutions – the minimum set of products and services necessary for the target customer to completely satisfy his or her compelling reason to buy. Knowing the customer ecosystem is critical for defining whole solutions that satisfy the multiple stakeholders within most business-to-business (B2B) and many business-to-consumer (B2C) customers.

Chapter 5. RTM Life Cycle. Explains the RTM Life Cycle in detail, showing typical routes and distribution channel structures for each phase. This chapter also explains disruptive versus non-disruptive innovation, and concludes with an analysis of different ways that vendors can respond to the forces driving commoditization.

Chapter 6. Constructing a Route. Provides specific guidelines for designing B2B and B2C routes, along with detailed examples including resource costs. This chapter also discusses issues in choosing and working with marketing agencies, distribution channels, resources for customer service, making media decisions, marketing to SMBs, and establishing a customer database. The chapter concludes with directions for monitoring the performance of a route.

Chapter 7. Go-to-Market Performance Assessment. Shows how to analyze and optimize the costs of resources for each step of the sales cycle. Several examples show the Expense-to-Revenue cost ratio, which is a key RTM metric. This chapter concludes with a case study of F5 Networks, Inc., showing how they assessed and then improved their go-to-market performance compared to industry best practices.

Chapter 8. Connecting RTM with Corporate Strategy. Presents a detailed case study of Adobe's RTM pilot project, which launched a major new product line and led to company-wide adoption of RTM.

Chapter 9. Implementing RTM Company-wide. Explains how to implement RTM company-wide.

Please visit the book's Web site, www.RoutesToCustomers.com, for more information including a library of case studies, checklists, implementation materials, and route-building and cost-calculating tools available at no charge.

Chapter 2
RTM Workshop

The purpose of this chapter is to show how the Routes-to-Market (RTM) methodology works by following a cross-functional RTM team as they build and operate a route. To do this, we continue the fictional story from the Prologue.

At the end of the Prologue, Bob Wilson joined Skyline Software, a company that develops and markets business management software. Bob is the marketing manager for one of Skyline's new products, code-named Evergreen, which is still in development and has not been announced yet. Skyline management chose the codename "Evergreen" because it implied that the software would be perennially fresh and enduring, like evergreen trees. They plan to pick a different name for the product before launching it, but for now, everyone at Skyline calls it "Evergreen."

Bob is on the cross-functional RTM team responsible for designing and implementing the routes for Evergreen. The other members of the RTM team for Evergreen are the product manager, the software development project lead, and managers from sales, customer service, and finance. During Bob's first week at Skyline, he received self-study training materials on the RTM methodology. He learned that there are eight decisions which need to be made to build a productive route for a product or service. A route is the combination of resources selected by the vendor to communicate, provide, or support the product or service to the customer at each step of the sales cycle. Most of the eight decisions will be made in the team's RTM Workshop, where all of the RTM concepts come together. The eight decisions are the following:

1. What product or service will be sold? This question is easy to answer except for new technologies that can be "productized" in potentially different ways. Existing products and services can be redefined to be sold in new ways, too. Normally this decision is made before using the RTM methodology.
2. What are the business objectives for the product or service (such as revenue, profit, unit volume, and market share)? These are usually set by upper management before the route is designed.
3. To whom will the product or service be sold? Segmenting the market and choosing a segment to target is normally how this decision is made for a new product or service. The RTM methodology includes guidance on doing this.

P. Raulerson et al., *Building Routes to Customers*, DOI: 10.1007/978-0-387-79951-3_2,

4. What are the compelling reasons for these target customers to buy the product or service? In RTM, understanding what compels target customers to buy is the foundation for building an effective route.

5. What phase of the life cycle is the product or service in? This is a key decision because each phase of the life cycle favors a different type of route. The remaining three decisions depend on the answer to this question.

6. What activities should be done to market, sell, and provide support for the product or service to the target customers? RTM is very tactical. A route specifies the activities that will be performed at every step of the sales cycle, from generating demand to providing support to the customer after the sale.

7. Who should do those activities? This decision selects the resources for the route.

8. How much should be spent to do each of these activities in order to achieve the business objectives? In RTM, budgets are built from the bottom–up.

As the product launch date for Evergreen approaches, the RTM team has been meeting frequently to share information and prepare for their RTM Workshop. Figure 2.1 shows the inputs and outputs for the RTM Workshop.

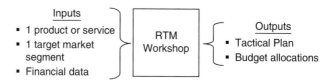

Fig. 2.1 The RTM Workshop's inputs and outputs

The inputs for the Evergreen RTM Workshop include a definition of Evergreen as a product or service, a complete description of the target market segment for Evergreen, and financial data including the revenue goal for Evergreen and cost data for all of the resource choices that will be considered for the routes. There are two outputs from the RTM Workshop. One is the Tactical Plan for launching Evergreen and establishing its initial customer base. The Tactical Plan specifies the routes for Evergreen – the activities and resources that will take customers through the sales cycle for Evergreen. The other output from the RTM Workshop will be budget allocations for these resources.

Preparing for the RTM Workshop

To run the RTM Workshop, the team needs to define Evergreen as a product, not as a technology or as a development project. Based on Evergreen's features and functions, they decided to define it as "e-marketing software" that captures leads from people visiting the customer's Web site, follows up with those leads automatically, tracks online referrals and affiliates, handles e-mail newsletters and all ecommerce functions (online shopping carts, credit card purchases, order confirmations, pick-and-pack lists, etc.). Evergreen was built on top of Skyline's salesforce automation software, so that both e-marketing and salesforce automation were included in the product.

Evergreen was developed so that it could be sold as either packaged software to be installed and operated on the customer's server computer or Software-as-a-Service that runs on Skyline's servers and is used by customers via the World Wide Web. The team realized that having these two alternatives meant that Evergreen was really two different products – a software product and an online service. They also realized that they needed to decide which product the route-to-market should focus on. They put that decision on hold, hoping that market data would clarify which package would be the right one to focus on.

Target Market Segment

To run the RTM Workshop, the RTM team must identify one target market segment for the product. If the team decides that they should target two or more market segments for the launch of Evergreen, they will need to run additional RTM Workshops for each additional segment.

In preparation for the RTM Workshop, Bob led the team through a sequence of steps to research market opportunities for the new product and prioritize market segments to target. One step in the research was interviewing Skyline's existing customers (companies using Skyline's other products) to determine if Evergreen would be a good fit for them. They gathered and reviewed published data and reports on markets for Customer Relationship Management (CRM) software and software for e-commerce, e-marketing, and related products and services. Then they hypothesized different ways to segment the market and reviewed these hypotheses with people who are knowledgeable in this product category. This was followed by conducting in-depth interviews with customers who fit the hypothesized segments, fielding a quantitative market study, and analyzing the results.

After examining all of the market data, they concluded that their target segment would be small companies with 5 to 20 employees, where the company owner or management has decided to expand their online sales aggressively. The data were mixed on which vertical markets within this segment would be most attractive, but a subsegment of companies looked very promising. It was companies whose products were already in electronic form, such as e-books, online training materials and training classes, and paid subscriptions to electronic information.

They found that companies with 5–20 employees strongly preferred the Software-as-a-Service model because they do not have the technical resources to operate their own servers in such a mission-critical application. The RTM team considered other market segments, but chose this segment because their market research showed that this segment was growing rapidly and that Evergreen's features would be very attractive to them.

They knew that, during the RTM Workshop, they would need to answer the following questions about the buying behavior of their target customers, so they included in their primary market research questions to resolve the following:

- What buying steps do the target customers typically go through?
- How do they make the transition from one step to the next in their buying cycle? What are the "gating items" for these transitions?
- Where do they turn for information about the type of need that our product meets, or for information about our type of product?
- Who influences the target customers?
- Where do they shop for our kind of product?
- What buying activities do they do, such as search the web, try out free samples, or do an ROI calculation?
- What features and benefits do they expect from products like Evergreen?
- What will compel them to buy Evergreen?

The Whole Solution

The primary market research conducted by the RTM team turned up the fact that many customers in their target market needed additional products and services beyond Evergreen to meet all of their e-marketing needs. The top three were the following:

1. Accounting software and services for their businesses, either new accounting software or some kind of data exchange between Evergreen and their existing accounting software.
2. Help in doing advertising, direct marketing, and telemarketing for their products.
3. Support for their entrepreneurial businesses, including advice on managing and growing their companies, getting loans and other financing, etc.

The "whole solution" for the customers in Evergreen's target market consisted of Evergreen plus these three products and services, which were complementary to Evergreen.

The research showed that most of their target customers already had accounting software, specifically QuickBooks, the most widely used accounting software in small businesses in the USA. So the RTM team asked the Evergreen development team to develop a way for Evergreen to exchange accounting data with QuickBooks. This turned out to be easy to do. This made it easier to sell Evergreen to target customers who used QuickBooks. Customers with other accounting packages could either convert to QuickBooks, use Evergreen without exchanging data with their accounting software, or wait for Skyline's development team to create a data exchange mechanism for their accounting package.

The RTM team followed the same logic for the other complementary products and services that were needed in the whole solution for Evergreen. To provide help in doing advertising, direct marketing and telemarketing for Evergreen customers, they decided to pursue relationships with the firms in these categories that focused on the kinds of companies in the target market segment for Evergreen. These relationships would provide two benefits for Skyline: (1) these firms could help Evergreen customers do more effective marketing, which would make them more successful and, consequently, better references for Evergreen; and (2) some of these firms would become Skyline business partners and resell Evergreen.

To provide product fulfillment services for Evergreen customers, the RTM team decided to establish relationships with companies in that business, along the same lines as the relationships with ad agencies. But in this case, there needed to be an electronic link between Evergreen and the fulfillment companies, to keep inventory data up to date and to automate the ordering and confirmation process. Like the QuickBooks situation, this was easy for the Evergreen development team to add.

At this point, the RTM team knew they had a compelling whole solution for Evergreen for their target customers.

RTM Life Cycle Phase

Another piece of information about the product is needed for the RTM Workshop: the phase of the RTM Life Cycle that the product is in. As shown in Fig. 2.2, there are four phases in the RTM Life Cycle. The phases are matched to groups of customers who share the same attitudes about buying innovative products and services.

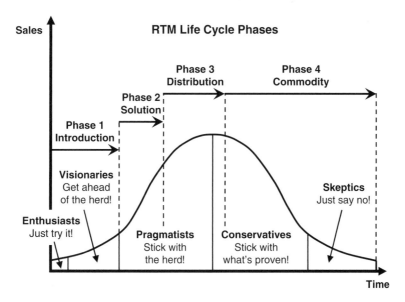

Fig. 2.2 RTM Life Cycle phases

Note that the assignment for the Evergreen RTM team, to do before their RTM Workshop, is to determine which phase of the RTM Life Cycle the product or service will be in during the time period that their Tactical Plan will be implemented. In other words, which phase of the RTM Life Cycle will they encounter in the market when they launch Evergreen?

Many people would look at Fig. 2.2 and say that, obviously, Evergreen will be in phase 1 Introduction when it is launched. But they would probably be wrong. The only products that enter the market in the RTM Introduction phase are so innovative that there is nothing like them in the market when they are launched. However, a new product cannot be very innovative if there are several similar products already in the market. Truly innovative products are "disruptive" in the sense that they change people's perceptions so much that the new products disrupt both strategy and behavior for the vendor and the customer.

To determine which phase of the RTM Life Cycle the market is in, the key question is: how innovative is the product or service perceived to be by people in its target market? If most of the people perceive the product to be very innovative, then only a few of them will buy it – the enthusiasts and perhaps the visionaries – and the product will enter the market in the Introduction phase of the RTM Life Cycle. On the other hand, if more than half of the people in the target market see the new product as providing no innovation over other products in the market, then the product is in the Commodity phase of the RTM Life Cycle.

For each of the four phases of the RTM Life Cycle, there is a different primary job that the vendor must do to succeed in that phase.

1. **Phase 1 Introduction.** The primary job in phase 1 is to *introduce* the product or service to the customers who will be the first ones in the market to buy it – enthusiasts and visionaries. Enthusiasts' response to an innovative product or service is "Just try it!" Visionaries' response is "Get ahead of the herd!", that is, obtain the advantage provided by the innovation before anyone else. The routes that accomplish this are largely direct sales and are focused on evangelizing enthusiasts and visionaries. A product is in phase 1 if it is so innovative that there are no other products like it in the market.
2. **Phase 2 Solution.** The primary job in phase 2 is to create and sell whole *solutions* to pragmatists, whose response to innovative products and services is "Stick with the herd!", that is, wait for other customers who are like themselves to buy the product or service. Pragmatists are interested in what the product or service does reliably and predictably to meet their specific needs. The way to get them to buy is to target a niche market of pragmatists who have no solution to a pressing problem, and provide a whole solution that completely solves their problem. Phase 2 routes differ from phase 1 routes by the addition of companies that provide the products and services that complete the whole solution. A product is in phase 2 if at least one niche market of pragmatic customers has bought it or a competitor's product, but most niche markets have yet to buy anything like the product.
3. **Phase 3 Distribution.** The primary job for this phase is to expand *distribution* as fast as possible, which requires building high-volume routes that cover all of the

pragmatists in the market, not just the ones in the niche markets targeted in phase 2. The routes must also cover the first conservatives to buy the product. Conservatives' response to innovative products and services is "Stick with what's proven!" They are price and option sensitive and think that, by waiting for products to mature and become well-established, they can minimize the cost and risk of buying them. Phase 3 routes differ from phase 2 routes by the addition of wholesale distributors and broader geographic coverage. A product is in phase 3 if several niche markets of pragmatists have bought it but sales are still growing rapidly.

4. **Phase 4 Commodity.** The primary jobs for this phase are to maximize market coverage while maintaining the profit margin, and to hold back the forces *commoditizing* the product as long as possible. Phase 4 routes sell to conservatives and skeptics. Skeptics' response to innovative products and services is "Just say no!" They buy products that are completely proven and risk free, products that they cannot live or work without, where they know that the cost of not having the product greatly exceeds the cost (and trauma) of buying it. Routes in phase 4 should maximize coverage while maintaining profitability. A product is in phase 4 if more than half of the market has bought the product or one of its competitors.

The key question for the RTM team is: which phase will they encounter in the market when Evergreen is launched? The answer to that question is critical because different activities and resources are needed to sell products in different phases.

The first thing the RTM team did to answer this question was to determine how innovative was the technology in Evergreen. Of course, every high-tech company wants to market innovative products, but the Evergreen RTM team concluded that the features and functions in Evergreen were not innovative. Other companies had been selling software or services that, individually, did one or another of all of Evergreen's functions. They also found about a dozen companies that sold products that provided all of Evergreen's functions in a single package, just like Evergreen. They needed to do a thorough competitive analysis of these companies and their products, but it looked like none of Evergreen's technical features or functions was innovative in the sense that it was distinctly different and superior to similar products in the market.

Innovation is not limited to the product or service, but can be in the go-to-market strategy, the supply chain, human resources, or finance. The RTM team felt that there was room to innovate in the go-to-market strategy for Evergreen in two areas: (1) branding, positioning, marketing messages, and marketing mix (selection of resources for marketing communications), and (2) distribution channels, sales models, and pricing. The competitors that they had identified in determining the product's level of innovation, appeared to be promoting the features and functions of their product instead of business and personal benefits to people in the customer's ecosystem (people who participate in, contribute to, and influence purchase decisions).

It looked like there might be good opportunities to partner with several types of organizations that provided complementary products and services to the target market for Evergreen, including ad agencies, direct marketing firms (which handle direct mail for small companies that need to enhance and integrate their online store with their print catalog), telemarketing firms (similar rationale), entrepreneur support groups and social networks, and other referral and affiliate marketing possibilities.

The last factor they considered was market growth rate. The highest growth rates are in RTM Life Cycle Phase 3 Distribution. Sales for the Evergreen competitors mentioned above were growing very fast. It seemed very likely that the majority of customers buying the competitors' products were pragmatists, based on the quarter-to-quarter growth rate. But there were no signs of two-tier distribution or significant penetration of any geographies outside the USA and Canada.

The RTM team concluded that the RTM Life Cycle phase for Evergreen at the launch date would be phase 2 Solution. However, they decided that as soon as they launched Evergreen, they would start planning for phase 3 Distribution so that they could move quickly if the market shifted in the near future.

Financial Data

The last input that the team needed for the RTM Workshop was financial data. They needed a revenue goal, of course, along with cost of revenue (cost of goods sold) figures for Evergreen, plus Skyline's costs for performing the different marketing, sales, and customer service activities that would be considered during the Workshop. The finance person on the Evergreen RTM team pulled the cost data together for them.

The RTM team shared the key findings of their preparation for the RTM Workshop with Skyline's executive team the week before the workshop. Skyline CEO Charlie Davis came back to the Evergreen RTM team 2 days later with the revenue goal for Evergreen. Charlie described the discussions he had had with his executive team and board members, and told them that the consensus was that the revenue goal for Evergreen's first year sales should be $25 million. That was aggressive compared to the level of revenue they had estimated for their competitors, but doable if they got the budget they needed for Evergreen's routes-to-market.

Charlie told them to come back with a solid tactical plan and he would get the funding for it. Everyone left that meeting charged up and ready to move forward.

During the RTM Workshop

The Evergreen RTM team started their RTM Workshop with all of the prerequisite data outlined above. Their first step was to translate the buying activities that their target customers were doing into the marketing, sales, and customer service activities that Skyline should do to sell Evergreen. Figure 2.3 shows the activities that would be needed for the Evergreen route-to-market.

Then the RTM team stepped through the following questions to identify which resources would be good choices for performing these activities.

- Which resources have the capacity to handle the volume of activity (such as the number of the telesales calls, or the number of installations) that needs to be performed?
- Which combination of resources perform these activities best?
- Which combination of resources is most cost-effective?
- Which combination of resources is available for your route?
- Which combination of resources work together versus compete?

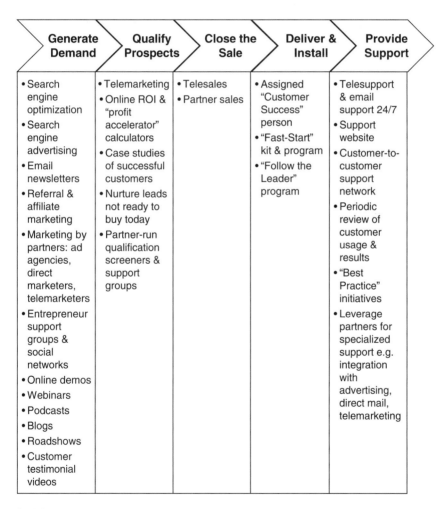

Generate Demand	Qualify Prospects	Close the Sale	Deliver & Install	Provide Support
• Search engine optimization • Search engine advertising • Email newsletters • Referral & affiliate marketing • Marketing by partners: ad agencies, direct marketers, telemarketers • Entrepreneur support groups & social networks • Online demos • Webinars • Podcasts • Blogs • Roadshows • Customer testimonial videos	• Telemarketing • Online ROI & "profit accelerator" calculators • Case studies of successful customers • Nurture leads not ready to buy today • Partner-run qualification screeners & support groups	• Telesales • Partner sales	• Assigned "Customer Success" person • "Fast-Start" kit & program • "Follow the Leader" program	• Telesupport & email support 24/7 • Support website • Customer-to-customer support network • Periodic review of customer usage & results • "Best Practice" initiatives • Leverage partners for specialized support e.g. integration with advertising, direct mail, telemarketing

Fig. 2.3 Activities to be performed on the Evergreen route-to-market

- How much time and effort will be needed to recruit, hire (or engage), train, and manage these resources, if they are not already on staff or engaged by your company as either contractors or channel partners?

After discussing the alternative resources and how they fit the above criteria, the Evergreen RTM team concluded that the best choices for resources to perform these activities were as given in Fig. 2.4.

Skyline had never worked with ad agencies as channel partners (instead of providers of creative and advertising services). They had no experience doing affiliate marketing or working with entrepreneur support groups. The RTM Team decided to bring in people with experience in these areas to help them understand how to make it work.

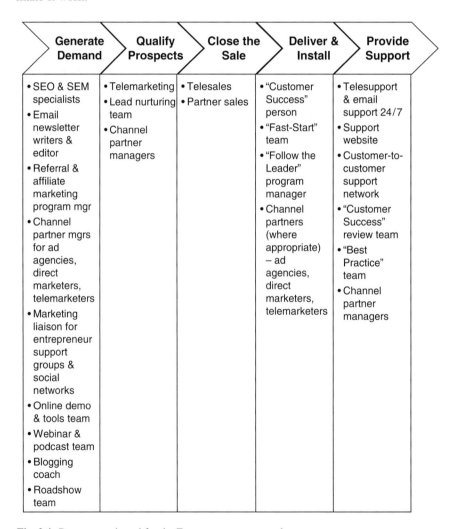

Generate Demand	Qualify Prospects	Close the Sale	Deliver & Install	Provide Support
• SEO & SEM specialists • Email newsletter writers & editor • Referral & affiliate marketing program mgr • Channel partner mgrs for ad agencies, direct marketers, telemarketers • Marketing liaison for entrepreneur support groups & social networks • Online demo & tools team • Webinar & podcast team • Blogging coach • Roadshow team	• Telemarketing • Lead nurturing team • Channel partner managers	• Telesales • Partner sales	• "Customer Success" person • "Fast-Start" team • "Follow the Leader" program manager • Channel partners (where appropriate) – ad agencies, direct marketers, telemarketers	• Telesupport & email support 24/7 • Support website • Customer-to-customer support network • "Customer Success" review team • "Best Practice" team • Channel partner managers

Fig. 2.4 Resources selected for the Evergreen route-to-market

The next step in the RTM Workshop was to cost out the route. They entered their resource selections and the costs for those resources into the Route Calculator spreadsheet, available at no charge at the book's Web site, www.RoutesToCustomers.com. The Route Calculator enabled them to easily project the impact on revenue of different resource mixes, and to calculate the cost of each mix.

Based on a first-year revenue goal of $25 million, the RTM team concluded that the optimal budget for the route would be $9 million for the first year of Evergreen sales (including the launch costs and the costs for market research prior to launch). This would result in an expense-to-revenue ratio for the route of 36% (=$9 million/$25 million), which is at the high end of the range of route expenses but acceptable for launching a new product in a competitive market.

The RTM team proposed allocating the $9 million expense budget as follows: 35% to sales cycle step 1 Generate Demand, 15% to step 2 Qualify Prospects, 18% to step 3 Close the Sale, 20% to step 4 Deliver and Install, and 12% to step 5 Provide Support.

The last step in the RTM Workshop was to document these decisions in the Tactical Plan. After the workshop, the team reviewed the Tactical Plan with the executive team and got their approval including the $9 million budget they requested.

Implementing the Tactical Plan

Before Evergreen was launched, the RTM Team conducted a Tactical Kick-off with everyone on the "extended team" – people who would be marketing, selling, or providing customer support for Evergreen, including Skyline's marketing agency and key business partners that they had already recruited, including people involved with referral and affiliate marketing and entrepreneur support groups. Bob's boss, Maria Lopez, VP of Marketing, was responsible for the revenue and profit of Evergreen, so she led the meeting. They had to rent a hotel conference room to accommodate the 45 people who participated.

In the Tactical Kick-off, Maria congratulated the RTM Team on the job they had done bringing Evergreen to the launch point, and told the extended team how excited she and the other executives of Skyline were about launching Evergreen. She said that they liked the Evergreen codename so much, that they decided to keep it as the product name, as long as it was OK with them (the extended team). This got a roar of approval from the group. She then explained the commitments that she and the other executive had made for visibility, funding, resources, and extra effort so that they could succeed. Then she led them through an exercise of giving personal commitments to each other that they would make their piece of the plan happen. This approach personalized each person's role in the team and energized everyone, which was the objective for the Tactical Kick-off.

Evergreen sales took off like a rocket. The RTM Team monitored performance carefully and made several mid-course corrections to the plan based on what they learned. They used the "feedback loop" mechanism in the RTM methodology – each planned activity has measurable inputs and outputs that can be monitored, enabling fine-tuning – to adjust priorities, spending, and the myriad of variables available in online marketing.

Sales at the end of the first year were $48 million, nearly twice the $25 million goal that everyone had thought was so aggressive 13 months previously. The expense budget was raised by 50% part way through the year to $13.5 million. At the end of the year, the expense-to-revenue ratio turned out to be 28%, 8 percentage points less than the original E/R ratio that had been budgeted. This meant that operating expenses for the route were 8 percentage points lower. The additional 8% of Evergreen's revenue, $3.8 million, flowed directly to Skyline's bottom line.

Bob's team became experts in using RTM to maximize Evergreen's revenue and profitability. It quickly became Skyline's biggest profit producer. At the end of the product's first year of sales, Bob was promoted to VP and general manager of the business unit that was formed for that product line.

Summary

As stated at the beginning of this chapter, there are eight decisions which need to be made in order to build a productive route for a product or service. The first two decisions are normally made before using the RTM methodology. Decisions 3 through 8 are made in the RTM Workshop, where all of the RTM concepts come together. The list below identifies the chapters that provide a detailed explanation of the RTM methodology for making each decision, along with examples.

1. What product or service will be sold? This question is easy to answer except for new technologies that can be "productized" in potentially different ways. Existing products and services can be redefined to sell them in new ways, too. Normally this decision is made before using the RTM methodology.
2. What are the business objectives for the product or service (such as revenue, profit, unit volume, and market share)? These are normally set by upper management before the route is designed.
3. To whom will the product or service be sold? This is discussed in Chap. 3: Market Segmentation.
4. What are the compelling reasons for these target customers to buy the product or service? This is covered in Chap. 4: Define Whole Solutions.
5. What phase of the life cycle is the product or service in? The phases of the RTM Life Cycle are explained in detail in Chap. 5.
6. For the product or service what activities should be done to market, sell, and provide support to them? This is discussed in Chap. 5: RTM Life Cycle.
7. Who should do those activities? This is also discussed in Chap. 5: RTM Life Cycle.
8. How much should be spent to do each of these activities in order to achieve the business objectives? Guidance for setting budgets and monitoring route expenses is provided in the following sections:

- "How to Monitor the Performance of a Route" section in Chap. 6: Constructing a Route.
- "Analyzing and Optimizing Go-to-Market Costs" section in Chap. 7: Go-to-Market Performance Assessment.
- "AlterCast Route Calculations" section of Chap. 8: Connecting RTM with Corporate Strategy.
- "Budgeting Costs by Department" and "Allocating Costs" sections in Chap. 9: Implementing RTM Company-wide.

The checklist above, along with other checklists from this book, is available as a free download from the book's Web site, www.RoutesToCustomers.com.

Chapter 3
Market Segmentation

The 360-Degree View

We learned in business school that segmentation is the process of dividing a market into distinct subsets that behave in different ways or have dissimilar needs. Because the customers in each segment are fairly homogeneous in their needs and attitudes, they will respond in the same way to a given marketing, sales, and distribution strategy.

We wish it were so simple. In fact, each dimension for segmenting the market presents only a slice of the company's reality. To get the 360-degree view, it is critical that segmentation include information for the external market and also for the company's internal operations and distribution partners. Otherwise, it is like a car with only one wheel – it will not go very far.

This is why all departments of the company should be involved in segmentation. It is the best way to overcome the pitfall of limiting the segmentation to a single view of the market. Defining and choosing segments is an excellent platform of communication within the company. This should allow everyone to align their objectives and to gain a complete understanding of their reality.

Companies with a Single Market Segment

Zipcar, Inc., founded in 1999, is the largest US car sharing company with a fleet of more than 5,000 vehicles that can be rented by the hour or day by its 180,000 urban customers in 48 US and Canadian cities. Zipcar's concept is that people who only occasionally need a car pay a membership fee to have access to cars positioned at fixed locations, typically around downtown or a university campus. Members typically use mass transit for work commutes, yet have access to a car when needed without the investment in buying, owning, and maintaining their own vehicle. Zipcar's founders had seen a car sharing cooperative while on vacation in Berlin. They decided to put an American spin on the concept by outfitting the cars with wireless key locks (to provide 24 × 7 vehicle access to Zipcar members), handling reservations online, and marketing Zipcar as an environmentally responsible lifestyle choice for urban dwellers.

P. Raulerson et al., *Building Routes to Customers*, DOI: 10.1007/978-0-387-79951-3_3,

Zipcar is an example of a company that focused initially on a single market segment. For such companies, their product or service usually comes in only one model or service plan. Features are the same with minor variations in color or other superficial differences between one unit and another.

It is actually quite rare for there to be a single, homogenous market segment for all of a company's products or services. Such a segmentation would imply that all customers want to buy the product for the same reasons and in the same places. This is unlikely to last long. The monosegment naturally leads to multiple subsegments.

Zipcar, for example, found that, by 2003, it attracted customers with needs and preferences beyond its original target market. Zipcar then broadened its marketing and operations to serve them. These customers include businesses with urban employees who need to drive cars occasionally to meet with their customers, and universities seeking to reduce demand for on-campus parking.

The problem for most companies with a single market segment is that, by treating all customers the same way, they could fail to meet the needs of many customers. They could also miss valuable opportunities with customers outside that segment, thereby limiting their revenue. The solution to these problems is to reevaluate the company's go-to-market strategy to determine if different approaches would be more productive with different customers. If so, these customers constitute different segments.

Traditionally, manufacturers segment the market on multiple dimensions, not solely on how their product will be used. For example, automobile manufacturers segment their markets based on style or appearance and on price: trucks, station-wagons, sports cars; low end, mid-market, or luxury – even if they use the same parts in these vehicles. They believe that people choose cars more by appearance and price than by use. Few customers who buy sports cars actually engage in any kind of automobile sport such as auto racing.

Everyone in a company should understand the positioning of the company's products, especially when different products are proposed.

Companies with Multiple Market Segments

Not many companies have a single market segment. Most offer different products or product lines so that they can meet the diverse needs of different market segments.

For example, large magazine publishers reach multiple segments of readers by offering multiple titles focused on different topics, each of which is of interest to a fairly homogenous set of readers. This enables the publishers to aggregate multiple sets of consumers for advertisers, which helps the publishers capture a larger share of the ad budgets of vendors who are targeting multiple customer segments. The largest magazine publisher in the USA and UK is Time, Inc., a subsidiary of Time Warner, Inc. Time publishes over 130 magazine titles including *Fortune* (read by business people), *People* (celebrity watchers), *Real Simple* (busy women who want quick solutions for everyday life), *Sports Illustrated* (passionate sports fans), and *TIME* (sophisticated readers). Advertisers with broad product lines, such as

General Motors (GM), Coca-Cola, Citigroup, Proctor & Gamble, and Microsoft, have traditionally placed ads in multiple Time titles in order to reach multiple customer segments.

Industrial products are organized into families of products corresponding to different types of customers. For example, tool manufacturers have a professional product line for experienced handymen, and a different product line for consumers (as opposed to professionals). The professional range is differentiated from the consumer range by adding "pro" to the product name, or by being marketed under a different brand name through a distinct distribution network.

For companies with multiple market segments, a thorough segmentation of the market is even more essential. Multiple products from the same manufacturer will compete with each other if they are not sufficiently differentiated. One speaks then about low-end products cannibalizing sales of top-of-the-line products, which reduces the manufacturer's top-end selling price and margin.

Automobile manufacturers are masters in the art of defining product lines intended for different customer groups but sharing common parts. Toyota markets their top-of-the-line vehicles under the luxury brand name Lexus, markets mid-range vehicles under the Toyota brand, and created the brand name Scion for a new line of small cars for the youth market. The three brands share parts, facilities, and even management, but are perceived by customers as distinctive from each other.

A product can fit multiple market segments. Traditionally, the person responsible for a product takes responsibility for the market segments associated with the product. This can result in overlooking segments that had not been previously identified, and can also create a barrier against targeting existing segments with additional products. In both situations, revenue will be missed and competitors who see the market differently could gain a foothold.

For example, call centers typically buy corded headsets that can be worn comfortably all day. They do not need cordless headsets because call center personnel work at fixed workstations. The product manager for corded, professional headsets "owned" the call center market. On the other hand, general office workers buy cordless headsets and wear them for shorter periods of time. The product manager for cordless, general office headsets "owned" that market. Neither product manager saw the market opportunity for cordless, professional headsets – headsets that could be worn comfortably by people who were on the phone all day but did not work at fixed workstations, such as technical support staff or call center team leaders.

A similar situation occurred with Bluetooth headsets, initially marketed only to customers with mobile phones. Many of those customers liked their Bluetooth headsets so much that they wanted to use them with their office phone. They did not want to switch headsets when they came into or left their offices. The product manager for general office headsets "owned" the office market, preventing the product manager for Bluetooth headsets from entering it.

To circumvent this problem, companies with multiple market segments should integrate product segmentation with customer segmentation in a collaborative way, as explained in the next section.

Product Segmentation Integrated with Customer Segmentation

In the examples cited above, the segments have been defined in different ways – by product use, by product appearance, or by price, and so on. On what criteria or dimensions should segments be defined so that they are operationally meaningful and effective?

Unfortunately, there is no single criterion which can be used to segment every market. There is no scientific method which makes it possible to define segmentation criteria completely and precisely. This is why segmentation is an executive decision and must fit the leaders' vision for the business. Segmentation cannot be just an exercise for market researchers.

We can however identify two basic approaches that have proven to be very successful:

1. Product segmentation – segment the market based on product features, capabilities, and other product attributes. Customer segments are identified by the products that are thought to be appropriate to them. This type of segmentation is often done by Product Management or Product Development as they define a product family consisting of multiple product models with different features and prices. This makes it possible to develop and manufacture products with common components, which improves the manufacturability and lowers supply-chain costs.

2. Customer segmentation – segment the market based on customer attributes such as demographics (objective characteristics such as age, gender, job title, and income level), psychographics (subjective characteristics such as needs, wants, personality, values, attitudes or interests), or behavior (habits or patterns of actions that affect their purchase, application or use of the product). Each segment is defined in terms of the customer's demographics and/or psychographics and/or behavior. The customer segmentation makes it possible to deploy marketing, sales, and customer service resources to obtain the best possible coverage of the selected customers. The customer segmentation is usually established by Customer Marketing working with sales, customer service, and other customer-facing organizations.

It is clear that a customer segmentation by itself does not make it possible to define product features and characteristics, and that a product segmentation by itself does not provide enough information to develop a marketing strategy. Companies need to do both types of segmentation – product segmentation AND customer segmentation – because these segmentations serve different purposes.

These two types of segmentation should be done together so that the people doing the segmentations can collaborate to make the two segmentations complementary. By "complementary," we mean that each product segment is mapped to one or more customer segments, and vice versa. This will result in every "segment" having two sets of attributes:

1. The products that are appropriate for, or targeted to, those customers, and how those products compare to the competition.
2. The demographic, psychographic, and/or behavioral characteristics of the customers in the segment.

These segments should divide the market into homogenous groups of people who have the same needs and buy the same products or services in similar ways, with the same motivations. Because each group is homogenous (everyone in the group is similar to each other), they will respond in similar ways to marketing, sales, and service. If they do not respond similarly, they belong in two different segments.

Many companies are trapped by the mistaken belief that one type of segmentation – product segmentation or customer segmentation – is better or more important than the other, or that they do not need to be integrated. As a result, their investments in product development are driven more by the preferences of engineering or manufacturing, than by customers' needs or market opportunities, or their sales and profits are constrained by a mismatch between supply and demand.

One way to integrate product segmentation and market segmentation is to ask the following two questions:

1. Step through every product and ask, which customers could use this product or a variation of it?
2. Step through every market and ask, which products (or variations of them) could meet the needs of these customers?

The integration of product segmentation with customer segmentation leads to the right decisions and actions because it brings people together from different departments to share their perspectives and create a common view that those departments can act on.

Segmenting by Company Size

For a business-to-business (B2B) market, segmentation is often based on company size:

- Large companies, which typically buy the biggest products in a product line or the largest volumes. There might be a single decision-maker (such as the CIO or manufacturing czar), a hierarchy of decision-makers (such as in IT or finance), or many distributed decision-makers (such as departmental customers). Sales cycles will be relatively long and involve a mix of products and services which might need to be customized.
- Small and mid-sized companies, which typically buy less powerful products or fewer units that are intended for more varied uses. These companies do not have a complex decision-making process as in the large accounts. Their decisions can be fast. On the other hand, their purchases are smaller and therefore the sales process must consume less resource in order to maintain profitability.

The danger in segmenting by company size is in assuming that large companies make centralized decisions and place centralized orders for all products and services that they buy. The downside of making this assumption is that marketing and sales may be erroneously focused on winning large orders from corporate-wide purchase decisions at large companies. In many large companies, the people at headquarters think they have the power to make centralized purchase decisions for everything, but purchase orders may actually be initiated and issued in a decentralized way at a departmental or plant level. Selling to headquarters may get the vendor onto an "approved vendors" list, but purchases are made when individual company departments or locations go through the buying process. For the companies in the target segment, the way to circumvent this danger is to understand the real purchasing process and the locations of the decision-makers for that process.

Geographical Segmentation

Segmentation can also reflect geographical realities.

In emerging countries like India and China, there is tremendous demand not only for high-end products like mobile phones and sophisticated microcomputers but also for low-end, extremely simple and low-cost products that are not sold in the USA or Europe.

In the 1980s, many multinational corporations used an organizational model in which they structured their business by country. If the products were developed in one place and sold worldwide, each country manager had the authority and the latitude to set prices, define a marketing mix, and choose its organization. At that time, each country was managed as a profit center or a subsidiary.

In the 1990s, this model was replaced by the creation of regional or continental structures such as pan-European or pan-Asian, to reduce costs. In Europe, the establishment of a single currency and the reinforcement of the European Community as an economic unit supported this approach.

The pressure on prices and thus on margins led companies to reconsider their marketing, sales, and distribution models and to resort to more specialized and sophisticated tools and methods including call centers, campaign-based marketing and sales, Internet-based communications, etc. Implementing these tools and methods required recruiting people with specialized competencies, but this could not be justified in each country, even major countries. Accordingly, competency centers were established at the continent level, above the national structures.

Similar constraints were encountered in logistics. To be able to deliver products to customers within 24 hours while controlling inventories of finished products, it proved to be necessary to create continent-level distribution centers (instead of national distribution centers). In some companies, a centralized distribution center was augmented with two or three satellite centers of smaller size, with all of the distribution centers managed together as a single system.

As a result, some countries were for the first time without local stock. They reduced or closed the departments which before had provided national logistics.

Finally, the need to reinforce the company's worldwide brand limited the missions of the local publicity and marketing communications teams. Their role was no longer the definition of local campaigns but the adaptation of international campaigns to the national market.

The people who are performing these international functions are no longer generalists who handled diverse assignments within their home country, but functional specialists able to work in heterogeneous teams of multiple cultures. Their role is not to innovate but to understand and apply locally strategies which are decided elsewhere, at the multinational or worldwide level. They might contribute to the strategy in some cases, but that is not their primary role.

The drawback in using geography as a segmentation dimension is in failing to take into account the company's organizational model. The evolution of the organizational structures of multinational firms since the 1980s has changed the roles and responsibilities of decision-makers and implementers for many geographies. It makes good business sense for the people with relevant geographic responsibilities to be involved in developing the segmentation.

For many companies, geographical segmentation is a pendulum that swings between making decisions at a worldwide level and making decisions locally, closer to customers. Different issues cause the pendulum to swing from one point to another. At each point, different people may be involved in making marketing, sales, and distribution decisions. For example, if executives perceive a need to brand a product uniformly across all geographies, they will pull decision-making away from local managers to a centralized or worldwide level, and the role of local personnel will largely be implementing decisions made elsewhere. If, on the other hand, executives want to maximize efficiency or market share in individual countries, they will push decision-making down to local managers as much as possible. As the pendulum swings from one point to another, it impacts head counts, job opportunities, and career progressions at each location. Unfortunately, the pendulum never comes back to the same initial position.

Segmenting by Industry Structure

Manufacturers of automobile tires distinguish three distinct market segments: auto manufacturers (who buy tires to sell on new automobiles), fleet managers (who control which tires are installed on the auto fleets they manage), and consumers (who buy replacement tires when the original tires wear out). It might seem that auto manufacturers act as a distribution channel for tire manufacturers, but from the tire manufacturers' point of view, car companies are a distinct customer segment. The challenge in this segment is to convince the auto manufacturer to establish a supply contract with the tire manufacturer. To do this, the tire manufacturer must work closely with auto manufacturers as they develop new cars and build their supply chains. The challenge in the fleet manager segment is to secure "preferred vendor" contracts for tires on new cars and also on a replacement basis. The challenge in the consumer segment is to build or develop a network of tire retailers that provide tire installation and service. The differences between these three market segments are significant, requiring different skills and investments for the tire manufacturer, even though the products sold to the segments are essentially identical.

This example illustrates the risk in assuming that the user or operator of a product is the purchase decision-maker for that product. In fact, the user is rarely the decision-maker in corporate markets. The user is often not the decision-maker in consumer markets, especially if the purchase is a "family decision" that involves parents, children, spouses, or partners.

Many industries have tiered distribution channels in which customers buy from retailers, which in turn buy from wholesale distributors which source products from manufacturers. This structure is present in the computer, telecommunications, office products, home mortgage, consumer packaged goods, and other industries. Manufacturers that gain more business with the channel improve their coverage of the market. So it is important for manufacturers to structure marketing, communication, and support for the channel to become the vendor of choice for them.

Every customer can be seen in multiple different views. A man named Tom might be a white, middle-aged manager in a life insurance company, who owns a dependable, low-cost automobile but wishes he had a flashier, more-exciting car. By that description, Tom fits segments on each of several dimensions – race (color), age, job (position), industry, industry structure, type of automobile owned, aspirations for next automobile purchase. One dimension does not exclude the others.

In 1908, Henry Ford rolled out the first Model T car. Ford wanted to produce a car that most people could afford. At the time, all other car manufacturers were focused on consumers who could afford high-priced cars. Ford's strategy was built around reducing production costs so that he could continue to gain market share by reducing the price of the car every few years, making it very difficult for competitors to match his price points. This strategy worked brilliantly – the model T became the first car to sell 1,000,000 units. By the time the last Model T rolled off the assembly line in 1927, over 15 million had been built.

Model Ts were designed to reduce production costs. Henry Ford used the fastest drying paint, which was black, thereby standardizing on one color to move production along quickly. He declared that "Any customer can have a car painted any color that he wants so long as it is black."

Tom, the middle-aged manager in a life insurance company, owns a Model T.

General Motors was a distant number 2 to Ford in size and wanted to surpass Ford. GM needed a different strategy than Ford because it could not easily catch up to Ford's level of production and cost efficiencies. GM's strategy, articulated by CEO Alfred P. Sloan in 1924 (at the peak of Model T sales), was "A car for every purse and purpose." GM pioneered breaking the automobile market into segments with a product and a price for each segment. Customers flocked to buy GM cars, cars which met their needs and appealed to their sense of style and taste, including a choice of colors. Within 3 years, GM surpassed Ford as the largest and most profitable auto company in the world.

Tom, the life insurance company manager, replaced his Model T with a GM automobile. Ford Motor Company lost sight of Tom while GM focused on him.

Using Categorization to Understand What Is Behind the Numbers

Most people think the word "segmentation" has meaning only when paired with "market," as in the phrase "market segmentation." They think that segmentation only applies to the external market for a company's products or services. But every transaction processed, product shipped, or service performed by a vendor involves the vendor's internal organizations. These organizations incur different costs depending on the complexity of the transaction processed, size or weight for the product shipped, level of effort for service performed, and so on. To maximize profitability, it is critical to understand all costs incurred in dealing with customers, with the costs grouped or segmented into appropriate categories. Segmenting the company's internal operations is just as important as segmenting the company's market.

In most companies, each department can identify the average cost for the work they do or the output they produce. Logistics can report the average cost for shipping a product. Administration can identify the average cost for handling a purchase order. Manufacturing or finance can calculate the average cost of goods the company produces.

Unfortunately, average costs mask disparities and ignore distinctions between categories. Reality can be misunderstood if the only data are averages.

For example, let us look at a company that sells products through different distribution channels. The administrative cost to process and fulfill a few large orders from wholesale distributors is small compared to the cost for handling many small orders from individual dealers. It is wrong to use the average cost for processing an order, computed across all distribution channels, as the typical order processing cost for all channels. It is also wrong to use the average cost for shipping an order, computed across all shipments, as the typical shipping cost for all channels. These two averages hide significant costs associated with each distribution channel – costs that impact profitability. To reduce costs, different kinds of optimization will be needed for each channel.

When marketing says that they plan to reach a customer segment through retail, they should keep in mind that retail-oriented packaging will be required for the product, and that will impact product costs. They should also make allowances for retailers' ordering procedures and shipping requirements, which will impact administrative and shipping costs.

Some retail chains replenish the local inventory in their stores weekly, but the number of units required by each store is low. Low unit volume shipments to individual stores will have a significantly higher shipping cost per unit than a single bulk shipment of all of the units to a central distribution point. In this case, it might make sense for the manufacturer to engage a wholesale distributor instead of supplying the retailer directly. Without understanding all of the costs involved, marketing will not be able to assess the trade-offs between different distribution channel structures.

How can marketing know all of the variations in costs that could affect the profitability of different combinations of products, segments, distribution channels, and terms of sale? The problem is not just in marketing. Each department breaks down their work or output into categories that have different requirements and costs.

The answer is: all departments need to communicate their categories of work and costs. In the example of reaching customers through retail distribution, marketing needs to talk with order entry and logistics to understand how they can handle retailers' requirements and the costs to do so. Marketing should not assume that the average cost for entering an order or shipping a product will be the appropriate figures when calculating the profitability of the retail market segment. For example, the sales department might recommend that quantity discounts for retailers start at 100 units per order, but the logistics department does not get any reduction in shipping costs until they fill a pallet with 108 units. It probably makes more economic sense for the discount order quantity to be 108 units.

It is dangerous to use average costs across different categories of work. Many companies sell low-cost, high-volume products and also high-cost, low-volume products. They manufacture the high-volume product at plants overseas where manufacturing has been streamlined for maximum efficiency and minimal cost. They manufacture the low-volume product closer to home to make it easier for engineering and manufacturing to interact, or because manufacturing has not been optimized for the low-volume product. Averaging the manufacturing costs across these products would produce a figure that does not represent either situation. It would be equally absurd to average shipping costs, order entry costs, and costs in other departments, across different categories.

It is critical to keep costs separate by category. However, categories will vary from one department to the next. The most straightforward way to know what the categories and costs are, is for the managers of all departments to meet periodically to discuss the categories and associated costs in their departments.

Many companies have adopted a scorecard system for performance management. The information systems that provide data for the scorecards typically use aggregated numbers in each category tracked by the scorecard. It is critical for these categories to be defined so that the aggregated numbers accurately represent the way the company operates, without masking the differences in how categories vary from department to department.

Segmentation and Categorization: Cultural Crossroads

Imagine cross-functional management meetings in which managers discuss their departments' categories along with the product segmentation and customer segmentation developed jointly by Product Management and Customer Marketing. The goals of the meetings would be to:

1. Establish a common platform or language for internal communications between departments, for talking about how they do business with customers.
2. Understand the things that drive costs in each department, in order to build a cost matrix that accurately represents the real world. This will enable them to make informed decisions as a group on reducing costs and increasing profitability.
3. To identify areas of improvement and innovation within departments and between them.

We will see in the following chapters that this kind of communication platform is a key ingredient in the success of Routes-to-Market (RTM).

Segmentation: An Executive Decision

Far from being reduced to a tiresome analysis of many Excel tables entrusted to some unhappy trainees, segmentation is a fundamental exercise which must be decided at the most senior level of the company.

In a start-up, the founders usually base their company on a single concept that they all know well. In this situation, the leaders of the company can provide good intelligence and decision-making for segmentation derived either from their knowledge and intuition or from systematic market research.

It is rare however that this level of personal knowledge and coherence continues as a company grows. When new employees join the company, they bring different knowledge and experiences. Going international or pursuing new markets via internal or external growth leads to serving multiple market segments. Each department of the company evolves its procedures and organization accordingly.

Amazon.com is an excellent example of this. Jeff Bezos did a study to determine which products consumers would buy on the Internet. His strategy was to build as quickly as possible a commercial Web site, warehouses, and other infrastructure to sell books. Having built a community of customers, he expanded his offerings to include other products: music CDs, movie DVDs, consumer electronics, toys, clothing, and so on. The expansion resulted in restructuring marketing, logistics, and other departments, and in changing Amazon.com's segmentation from consumers who buy books to multiple segments of consumers who buy other kinds of products.

Questioning the "Business Case"

In almost every company, the viability of each investment or new expenditure must be evaluated and documented in a business case. If the evaluation is positive, the new project will be added to a list of projects to be prioritized. Only the top priority projects are implemented.

The walls of the company's conference rooms can testify to the impassioned debates during this process. Product development teams propose projects to create new, wonderful products based on innovative technology whose development presents a minimum risk. Marketing and the sales teams recommend a huge marketing campaign and expansion of the salesforce to rapidly ramp up sales of the new products. The finance and production people in the meeting wonder how realistic the projections are and what the consequences will be on their own departments.

The final decision is driven by the magic of the "business case." Sound analysis and financial assessment are important elements of the business case. But two things limit the decisions made by the business case approach:

1. Often, all the assessments in a business case are favorable, especially when they are presented by those who will be funded by it. Unfortunately, the real world is not so perfect.
2. More basically, the direction of the company cannot be determined from a list of the business cases with the most favorable assessments. Top management must first define a strategy and priorities for the company.

For example, the top management of General Electric has established the goal of being the leader or number two in each segment in which the company participates. GE business units must have a plan to achieve that goal or leave the segment.

General managers make a strategic decision to give priority to a product-centric approach or a customer-centric approach.

With a company strategy and priorities established, management teams will not have to rebuild the world at each meeting in order to make decisions on investments. They can make decisions on resource allocation by considering how the proposed investments achieve the strategy and not according to an abstract business case.

Questioning a Segmentation

In spite of its quality and its relevance, a segmentation can be reconsidered or abandoned as a result of technological development, the arrival of new competitors, the loss of market share, or drop in profitability. Whatever is the cause, changing a segmentation can be an excellent source of progress.

For many years IBM segmented its market based on customer size, as shown in Fig. 3.1. (IBM's customers were companies, government agencies, and other organizations, not consumers.) Each segment corresponded to a different type of sales coverage:

- Direct, face-to-face sales for the largest customers
- Indirect distribution channels for mid-sized customers
- Telesales and direct marketing for the smallest or prospective customers

Over time, many customers began to be contacted by different parts of IBM or IBM's distribution channel, be the target of various IBM marketing campaigns, providers of software, or services for IBM computers, and so on. Everyone claimed

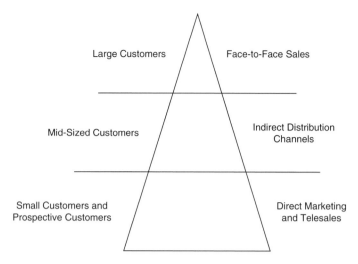

Fig. 3.1 IBM's market segmentation pyramid before 1995 – segmentation by customer size

to "own" the customer, to be the primary contact between them and IBM. At the same time, other customers or prospects did not receive any attention from IBM.

This multiplicity of contacts became a problem for the customer because he did not know which one to hold responsible for his business with IBM. Some of IBM's sales resources lost their effectiveness because they were deployed to cover customers who were not very receptive to IBM at that time. Another problem was that companies in the top section of the pyramid model got 80% of IBM's attention, while companies in the bottom two sections accounted for more than half of the market opportunity for many IBM products and services.

In 1995, a new segmentation approach was developed and the pyramid was banished. The segmentation by customer size was replaced by a segmentation based on the type of customer relationship illustrated in four squares or quadrants, as shown in Fig. 3.2.

- Quadrant 1 is the segment for customers involved with complex projects. Whatever the size of the customer, an IBM salesperson will maintain a face-to-face relationship with the customer throughout the project.
- Quadrant 2 is the segment for active customers who do not have a complex project but want to have an ongoing relationship with IBM. IBM salespeople located at a call center will maintain the relationship by telephone. Telesales people can communicate with ten or more customers per day, compared to only two or three for face-to-face salespeople.
- Quadrant 3 contains the customers who are installing applications software and therefore have a relationship with the software provider or systems integrator of the applications software. As the manufacturer of the computer on which the software will run, IBM has a small support role with the software provider or systems integrator.
- Quadrant 4 gathers all the customers and prospective customers who do not have an ongoing relationship with IBM, but are targeted by IBM for marketing campaigns.

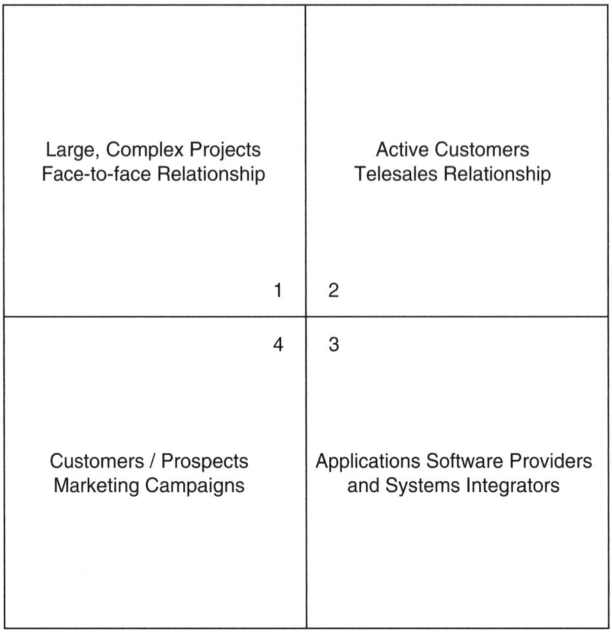

Large, Complex Projects Face-to-face Relationship 1	Active Customers Telesales Relationship 2
4	3
Customers / Prospects Marketing Campaigns	Applications Software Providers and Systems Integrators

Fig. 3.2 IBM's market segmentation quadrants in 1995 – segmentation by customer relationship

They could be targeted based on their industry, existing computer equipment, or other criteria. The leads generated from these campaigns will be qualified and transmitted to the appropriate internal sales or external distribution channels.

After IBM's top management replaced the pyramid segmentation approach with the quadrant model, a lot of work had to be done to persuade hundreds of IBM marketing and sales personnel and thousands of external partners (channels of distribution) to reorganize and refocus their organizations. Call centers were created with Customer Relationship Management systems and staffed with people reassigned and retrained from other sales and service groups. It took 6 months to switch over, during which the day-to-day work of selling customers continued unabated.

Nine months after the decision to adopt the new segmentation, revenue growth increased by double-digit percentages and the ratio of expenses to revenue decreased several points. The new segmentation had enabled IBM to achieve the financial goals set by top management.

Obstacles to Segmentation

There are several issues that can make it difficult to produce a rigorous and systematic segmentation.

Segmentation Is Boring for Action Freaks

Many business executives have little interest in segmentation or market analysis because they are action oriented.

For many engineers and salesmen, taking part in a meeting to discuss the results of market research, is absolute torture. For them, market research is a bureaucratic exercise that has no impact on real life.

To escape from the meeting, engineers will pretend they have an urgent project to finish. Salesmen will say that it is much more productive for them to do an important sales call since customers pay the bills, implying that the investment in market research only ran up the bills that had to be paid.

When experienced sales professionals take on responsibility for marketing, they are tempted to generalize their personal sales experience and to believe that it applies to the entire market, without seeking validation. They think that their successful individual experience is sufficient and no market research is required.

We have observed these attitudes at all levels of management, in all sizes, nationalities, and ages of companies. People do not like doing segmentation, but it is like a lot of things in life such as personal hygiene – people still have to do it.

The 80/20 Myth

Another substitute for doing a thorough segmentation consists in using a seemingly powerful, but simple concept of the "80/20" rule.

Many people believe that since 20% of a company's customers produce 80% of the revenue, it is therefore useless to develop any other form of segmentation than to identify those top 20%. This analysis is often made by managers who are action oriented, as mentioned previously. Their recommendation is to focus on the top 20% of customers, to reinforce the company's relationships with them via regular review meetings, and for management at all levels to ensure that the projects with them are proceeding smoothly.

Careful tracking of opportunities and projects with the top 20% can help to maximize the company's business with them. However, there can be unfortunate consequences to focusing exclusively on the top 20%. In the short term, it ignores fundamental questions about what the competition is doing, where new sources of growth are, and whether a different positioning or channel strategy would be more profitable. It can also blindside management to "big picture" trends in technology, the economy or the market that might affect their customers, their industry, or their company.

Another risk in applying the 80/20 Rule is that tracking the top 20% becomes an end in itself, even more important than selling. Putting more effort into tracking the top 20% can drive up sales costs without increasing revenue or profitability.

A more significant problem with the 80/20 Rule is that it is focused on customers who contribute 80% of the revenue, rather than 80% of the profit. Large customers are often very demanding and ask for special treatment, dedicated resources, and contract conditions with higher risks. Profit margins can be higher on transactions with smaller, less demanding customers. For example, consumer electronics retailer Best Buy focuses specifically on customers whose purchases have higher profit margins, and avoids customers generating lower profit margins; it regularly reports substantially higher net profit than its direct competitors.

One variation of the 80/20 Rule is to limit resources to major countries. In Europe, the cost of setting up to do business in every country can be significant, and it turns out that five major countries represent more than 70% of the European market for many products.

It can be tempting to limit marketing to just a few big countries. Translating marketing materials and product information into just a few languages, and cultivating contacts for marketing communications in a handful of locations, can reduce complexity and costs.

However, limiting resources to a few major countries can be suicidal, especially when the opportunity is in countries with high growth rates, which are typically not the largest countries. For example, the growth rate of young European countries has been much higher than that of "Old Europe." Companies which invested in countries like Spain or Ireland had better performance that those which focused on the five major European countries.

Over the last 35 years in the USA, many retailers expanded nationwide by opening stores in high-population urban centers and big-city suburbs. They also grew by acquiring competitors with similar customers in other regions of the country. However, Wal-Mart grew much faster to become the largest and highest profit retailer by focusing on small towns and rural locations surrounding suburbia, locations that other large retailers ignored. It is clear that pursuing geographies with higher growth rates can improve revenue and profit faster than limiting investment to geographies with large but slow-growing markets.

Absence of Segmentation

Sometimes it is necessary to launch a product or technology just to test market reaction. Segmentation cannot be done in these cases without testing the market, which also provides opportunities to educate customers, business partners, and other participants.

A famous example is that of the Sony Walkman, a product which had been developed to satisfy Akio Morita, the chairman of Sony, who wanted to listen to music while playing golf. At the time, the technology was so new that it was not really possible to test its potential by traditional methods such as customer focus groups or surveys. The upside of creating a new product worth billions of dollars to Sony, justified the risk of developing the Walkman even though there was no data on the market potential for it.

Even after conducting extensive market research, the largest companies make mistakes in estimating market reception for new products. When IBM's PC division showed its TrackPoint device (a finger-controlled mouse located in the center of the keyboard) to customers in focus groups, the customers loved it. But IBM product management was skeptical, even when the positive response was confirmed in more focus groups. So they defined the TrackPoint as an option on a limited number of models. Market reception was so enthusiastic that IBM put it on all of its notebook PCs. IBM's competitors sought to duplicate or license IBM's patented TrackPoint technology. Over time, IBM generated significant profit from licensing TrackPoint to Dell and Toshiba.

People who start new companies must not only develop a new product but also evaluate the potential without having the means to research markets as large companies do. Actually, most start-ups bet their success on a small number of customers and not on systematic analysis of a large market. Rare, however, are the start-ups which can metamorphose their cultures from concentrating initially on developing and securing a beachhead for their products, to focusing later on expanding their product lines and conquering multiple market segments. Many companies make this transition by bringing in executives from the outside to run the business.

Product-Driven Versus Market-Driven

We previously discussed the two market segmentations carried out by Product Management and Customer Marketing. We showed that these two types of segmentation should be done together so that they can be integrated, and that the integrated segmentation leads to the right decisions and actions.

There is another dichotomy that splits companies into two cultures which reflect their orientation and priorities. One culture, "product-driven," is centered on the company's products, as opposed to "market-driven," which can be described as obsessed by listening to customers and focusing on their satisfaction.

Management and employees in product-driven companies focus on products first and customers second. They spend the vast majority of their time working to make their products better than competitors, and to grow their product sales faster than competitors. They may say that they are "customer focused" but the truth is that they spend far more time talking about products than they spend talking about customers.

In contrast, management and employees in market-driven companies focus on customers first. They spend the vast majority of their time tying to make sure that their customers are completely satisfied. They measure sales performance by customer satisfaction and share of their customers' total spending, not by how many units they have sold.

Michael Treacy and Fred Wiersema, in *The Discipline of Market Leaders* (published in 1995), made the case that market-leading companies succeed by first choosing one of three "value disciplines" and then focusing their organizations on excelling in their chosen discipline. They characterized the three disciplines as: operational excellence (delivering the lowest cost products), product leadership (delivering the most innovative or superior products), and customer intimacy (delivering the highest level of service and customization).

In Chap. 8 of their book, Treacy and Wiersema described IBM's customer-centric operations in the 1970s and 1980s as the number one example of a market-leading company succeeding by excelling in the discipline of customer intimacy. Their very positive, multipage profile of IBM's market-driven strategy was followed by, "Of course, more recently IBM has lost its way."

When Treacy and Wiersema wrote those words in 1994, IBM had just completed a third year of declining sales and losses which by then totaled $16 billion. The board of directors had brought in Lou Gerstner from outside the company to be CEO in March 1993, but the evidence of a turnaround would not be visible until the end of IBM's 1994 fiscal year.

After Gerstner joined IBM, Wall Street analysts urged him to split the company into 12 independent companies, one for each major product line. Instead, he bet that customers would increasingly value a supplier that could integrate a wide range of technologies into their businesses. He thought that the information technology industry would be services led, not technology led, in the future. He concluded that IBM should rededicate itself to being market driven.

As we pointed out earlier in this chapter, segmentation is a fundamental exercise which must be decided at the most senior level of the company. The starting point or framework for segmentation is the company's basic orientation, what Treacy and Wiersema called "value disciplines." For a market-driven or "customer intimate" company, segmentation starts with customers and how to satisfy them. For a product-driven or "product leadership" company, segmentation starts with products and how to drive those into the market.

RTM has been used successfully by both product-driven and market-driven companies. This is easiest to see in the context of the changes that occurred at IBM during its turnaround.

IBM's Turnaround

When Gerstner concluded that IBM should rededicate itself to being market-driven, he demanded that IBM executives work together to reestablish IBM's mission as a customer-focused provider of computing solutions. He told his direct reports to document their discussions with customers in their regular monthly reports. The direction that he gave to his direct reports spread rapidly throughout the company and had an enormous impact on IBM's culture and processes.

Another Gerstner initiative was establishing a "managing director" for each of IBM's top 50 customers, whose role was to advance the customer's needs throughout IBM. This approach placed executives responsible for key customers at an equal level to executives responsible for product development, manufacturing, marketing, finance, etc.

IBM reorganized into a matrix management structure with a general manager for each customer industry (banking, insurance, manufacturing, government, etc.). The other dimension of the matrix was IBM's product and service lines. The net result was that the general manager for the banking industry, for example, could choose from a full range of products – from PCs to mid-range computers to mainframes, with many different types of software and services – to assemble offers specifically for banking customers. If he needed something that IBM did not produce, he could go outside the company for it.

At the same time, if the general manager for communication software products, for example, wanted to pursue opportunities in different industries, she could work with the general managers of those industries to prioritize opportunities and develop routes that were customized to fit each targeted industry. If she needed something that the industry executives could not provide, she could go outside the company to establish relationships with other firms to provide it. This included products and services that IBM did not have, and also distribution channels that IBM did not have.

Gerstner's services-led strategy worked well for large companies. They needed (and still need) services to help them deal with the enormous complexity of their existing IT infrastructure and business operations. IBM's services division was a good fit for Gerstner's strategy because it was already the number one provider of information technology services to large companies.

However, Gerstner's services-led strategy was difficult to implement for the fastest growing segment in the IT industry, small and mid-sized companies. Unfortunately, IBM's direct salesforce was too costly to sell IBM's products and services to small and mid-sized companies. An internal study concluded that IBM's selling, general, and administrative expenses (SG&A) had to be reduced by 25% in order to restore profitability. This was not achievable if the direct salesforce was the only way to close sales.

Ned Lautenbach, IBM's Senior Vice President of Worldwide Sales and Services, who reported directly to Gerstner, asked his team for their ideas for quickly transforming IBM to make more use of cost-effective direct marketing, call centers, and indirect distribution channels, instead of relying on the more-costly direct salesforce. From several proposals, Lautenbach chose RTM, which had been developed and piloted in IBM Europe.

Lautenbach fast-tracked the roll-out of RTM across all of IBM's operating divisions and geographies worldwide. RTM began as a way to use lower-cost resources to reach small and mid-sized businesses, but it quickly spread to IBM organizations that focused on large companies as well, because it enabled every route to be optimized. RTM was adopted by the general managers of each customer industry, and by the general managers of each product and service division, as well as the functional areas of marketing, sales, distribution, and customer service.

RTM contributed directly to IBM's turnaround by enabling marketing, sales, and brand managers to tailor go-to-market plans for each product or service, and each market segment, by objectively choosing the mix of internal and external resources that maximized sales and profit. With RTM, IBM reduced SG&A by the desired amount, 25%, while growing sales.

IBM's revenue increased 12% year-over-year in 1995, the first year that the company used RTM, exceeding the previous high set in 1990, which was just before the 3 years of losses. In 1997, 2 years after rolling-out RTM company-wide, IBM's profit exceeded the previous profit peak of $6 billion, also set in 1990. IBM has used RTM continuously since 1995, and has published a summary of the company's "Internal Routes-to-Market" and "Business Partners Routes-to-Market" in IBM's annual report each year.

The combination of Gerstner's services-led strategy for large companies and Lautenbach's reengineering of IBM's go-to-market model restored IBM to profitability and a strong competitive position. Consultant Michael Hammer, author of *Re-engineering the Corporation*, said in 2005 that IBM's turnaround was "the single greatest turnaround in modern business history."

Summary

The framework for segmentation is the company's basic strategy for creating value. Market segmentation is a fundamental exercise which must be decided at the most senior level of the company.

Segmentation is an important step in building routes to market because it enables management to focus resources to best meet the company's business objectives. There are many ways to segment a market: by company size, geography, industry structure, customer attitudes, etc. When product segmentation is integrated with customer segmentation, every segment will have the two pieces of data needed for designing effective routes:

1. The products that are appropriate for, or targeted to, those customers, and how those products compare to the competition.
2. The demographic, psychographic, and/or behavioral characteristics of the customers in the segment.

RTM can help product-driven companies develop a customer focus and make the right decisions about which customers to pursue and how to succeed with them. RTM can help market-driven companies optimize their customer-facing resources (marketing, sales, and services) to best achieve their goals.

Chapter 4
Define Whole Solutions

This chapter discusses the customer ecosystem and explains how to define whole solutions. The customer ecosystem is the collection of people and organizations that influence the decision-makers; provide information, products, or services related to the purchase decision; make the decision; or use the product or service.

A whole solution is the minimum set of products and services necessary for the target customer to completely satisfy his or her compelling reason to buy. Understanding the customer ecosystem is critical for defining whole solutions that satisfy the multiple stakeholders within most business-to-business (B2B) and many business-to-consumer (B2C) markets.

Who Is the Customer?

Ask the members of a company's management team: who is the customer?

This question is not as commonplace as one would think. In fact, different departments communicate with different people in the customer's organization. This is certainly true for business-to-business markets, but it is often the case for consumer markets when products or services are sold to families, such as groceries, clothing, vacation destinations, and mobile telephone services.

To the logistics department, "customers" are the people to whom products are shipped, such as wholesalers, retailers, or other distribution channels. Confusion between external channels and end-user customers is quite common, but their needs and interests are basically different.

The product development department worries about the end-user. The sales department is focused on the person who makes the purchase decision, usually a different person than the end-user, with different needs and issues. The accounting department sends invoices and follows up with the person who pays the bills. Sales management wants to build a relationship with the customer's executives.

Misunderstandings often occur when the managers of these functions meet because each one has his own vision of the "customer."

P. Raulerson et al., *Building Routes to Customers*, DOI: 10.1007/978-0-387-79951-3_4,
© 2009 Peter Raulerson, Jean-Claude Malraison and Antoine Leboyer

Customer satisfaction surveys produce wildly different results depending on which list of "customers" were sent the survey – the list of trade partners from logistics, purchase decision-makers from sales, or invoice payers from accounting.

Generally speaking, the less one meets with customers, the more one talks about them without naming them. This is why a good response for a general manager is to ask people to name the customer when they talk about "a customer," to establish the origin of the information and the context. This can avoid the accident of assigning to the "customer" opinions which were never expressed by the customer.

Because of the multiplicity of customer contacts, answering the following questions is important:

- Who will use the product or service?
- Who will buy the product or service?
- Who will make the decision to buy the product or service?
- Where will the product or service be bought?
- Who will need information before, during, or after buying the product or service?
- To whom will the product or service be delivered, and who will deliver it?
- Who will be invoiced for the product or service, and who will provide the invoice?
- Who will request or receive service after the product or service is delivered?

Let us consider the example of telephone headsets used in call centers:

- The user is the call center agent. However, the agent does not carry out the acquisition of the headset. That is the role of the purchasing department. But the agent's needs and satisfaction are taken into account, perhaps through a formal representative (if the agents are unionized).
- The decision concerning the model of the headset to buy, and any associated options, is made by the operations manager in collaboration with the IT department, after analyzing the agents' assignments and needs, and possibly conducting evaluation tests. The human resources manager may have a voice in the decision due to health, safety, or workplace issues.
- Information on headset products, compatibility with telephone systems, and demonstration or evaluation equipment, are needed by the IT department. Sometimes the information can be provided by telephone installers, but mainly it is provided by salespeople who specialize in headsets or telephony equipment (employed by the retailer or possibly by the manufacturer).
- The headsets will ultimately be delivered and installed at each agent's telephone. An interim delivery may be made to the IT department which then installs them for the agents. Alternatively, the interim delivery may go to the telephone installer, who then installs them for the agents. In either case, the headsets come from a retailer or the telephone installer (if the installer sold the headsets). It is possible that a wholesaler "drop shipped" the headsets directly to the call center from his warehouse instead of shipping them to the retailer or installer's facility.

- The invoice will be sent to the accounts payable department or possibly the IT department, from the retailer or the telephone installer (if the installer sold the headsets).
- An individual agent who runs into a problem with his or her headset will be helped by the IT department, which keeps spare headsets on hand for this purpose. In turn, the IT department will get service from the retailer or installer (if the installer sold the headsets) and the manufacturer, typically by returning malfunctioning headsets for replacement under warranty.

All these people contribute to the commonplace decision to buy headsets for users. Each participant at various stages of selling and servicing the headset is a "customer" of the vendor – call center agent, operations manager, IT staff, purchasing agent, retailer, installer, wholesaler.

The vendor's communications must be defined, adapted, and targeted appropriately to these people, and the vendor must understand their interactions.

Figure 4.1 illustrates the concept of the ecosystem of people who participate in, provide information or products or services for, or influence purchase decisions.

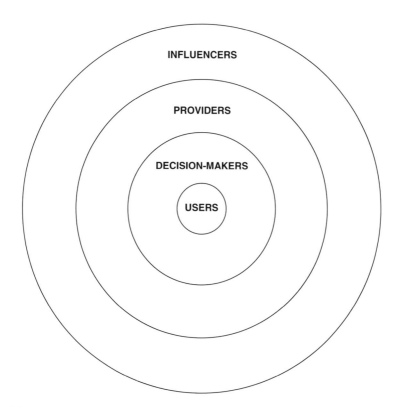

Fig. 4.1 The customer ecosystem

The Ecosystem of Call Centers

Let us continue with the example of selling telephone headsets to call centers. Figure 4.2 diagrams this ecosystem and reveals the important role that the Purchasing Manager, Operations Manager, IT Manager, Human Resources Manager, and Facilities Manager may have in making the decision. Whether all of these people participate in making the decision will vary from company to company. The purchase order will be prepared by someone who reports to the Purchasing Manager. The users – call center agents – are managed by the Operations Manager, who is sometimes known as the Call Center Manager. The IT Manager (or someone reporting to the IT Manager) is responsible for the call center's telephone systems, to which the headsets will be connected. In some companies, IT and telephony products are chosen by the IT organization, but in other organizations, they play an advisory role. Headsets can have a significant impact on hygiene, safety, and ergonomic issues. Some companies assign these to the Human Resources

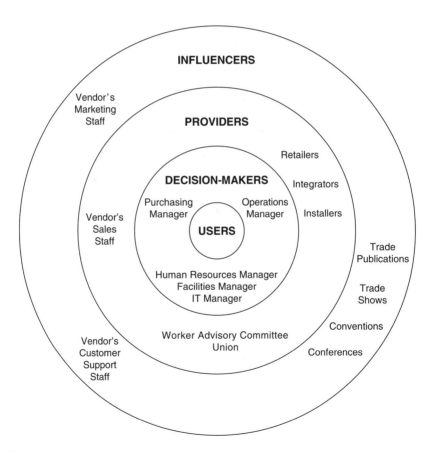

Fig. 4.2 The call center ecosystem for headset customers

Manager and other companies, the Facilities Manager, so both are positioned on the ecosystem chart.

The justification for purchasing headsets might be based on those issues, or it might be based on enabling "personal" or "confidential" conversations with customers, which requires good sound quality and elimination of background noise and distracting hubbub.

Putting forward these arguments is the role of the trade press and also of conferences and trade shows in the call center industry. These media are influencers of decisions to purchase headsets for call centers. Headsets are now perceived to be essential ergonomic accessories for all employees who spend more than 2 hours per day on the telephone. More and more companies now provide new employees with a badge, a PC, a mobile phone, and a headset for the office phone.

Knowing the ecosystem of the headset customer in the call center segment enables the manufacturer to focus resources where they are needed.

The sale of applications software is much more complex than headsets because there are more people who are involved:

- the manufacturer of the computer that the software will run on,
- various suppliers of software used in the customer's organization, that may need to be connected to (or integrated with) the applications software in some way,
- the integrator (the company that will integrate the applications software with the company's other systems and applications),
- trainers,
- installers,
- management,
- the users of the applications software.

The software vendor must treat all of these people as "customers." They form an integral part of the ecosystem. They will need different information and messages about the application software, depending on their role:

- The user wants a solution to his or her need.
- The integrator wishes an easy installation which requires only a minimum technical investment as well as readily available technical support.
- The trainers want good documentation and support.
- The retailer wants to maximize his margin, and to minimize any pressure on prices.

The best product will not be the most successful if the ecosystem is not well understood.

The concept of ecosystem applies in consumer markets as well business-to-business markets. In both cases, it is necessary to identify all of the people who will participate in the purchase decision and the implementation (or consumption) of the product or service. The person who will make the decision to purchase a product or service is not necessarily the person who will use it.

Products are designed for users. Users are at the center of market segments. Ecosystems identify the people who participate in the purchase decision: influencers, providers, decision-makers, and, finally, users. Each category of participant looks at the product differently and is interested in different attributes of the product. Communication campaigns must direct different messages to each category.

What Is a Whole Solution?

In *Crossing the Chasm*, Geoffrey Moore defined the "whole product" as the minimum set of products and services necessary for the target customer to completely satisfy his or her compelling reason to buy. We prefer the term "whole solution" because it conveys the idea of solving the customer's problem. Moore observed that many customers would not (or could not) buy a product without the additional products and services that they needed in order to use it successfully, like installation or training (if the product is a business computer system), or a license and fuel (if the product is an automobile).

The "whole solution" phrase also resonates with Clayton Christensen's idea in *The Innovator's Solution* that customers (people and companies) have "jobs" that arise regularly and need to get done, and for which they look around for a product or service that they can "hire" to get the job done. Christensen recommends that vendors target their products and services at the circumstances in which customers find themselves, rather than at the customers themselves, because the functional, emotional, and social dimensions of the jobs that the customers need to get done constitute the circumstances in which they buy. In other words, sell products as solutions to customers' problems.

In Moore's definition of "whole solution" and Christensen's "hire to get the job done" model, there are two dimensions that the vendor needs to understand thoroughly in order to beat the competition:

1. Who is the customer? As we saw earlier in this chapter, there are potentially several groups of people who have some voice in a purchase decision. Each person may prioritize the requirements for the solution differently, or may rate the features and benefits of a proposed solution differently. In Christensen's model, different decision-makers have different jobs to do. In a call center, the purchasing manager is "hiring" headsets to meet specifications and cost constraints, while the operations manager is more concerned about minimizing disruptions in the workplace, and so on. The circumstances of each participant in the purchase decision include their responsibilities, personal preferences, and emotional "hot buttons."
2. What will compel the customer to buy one solution over another? To a computer geek, the microprocessor and the operating system are the two chambers of the heart of a personal computer, the most important things to him. To a consumer who is not a geek, the attractiveness of the screen and the feel of the keyboard are far more important than the microprocessor and operating system – she would say "obviously more important." If both customers bought exactly the

same personal computer, then it would seem that the whole solution was the same in both cases. But they did not buy the same whole solution – the geek was compelled to buy the personal computer because of its microprocessor and operating system, and the non-geek because of its screen and keyboard. The geek was hiring the computer to do a job, and the consumer was hiring the same computer to do a different job.

To sell a product or service to a customer, it is critical to understand the first dimension – who influences the decision-makers; provides information, products, or services related to the purchase decision; makes the decision; or uses the product or service. It is equally critical to understand the second dimension – the circumstances of each person who participates in the purchase decision: the jobs they are hiring the product or service for, the needs or wants they are trying to satisfy.

The first step in defining a whole solution is to establish both of these dimensions, with a list of the participants in making the purchase decision (dimension one) and the jobs, needs, and wants they have (dimension two). The second step in defining a whole solution is to list the elements or components of a potential solution that will (1) do the jobs and satisfy the needs and wants of the participants in making the purchase decision, and (2) be perceived by the participants as important to their role in the decision-making. The latter are often called "decision criteria" or "customer preferences" or "purchase hot buttons."

In the example of call center headset purchases, the purchasing manager, operations manager, and installers all need to know the delivery date for the headsets because that could potentially interfere with a high-priority call center campaign. In fact, the purchase might be awarded to the vendor who can schedule delivery for the customer's preferred delivery date, if all other things are equal between competing vendors.

Figure 4.3 illustrates the idea that two different whole solutions can be constructed for the same product. The large left circle represents a hotel room for vacation travelers.

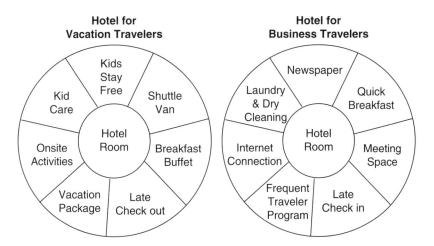

Fig. 4.3 Two different whole solutions constructed from the same generic product

The small circle in the center of the hotel room for vacation travelers represents an ordinary hotel room that is identical to the hotel room in the small circle in the center of the hotel room for business travelers on the right of Fig. 4.3.

The small circles represent the vendor's product – a generic hotel room. The large circles represent two different whole solutions that can be created by adding different products and services to the same generic product.

Figure 4.4 is a template for a whole solution for a computer product or service. The center circle in the diagram is the vendor's product or service, and the larger circle adds other components that the customer needs in order to buy the product. The vendor's basic product could be a microprocessor or a display (screen), or a computer program, or even a cable or an antistatic tissue for cleaning the display.

To fill in the template, one simply writes a list of components that the target customer needs, along with the criteria and preferences the customer has. If these are unknown, then it is time to do market research, either by reviewing research already available to the vendor, buying a report based on research conducted for multiple vendors, or doing primary research specifically for this purpose.

This is not as simple an exercise as it might seem. Any list of product components and customer criteria or preferences can quickly become the "gospel" – something regarded as true and to be believed without question. The list must be tested by asking (or observing) target customers and the other people who have a stake in the accuracy of the list, such as the vendor's ad agency and distribution partners, whether they would buy the whole solution, how important each component is to them, what alternatives can they think of that would also meet their needs, and whether they would respond differently under different circumstances.

Even after testing the list of components, it is important to challenge the accuracy of the list again and again from different perspectives and with different testing

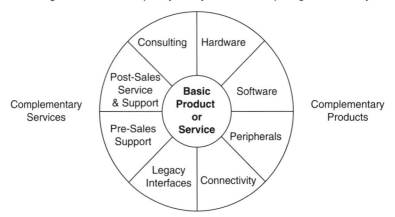

The Whole Solution for a B2B Computer Systems Customer

The Whole Solution is the minimum set of products and services necessary for the target customer to completely satisfy his or her compelling reason to buy.

Fig. 4.4 Template for a whole solution for a computer product or service

strategies, because the world is not static, people change, new alternatives appear, and the vendor's best opportunities may shift to other market segments.

The good news is that testing the list of components, criteria, and preferences can be done automatically and continuously on a Web site, producing an ongoing stream of test results. This assumes that the target customers can access the Web site that is running the test, and that their actions on the Web site are representative of their actual purchase actions in real life. These two conditions are true for a very large number of customers and products or services in developed countries, and becoming more feasible in under-developed countries due to their rapid adoption of mobile phones.

The methodology for conducting the Web site testing can be described simply, and there are several products and services available that can be used to set up and run the tests and analyze the results without understanding the mechanism. Basically, the methodology requires that target customers visit a webpage that gives them a choice between one component on the list or another, alternative component. The choices that the customers make are recorded and analyzed. The most-chosen components are the ones the vendor should promote and deliver. More sophisticated analysis is needed to resolve dependencies between different components.

The mechanism can be an online survey, but more accurate results are attainable when the choices are actual purchases, or a sequence of choices made by customers that lead to a purchase. For example, let us look at testing online a list of whole solution components, criteria, and preferences for product X (it does not matter what the product is in this example).

The product manager and marketing manager responsible for product X have constructed a list with five different components, four criteria, and three preferences, which totals 60 ($=5 \times 4 \times 3$) different combinations of one choice from each of these three categories. The question is: which of these combinations sells product X best? It is important to know the answer to this question before buying expensive print advertising space, because the top-selling combination should be featured in the ads, which cannot be changed after the print publication has been mailed to subscribers.

To conduct the test, the marketing manager arranges for the e-mail newsletter sent to prospects to contain the introduction to an article, but not the entire article. When someone reads the introduction to an article in the e-mail newsletter, and is interested enough to read more, he or she clicks through to a webpage that automatically records the unique ID of that prospect as a subscriber to the newsletter. Tracking each user who clicks through to the webpage from the newsletter enables the testing software to accumulate results for each newsletter recipient that show the vendor's marketing and sales people what the recipient looked at on the vendor's Web site, in what order, and for how long (which is called the visitor's history).

This tracking data can be analyzed across all people who visit the vendor's Web site, whether they start from the vendor's newsletter, or an article in an online publication, a partner's Web site, an ad or search result, and many other sources. Each person clicking through to a landing page will see different information generated dynamically to randomly present one of the 60 different combinations. All of the pages give the visitor choices for where to click next. Visitors who click on positive links ("buy now," "tell me more," "sign up for free trial," "register for a webinar," "post a question," etc.), are in effect voting for the combination on that page. Visitors who click on negative links ("remove me from your newsletter subscriber list") or who leave the page without clicking on any links, are in effect voting against the combination on that page.

With this kind of testing, if enough people participate in the test, the results can be accurate enough to act on – put the highest clicked-on product components, customer criteria, and preferences into the product and market it that way. The net result will be increased sales, more sales than the other combinations would produce.

In this way, off-line marketing and sales actions – such as ads in print magazines, or presentations made face-to-face with prospects, or price points, or terms and conditions included with product quotations – can all be tested online, where the testing is quick and inexpensive.

Figure 4.5 presents a whole solution for a sports fan, someone who spends money to watch sporting events. The sport in this case is played in a stadium. The vendor is the team owner.

Some of the complementary products and services shown in the perimeter of the larger circle are sold to the fan (a ticket for a seat in the stadium, food and drink at the stadium, sports memorabilia). The other complementary products and services are provided at no charge to the fan, but may generate advertising revenues, such as ads on the scoreboard. There may be promotional or charity opportunities with the "Meet Players" option: a local charity could hold a fund-raising auction or other participatory event (such as a golf tournament), in which players from the team participate, donating their time, and attracting fans to participate in the event.

Innovations in whole solutions can take many forms. Several US sports teams have discovered that they can sell the least-attractive seats in their stadiums (which

The Whole Solution for a Sports Fan

The Whole Solution is the minimum set of products and services necessary for
the target customer to completely satisfy his or her compelling reason to buy.

Fig. 4.5 Whole solution for a sports fan

usually go unsold in many games, even at very low prices) by offering a combination ticket that bundles the seat with unlimited food from a stadium restaurant at a fixed price. The previously unsellable seats have been fully sold, at a very attractive profit, to young men who apparently find it irresistible to spend a lot of money to overeat along with their peers while watching a game that they would not have attended otherwise. Perhaps it is the allure of participating in a public eating contest while watching the game.

Two of the sports clubs that have had a lot of success with this kind of combination ticket, the Boston Red Sox baseball team and the New England Patriots football team, have used the Web site-based testing methodology described above to determine the optimal pricing and combination of the components for the whole solution (which menu items to offer in unlimited quantities for a fixed price, which seats to bundle into the package, etc.), along with the promotional information. They have found that dynamically setting the pricing, components, criteria, and preferences leading up to the start time for the game (and even after the start time), enables them to maximize profit. This is the power of defining the perfect whole solution for a target customer: the vendor can make much more money by combining things that, when sold separately, made only a little money.

Summary

Vendors make contact, directly or indirectly, with multiple people in the customer's organization, and with people in other companies who are involved with the customer's organization. It is not always clear what their roles are, nor how they could impact the vendor's business. It is important to resolve this in order to direct the right communication or action to the proper person. The customer ecosystem is an excellent model for understanding the collection of people and organizations that influence the decision-makers; provide information, products, or services related to the purchase decision; make the decision; or use the product or service.

A whole solution is the minimum set of products and services necessary for the target customer to completely satisfy his or her compelling reason to buy. Understanding the customer ecosystem is critical for defining whole solutions that satisfy the multiple stakeholders within most B2B and many B2C markets. The vendor needs to understand two dimensions thoroughly in order to beat the competition:

1. Who is the customer? That is, what is the customer ecosystem?
2. What will compel the customer to buy one solution over another? That is, what is the whole solution for that customer?

The concept of a basic product surrounded by complementary products and services is a good model for the whole solution. Each element of a whole solution can be evaluated for its contribution to compelling the customer to buy the whole solution.

Chapter 5
RTM Life Cycle

This chapter explains the RTM Life Cycle at the level of detail needed by the person who is in charge of implementing RTM in your company, or who will be your internal RTM expert. Everyone else should read this chapter quickly, not deeply, to become familiar with the RTM Life Cycle concepts. This chapter starts by recapping the overview in Chap. 1 about the adoption of innovation and the phases of the RTM Life Cycle. This is followed by an explanation of disruptive versus non-disruptive innovation. Then detailed guidance is provided for understanding the customers in each of the four phases of the RTM Life Cycle, and for designing effective and efficient routes for each phase. Also covered is how to transition smoothly from phase to phase. At the end of the chapter there is an extensive discussion of the ways that vendors deal with commoditization in the last phase of the RTM Life Cycle. On the book's Web site, www.RoutesToCustomers.com, you will find free diagnostic tools for determining which phase of the RTM Life Cycle your product or service is in.

The Adoption of Innovation

People react differently to innovation. A few people are enthusiastic about buying an innovative product or service as soon as it is available. Others want to wait until the product or service has been proven. The adoption of innovative products and services proceeds over time through a sequence of customer groups distinguished by their reactions to innovation. Everett Rogers conducted extensive research that laid the foundation for understanding how innovations spread through society in his book *Diffusion of Innovations,* first published in 1962 and most recently updated in 2003. Geoffrey Moore drew from Rogers' work to show that marketing strategies for technology products depend on the customers' attitudes about adopting the innovation in those products in his books, *Crossing the Chasm* (published in 1991), *Inside the Tornado* (1995), and *Dealing with Darwin* (2005).

In Rogers' and Moore's model, shown in Fig. 5.1, the first people to adopt an innovation are enthusiasts whose attitude about the innovation Moore summed up as "Just try it!" Innovations must first be adopted by enthusiasts before they can spread to the next group, visionaries, whose attitude about the innovation is "Get

P. Raulerson et al., *Building Routes to Customers*, DOI: 10.1007/978-0-387-79951-3_5,

ahead of the herd!!," that is, get the advantage provided by the innovation before anyone else. Visionaries look to enthusiasts to identify innovations that are worthy of their consideration and adoption. The same influence pattern applies to each successive group: from visionaries to pragmatists, then to conservatives, and finally to skeptics. People within a group also influence adoption by other members of their group.

The transition from one group of like-minded adopters to the next group forces vendors to adjust their routes-to-market to fit the buying behavior of each successive group, resulting in four distinct phases in the life cycle of a route: Introduction, Solution, Distribution, and Commodity, as shown in Fig. 5.2. Each of these phases, along with Rogers' and Moore's terminology, is discussed in detail later in this chapter.

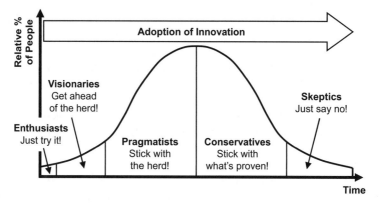

Fig. 5.1 Adoption of innovation over time

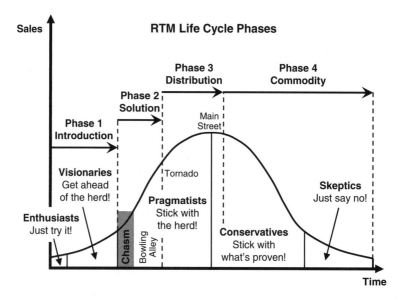

Fig. 5.2 RTM Life Cycle phases

Innovation is widely seen as the solution to the competitive challenges that companies face in today's globalized, commoditized, rapidly changing marketplace. Many executives think that a steady stream of innovative products and services, or just one revolutionary innovation that hits the jackpot, is needed to drive their company's revenue and profit growth into the foreseeable future.

Innovation is indisputably important. Understanding how to successfully market and sell innovative products and services throughout their entire life cycle – from the time they were launched, to the time they are no longer offered for sale – is obviously critical to maximizing the revenue and profit from these products and services.

The challenge is that people respond to innovations in different ways. According to Rogers, on average, only 2.5% of the population are so enthusiastic about innovations that they rush to buy innovative new products or services as soon as they are available. Over 97% of people hold off their purchases of innovative products and services until other events or conditions occur. Making these events and conditions occur successfully is one of the keys to maximizing revenue and profit.

Disruptive Versus Non-Disruptive Innovation

Most new products are "new" because they provide a small, incremental change from a previous product or from competitive products. These changes could be in physical attributes (size or weight), performance (speed, power, energy consumption), process (simplification, time, quality), usage (ease of use, ease of learning) or cost (purchase or operating cost), or any combination of these, such as price/performance.

In many companies, the product development organization dedicates most of its resources to making incremental changes to existing products to produce new products. However, the new products do not significantly change the way that customers view the product.

Small, incremental changes are continuous innovations in the sense that there is a strong degree of continuity with the previous product.

Very few "new" products or services are new because they have a discontinuous (disruptive) innovation. Such an innovation produces a significant improvement in physical attributes, performance, process, usage, or cost. These advantages open new markets to the product or service that competing products are unable to address.

What sets discontinuous innovations apart is that the innovation disrupts both strategy and behavior for the vendor and the customer. When a product or service that incorporates a discontinuous innovation is first introduced, it can be a "game changer" that alters customers' perceptions of their priorities and also of competing products and services. The discontinuous innovation "tilts the playing field" to the disadvantage of products that lack that innovation.

The key to distinguishing between continuous and discontinuous innovation is to determine if the innovation causes a small jump versus a "quantum leap," or

Table 5.1 Disruptive versus non-disruptive innovations in the automobile industry

Disruptive Innovations	Non-disruptive Innovations
The first automobile, invented by Nicolas Joseph Cugnot of France in 1769. Powered by a steam engine, it proved that a horseless, self-propelled vehicle was feasible. It began the disruption of horse-drawn vehicular transportation which was originally invented in pre-historic times.	New, more elegant and comfortable horse-drawn carriages in 1769. Production of horse-drawn carriages, buggy whips and related products and services peaked around 1900. None of the manufacturers of horse-drawn carriages became a successful automobile manufacturer.
The first gasoline-powered automobile, invented by Gottlieb Daimler of Germany in 1885. It could carry significantly more goods farther and faster than steam-powered vehicles, and was much easier to maintain and operate. It disrupted the market for automobiles powered by steam and other energy sources.	New models of steam-powered automobiles in 1885, available from dozens of manufacturers. Production of steam-powered automobiles peaked in 1909. The remaining manufacturers of steam-powered automobiles went out of business shortly after that.
The first moving assembly line for manufacturing automobiles, put into practice by Henry Ford in 1908. It opened the mass market for automobiles, and revolutionized manufacturing as well as transportation. It disrupted the manufacture of automobiles one-at-a-time, and accelerated the disruption of other forms of transportation such as trains and horse-drawn vehicles.	New models of automobiles manufactured one-at-a-time by nearly 100 different companies in the US and Europe in 1908. Manufacturing automobiles one-at-a-time was displaced by assembly line production in 1920. Automobile manufacturers that did not embrace the assembly line model went out of business or became limited to niche markets.

business-as-usual versus a "paradigm shift," or is a "me-too" product versus a "breakthrough." A tell-tale clue is whether customers are buying competing products or services that include the same innovation. If they are, then the innovation did not make the product or service unique.

If the discontinuous innovation wins favor with enough customers, it can disrupt an established product category as customers flock to the new product and stop buying the products in the old category. Discontinuous innovations form the basis for a new category of products. That in turn provides an opportunity for new companies to emerge and take the lead in the new category, or for existing companies to jump ahead of competitors. Table 5.1 gives some examples of disruptive and non-disruptive products and services in the automobile industry.

Driving the Adoption of Innovative Products and Services

The bell-shaped curve in Figs. 5.1 and 5.2 graphs the sizes of the five groups of adopters. According to Rogers, approximately 2.5% of the population are enthusiasts, 13.5% are visionaries, 34% are pragmatists, 34% are conservatives, and 16% are skeptics. We have confirmed these percentages (plus or minus a few percentage points) in several broad-based market research surveys in North America, Europe, and Asia, and in thousands of interviews of people just after they have adopted an innovation.

In Fig. 5.2, the Chasm between visionaries and pragmatists, as defined by Moore, is the period in which adoption often stalls. Visionaries have adopted as much of the innovation as they need and are no longer interested in more of it. Pragmatists, with their stick-with-the-herd mentality, are not yet convinced that it is safe to adopt the innovation. Moore pointed out that the only reliable way for the innovation to cross the chasm is to target a niche market composed of pragmatists who share a common problem for which there is no known solution. These pragmatists unite to adopt the innovation if, and only if, it is packaged as a whole solution to their problem.

Moore extended his crossing-the-chasm analysis to define his Technology Adoption Life Cycle model. He used the expression "knocking over a bowling pin" for when an innovation crosses the chasm and gets adopted by a niche market of pragmatists. He referred to other pragmatists as the "Bowling Alley" in which each niche of pragmatists waited until a whole solution, based on the innovation, was prepared for them. He called the rapid adoption that occurs as more and more pragmatists come on board, the "Tornado." The period in which the rate of adoption flattens out at the transition from pragmatists to conservatives is "Main Street."

When a vendor first introduces a disruptively innovative product or service, it enters the market in phase 1 (see Fig. 5.2). Many vendors modify their innovative products and services in phase 1, as they try to find the combination of features and attributes that deliver the "breakthrough" they believed that the innovation would provide. These modified products or services are variations or derivatives of the first version of the product or service. They enter the market in phase 1, but, in many cases, simply continue the progression of the first product through phase 1 instead of restarting at the beginning of phase 1. This happens because the variations and derivatives provide only minor, non-disruptive changes to the original product or service, while continuing to include the disruptive innovation of the original.

After a disruptively innovative product or service progresses into later phases of the RTM Life Cycle, vendors introduce "new and improved" versions of them. Vendors are motivated to bring out successor products that continue to leverage the disruptive innovation of the original product while at the same time improving on the original product's competitiveness, or expanding the market beyond the original product.

The Computer Industry: A Series of Disruptive Innovations

The history of the computer industry is the story of disruptive innovations establishing new product categories in which new companies became dominant, but then were threatened by other companies that exploited later disruptive innovations.

In the 1970s, minicomputers disrupted mainframes because they could do departmental tasks at much lower costs, enabling departmental decision-makers and smaller companies to buy their own computers. This allowed Digital Equipment Corporation (the leader in minicomputers) to establish and dominate a new category, not IBM (the leader in mainframes).

In the 1980s, personal computers disrupted minicomputers because users could do individual tasks independently instead of sharing a departmental computer. This allowed the personal computer category to emerge and become the largest segment in the computer industry, evolving from hobbyists to mainstream customers who made Microsoft and Intel the dominant vendors in the category, along with other companies allied with them, not Digital Equipment (the leader in minicomputers).

In the late 1990s, networking computers together via the Internet disrupted every category of standalone computers because users could communicate instead of just compute. This allowed AOL, Netscape, Cisco, and other Internet-centric vendors to gain a share of customers' budgets, effectively redirecting purchase dollars away from standalone computers. As a late entrant, Microsoft captured a small share of the Internet category by giving its Internet product away free in order to defeat Netscape.

One of the most recent disruptions is search engines. People search for every kind of information on the Internet because they believe that everything is there somewhere. Google has innovated its search engine to outperform competitors from both the end-user's (the searcher's) point of view and also the advertiser's point of view. Google's revenue, profits, and market capitalization indicate its dominance of this category, far outdistancing their competitors, which today (as this is written) are Yahoo, Microsoft, and AOL.

The holy grail for technology companies is innovation that disrupts established products and markets. With the holy grail in hand, a technology company tries to win followers (customers) in order to establish, grow, and dominate a new market.

Markets that grow via continuous innovations expand slowly, approximately at the rate of growth of their entire industry. Markets that are created with a discontinuous innovation grow substantially faster for several years, ranging from twice to ten times higher growth rate than the overall industry. The dominant vendor in a market that was launched with a discontinuous innovation, captures a disproportionate share of the profits in that market, fueling their expansion into other markets.

IBM used mainframe profits to expand into every other market in the computer industry. None of IBM's mainframe competitors survived and did that. Digital Equipment used minicomputer profits to expand into PCs, networking, and services, but was acquired by the then-dominant PC manufacturer (Compaq). Only one of Digital's minicomputer competitors survived, and that is Hewlett-Packard, which used profits from dominating the desktop printer market to prop up its computer business before acquiring Compaq.

Microsoft and Intel used PC profits to fund forays into other markets such as networking, video games, personal digital assistants, cable TV systems, and Internet advertising. Microsoft and Intel achieved modest success in these markets while competitors with disruptive innovations, such as Cisco, Nintendo, Palm, Research in Motion (Blackberry), and Google, came to dominate them.

Disruptive Innovations in Every Industry

Disruptive innovations are at the heart of every fast-growing market sector in the world today, not just in the technology industry. Agriculture, banking, clothing, communications, construction, energy, entertainment, food, health care, insurance, publishing, raw materials, retailing, transportation, and every other business sector, even politics, are all witnessing the impact of disruptive innovations on their markets.

The disruption in these sectors is not always caused by new technology. The disruption can be caused by business model innovation, capital investment innovation, labor innovation, supply chain or distribution chain innovation, instead of (or in addition to) technology innovation.

Phases of the RTM Life Cycle

There are several things that a vendor must do to succeed in phase 1 of the RTM Life Cycle. If the vendor's product or service fails to win customers in phase 1, it will have a short life, and the vendor will lose money on it. To extend the life of the product or service, and to maximize the number of people who buy it (which results in maximizing revenue and profit), the vendor must succeed in phase 1 and then successfully cross the chasm into phase 2 and accomplish the transitions to phases 3 and 4.

For each of the four phases of the RTM Life Cycle, the vendor must perform two tasks:

1. Operate routes to the customers in the current phase.
2. Prepare routes for the next phase.

The second task often requires recruiting, training, supporting, and managing new resources before the next phase starts, because it can take many weeks or months to do this. If vendors wait until the end of the current phase to begin recruiting resources for the next phase, they will not have enough time to find, engage, train, and ramp up those resources so that they are productive at the start of the next phase. This is particularly true when the resources are any of the following types of businesses:

- Specialized retailers who must master the vendor's technology in order to sell, install, and support it. They normally have a store where customers can see and buy vendors' products. This category includes "specialized retailers" in the consumer electronics industry, and "resellers" or "dealers" in the computer industry. It also includes telecommunications companies which integrate the vendor's technology into their infrastructure and resell it as a product or service to the customer.
- Software development companies, value-added resellers, systems integrators, consultants, and other professional services firms which provide the products and services that constitute (along with the vendor's product or service) the

"whole solution" for the customer. These firms are collectively called "solutions providers" in the IT industry, and that is also how we refer to them in this book. They normally do not have a store front.

- Financial, legal, and medical specialists who must study for and pass exams in order to advise customers about the vendor's product or service. These resources are often used on routes for financial services products, investments, legal services, drug prescriptions, medical procedures, and other types of restricted or regulated products or services.

Every route-to-market uses one or more of the four distribution channel structures shown in Fig. 5.3 for the resources engaged in step 3 Close the Sale. A distribution channel structure connects the vendor to the target market segment either directly or through one or more levels of intermediaries which constitute the vendor's indirect distribution channels.

Figure 5.3 diagrams the flow of product shipments from the vendor to each level of different distribution channel structures. In addition to product shipments, each

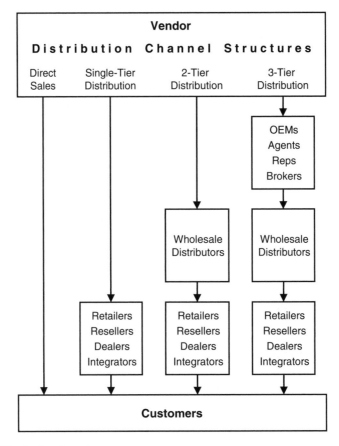

Fig. 5.3 Distribution channel structures

level is normally responsible for recruiting, training, supporting, and managing the companies in the level below it. For example, in Two-Tier Distribution, wholesale distributors are normally responsible for recruiting, training, supporting, and managing the next level down, which are retailers, resellers, dealers, and integrators.

However, some vendors have decoupled one or more of these responsibilities (recruiting, training, supporting, and managing) from the flow of product shipments, so that they can assign those responsibilities to themselves or to companies at other levels of the distribution channel structure. Assigning responsibilities to specific companies in a distribution channel structure (not just to those handling product shipments) can minimize costs, increase communications and agility, speed up recruitment, improve the delivery of training or support, and manage each level more effectively.

For example, some vendors have implemented Partner Relationship Management systems that enable bi-directional communications between the vendor and all channel members (regardless of their level in the distribution channel structure), and also among channel members. These systems enable vendors to distribute leads quickly to appropriate channel members, instead of routing them through intermediate levels in the structure, and to monitor how those channel members follow up on the leads. This has created a feedback loop between the vendor and its channel members for training (coaching), lead nurturing and qualification, and future demand generation campaigns. Enabling channel members to contact and communicate with each other has fostered partnering arrangements between them that have strengthened their competitiveness versus channel firms representing the vendors' competitors.

RTM Life Cycle Phase 1: Introduction

The primary job in RTM Life Cycle phase 1 Introduction is to *introduce* the product or service to the customers who will be the first ones in the market to buy it – enthusiasts and visionaries, as shown in Fig. 5.4. Enthusiasts' response to an innovative product or service is "Just try it!" Visionaries' response is "Get ahead of the herd!," that is, obtain the advantage provided by the innovation before anyone else.

Phase 1 of the life cycle deals with products and services that are "new" because they contain a discontinuous (disruptive) innovation. If a product or service is "new" only because it contains one or more continuous (non-disruptive) innovations, then it is not in phase 1.

It can be very difficult to grasp the concept that only disruptive products are in phase 1 of the life cycle model. Most people automatically think that everything starts at phase 1 or step 1 in a diagram or on a time line, because that seems natural. But the RTM Life Cycle is driven by people's attitudes about innovation. Phase 1 is reserved for products that are truly innovative and therefore radically different from other products in the market, from other solutions to the same problem, from other ways to meet the same need or satisfy the same desire.

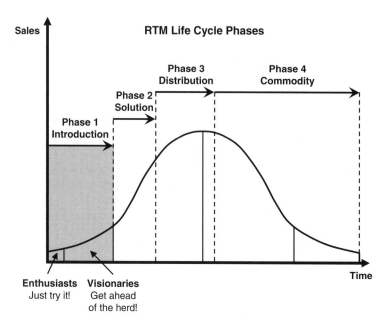

Fig. 5.4 RTM Life Cycle Phase 1 Introduction

Phase 1 is characterized by both excitement and uncertainty in the minds of vendors and customers. No one knows whether the product will work or not, whether the innovation will be valuable or not, whether the innovation is truly disruptive or just a minor change.

At the start of phase 1, the product is not yet known to anyone in the market, unless it has been publicized to people who are on the lookout for new products. The innovation may have been described in a research journal or documented in a patent application. But the innovation has not been offered as part of a product or service before, not in the form or purpose for which it is being offered at this point.

Two groups of customers buy in phase 1: enthusiasts and visionaries. All other customers buy in later phases of the RTM Life Cycle.

Enthusiasts: Just Do It!

Enthusiasts operate on the principle that an innovation is, at it core, superior to what is currently available. Disruptive innovations are much more interesting to enthusiasts than continuous innovations. Enthusiasts seek out innovations, explore them, and share their knowledge with other enthusiasts.

Enthusiasts are interested in innovations because they are new, not because the innovations can be exploited to produce tangible results. They are not interested in gaining a competitive advantage from a disruptive innovation, except to the extent that it gives them something new to explore or talk about.

Enthusiasts are only 2.5% of the total number of customers across all phases of the life cycle for the product. Enthusiasts typically purchase only the minimum number of units to try out an innovative product. The revenue potential among enthusiasts is generally not enough to justify the development of a truly innovative product.

However, without enthusiasts, new innovative products would have no customers at all, and these products would not progress to later phases of the life cycle because the customers at those phases would not have heard any pronouncements from the enthusiasts about the new product.

Enthusiasts are willing to pay to use innovative products. Sometimes they "pay" by investing their time in exploring the product and providing their feedback to the product's developers. If there is a cost for them to buy the product before they can test it, enthusiasts will pay that cost unless it is totally out of line with the cost for other products that perform a comparable function.

"Beta test" (or "beta") software that is truly innovative, is in phase 1, just like any innovative product or service. The decision to end a beta test and release an innovative software product to customers may depend on whether the product has achieved an acceptable level of quality. The more one wants to improve the product, the longer the beta testing period. Conversely, a product that has been insufficiently tested can damage the vendor's reputation for quality. Microsoft, in particular, is very skillful in using the concept of "good enough" when deciding to release beta products to enthusiasts (who tolerate software bugs), while delaying release to general users (who would be very dissatisfied with the same level of quality).

One should not make the mistake of confusing the reactions of enthusiasts with the reactions of other customers who are present in the market in later phases. They have different attitudes and behaviors. Enthusiasts are not representative of the overall market, and cannot be substituted for doing real market research to understand the needs and wants of other customers in the market.

Visionaries: Get Ahead of the Herd!

Visionaries are the second group of customers who buy in phase 1 of the RTM Life Cycle. They see innovations as opportunities to gain an advantage for themselves or their companies. They are motivated to buy products with disruptive innovations because they expect disruptive innovations will give them a significant competitive advantage, which has much more value than the advantage they could get from a continuous innovation. In fact, if visionaries are offered two products, one with a continuous innovation and the other with a discontinuous innovation, they will almost always choose the discontinuous innovation to invest their time and money in, because they expect the return on that investment to be much higher.

Unlike enthusiasts, visionaries are not interested in an innovation by itself. Their interest is in what they can do with the innovation, and they are adept at envisioning how they could use a truly innovative product to their advantage.

Visionaries want to be confident that they can successfully use an innovative product or service before they buy it, but their confidence comes from their ability to envision how it will work for them, not on proof that someone else has used it successfully. Visionaries are willing and able to take an innovative offer and use it without waiting for proof from other customers. In this sense, visionaries take risks that other customers will not take. From the visionaries' point of view, these calculated risks are worth taking in order to obtain the significant competitive advantage that they will gain from the offer.

There are three to five times as many visionaries as there are enthusiasts, about 13.5% of the total number of customers across all phases of the life cycle for the product.

Some visionaries will buy many units of a new product to deploy in their company in order to maximize the advantage they get from it, once they become convinced that the new product does provide an advantage. Note that their "conviction" is critical, not "proof."

Visionaries will also advocate to other decision-makers in their organization that they should buy the new product, but first they need to be acknowledged within their organization as the visionary who achieved a significant advantage with it. Until that acknowledgement (and the reward or satisfaction that accompanies it) occurs, many visionaries will keep the new product a secret so that their rivals in other departments and competitors in other companies do not discover it, thereby eliminating the competitive advantage that they had obtained from being the first to exploit it.

This aspect of the visionary's attitude means that one should view visionaries as though they were rival princes in a kingdom. Within a specific kingdom (such as a company or an industry), only one prince can be the first to buy and exploit a particular product. One must then search other kingdoms to find princes who could be the first in their domain to buy it. After a prince has been recognized by his rivals for obtaining a noteworthy advantage with the product, the other visionary princes in that kingdom will not be interested in the product because it cannot give them an advantage over their rivals.

Many large companies maintain an "advanced technology" or "advanced techniques" department whose role is to evaluate innovative products that could give the company a competitive advantage. Boeing, General Electric, Royal Dutch Shell, and JP Morgan Chase are examples. Unfortunately, these departments often act as "innovation prevention" organizations by taking months to test a product while holding up purchases by visionaries who could actually take advantage of it. In many cases, their tests are designed to minimize the risk of failure as opposed to determining if the innovation has value, so the net result is that many innovative products are deemed to be "not ready" for the company to buy. One should not confuse a department that is assigned the bureaucratic role of investigating new products, with visionaries whose psychology drives them to seek out and obtain innovative products.

Spending by visionaries on new products can sustain the first vendor of those products as it refines and broadens them, but it also brings other vendors into a fledgling market. If the limited early market demand for a product has been satisfied, but mainstream customers have not started buying it, then the product is stuck in phase 1 and cannot progress to phase 2 of the life cycle. At this point, sales will drop off because all of the phase 1 market demand has been satisfied.

Note that the newness of the innovation in the product is the buying motivation for both enthusiasts and visionaries. The longer that a product is in the market without progressing to mainstream customers in phase 2, the older that innovation becomes. As time goes by, the attention of enthusiasts and visionaries moves on to other products and other innovations. One should try to win as many enthusiasts and visionaries in phase 1 as quickly as possible, rather than count on them continuing to be interested in the new product for an extended period of time.

Building and Operating Routes to Phase 1 Customers

Narrowly targeted "awareness" campaigns can be very successful in reaching enthusiasts. Public relations via niche publications, Web sites, and conferences can be effective. Enthusiasts can be identified by buying lists of subscribers to publications that focus on new technologies or innovations, and buying lists of attendees at similarly focused conferences. Enthusiasts can also be identified by their posts in discussion forums and blogs about new technologies or innovations.

Making and communicating judgments about the innovation's value, uniqueness, "coolness," and fitness for adoption by other customers, are the principal purposes in life for enthusiasts. They need to understand how the innovation works, how it sets the new offer apart, and why it is valuable. It is important for the vendor to engage enthusiasts in a dialog about the new offer, and get the offer into their hands so they can explore it and put it to work.

In addition to face-to-face meetings with enthusiasts in their offices and in stores, conventions and trade shows, vendors have found that online communications, such as e-mail, discussion groups, forums, social networks, blogs, video, and/or web conferences, can be very helpful in giving them opportunities to interact with enthusiasts, and for enthusiasts to interact with other enthusiasts interested in the same innovation. For example, Engadget (http://engadget.com) is a blog-based web magazine with obsessive daily coverage of everything new in gadgets and consumer electronics. Engadget has millions of passionate readers and is a very popular hang-out for technology enthusiasts. Readers can post comments to add their opinions about new products and services. In almost every product or service category, there is at least one Web site that, like Engadget, provides announcements, reviews, and opinions about disruptive innovations in that category, and also enables readers to add their own comments and form a community of like-minded enthusiasts.

Without enthusiasts, truly new products would have no customers at all, and would not progress to later phases of the life cycle because the customers at those phases would not have heard any pronouncements from enthusiasts about the new product.

The typical route for phase 1 is shown in Fig. 5.5, and the distribution channel structure for this route is highlighted with a gray background in Fig. 5.6.

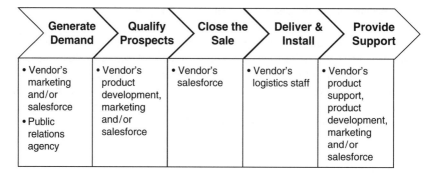

Fig. 5.5 Vendor direct route for RTM Life Cycle Phase 1 Introduction

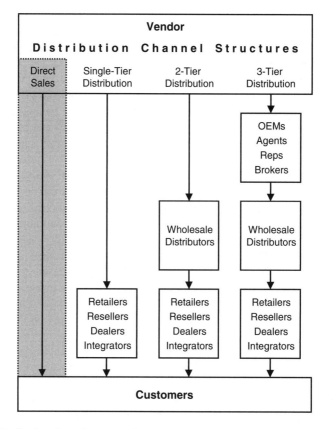

Fig. 5.6 Distribution channel structure for RTM Life Cycle Phase 1 Introduction (highlighted in gray)

In phase 1, the vendor's entire company (or division) must be dedicated to evangelizing the target market segment. Their mission is to identify, contact, persuade, motivate, and follow up with all potential enthusiasts and visionaries for the offer. The employees undertaking this mission must be passionate about the product. It should not be up to the company's salesforce alone. Other people, including the CEO, product manager, product designer or developer, customer support staff, and even manufacturing and finance people, should participate, if they are passionate about the product.

The goal is to get conversations going with potential enthusiasts and visionaries, not product volumes. The costs of the route are essentially the expense of dedicating people to the evangelism. Unfortunately, revenue is low during phase 1, while sales costs are high. The expense-to-income ratio is not attractive, but the investment in establishing enthusiastic references is required for launching new offers that are based on disruptive innovations.

The success or failure of this route is easy to see if more than 50% of enthusiasts and visionaries who are focused on the product category buy the product or endorse it. Even better would be for the majority of enthusiasts and visionaries to endorse the product for the same reasons. That result would be declared a major victory for the vendor.

Unfortunately, many innovative products get negative or mixed results in phase 1 – the enthusiasts and visionaries are split over whether the innovation makes the product significant and valuable compared to other products, or they disagree about the importance of different product features and benefits. The lack of consensus creates confusion for customers in phases 2 and 3 who are looking for endorsements from enthusiasts and visionaries to help them separate viable products from long shots they should avoid.

The lack of consensus can also make it difficult for the vendor's management to determine which features they should continue to invest in or promote to customers, and which should be dropped from the product. Some companies have solved this problem by expanding their contacts with enthusiasts and visionaries to the point where trends were clear, but this can take many months. Other companies have stuck with their original vision and feature set, and filtered out the feedback that did not fit their vision. They sold successfully to enthusiasts and visionaries who "bought" their vision, and ignored those who did not like their offer.

Regardless of how the company interprets the feedback from enthusiasts and visionaries during phase 1, it is critical that some of them buy the offer and pronounce it worthy of purchase by others. Strong endorsements are clearly preferred to mixed or lukewarm ones.

Preparing Routes for Phase 2

During phase 1, many companies focus all of their efforts on building and operating their routes to phase 1 customers, and wait until phase 2 to build routes for phase 2. This is a mistake. The work to decide which routes should be used in phase 2, and to construct those routes, must begin as early as possible in phase 1. This is particularly true when the routes in phase 2 will involve other companies that the vendor must recruit, train, support, and manage, because that can take many weeks or months. Starting that in phase 1 will accelerate the transition from phase 1 to phase 2 and propel the vendor into the market leadership position ahead of competitors.

The task for preparing routes for phase 2 is often referred to as figuring out how to cross the chasm. Many established, industry-leading vendors were once part of a peer group of small companies in their industry in phase 1, but then outperformed their competitors in phase 2 to become the market leader. Because the phase 2 market is much larger than the phase 1 market, becoming the market leader in phase 2 made these companies the "gorillas" of their industry segments, such as IBM (which raced ahead of Burroughs, Univac, NCR, Control Data, and Honeywell in phase 2 of the mainframe market), Microsoft (which leaped ahead of WordPerfect, Lotus, and Harvard Graphics in phase 2 of the office software market when Windows replaced MS-DOS), Yahoo (which eclipsed AOL and other portal companies in phase 2 of the consumer web services market), Google (which zipped past Overture, AltaVista, Inktomi, and other providers of search engine services in phase 2, when search engine advertising took off), and Apple (which jumped ahead of Rio and other manufacturers which preceded it in the digital audio player market). The key learning is that companies that do not prepare for phase 2 while the market is still in phase 1, fall behind competitors that use phase 1 to prepare for phase 2.

If all of the vendors in phase 1 are unable to build routes for phase 2 for any reason, such as not being able to determine which resources to engage or how to motivate those resources to work with them, the market will languish in phase 1 for an extended period of time, until one competitor or another figures out how to ignite phase 2. In this scenario, the extended period of time during which the market languishes at the end of phase 1 is the chasm.

During the transition from phase 1 to phase 2, the vendor must shift the focus from the offer's features to the benefits that customers will obtain by buying or using the offer. This is the first of several important shifts that the vendor must make during the RTM Life Cycle.

RTM Life Cycle Phase 2: Solution

The primary job in RTM Life Cycle Phase 2 is to create and sell whole *solutions* to pragmatists, as shown in Fig. 5.7.

Pragmatists: Stick with the Herd!

Pragmatists' response to innovative products and services is "Stick with the herd!," that is, wait for other customers who are like themselves to buy the product or service. Pragmatists are interested in what the innovative product or service does

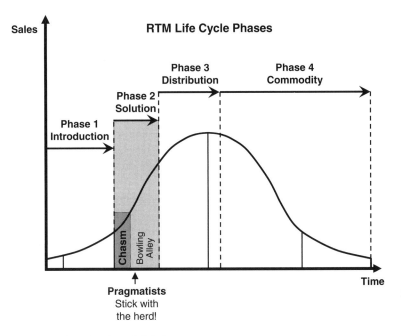

Fig. 5.7 RTM Life Cycle Phase 2 Solution

reliably and predictably to meet their specific needs. They need demonstrable evidence that buying the new product will pay off for them, and that other people like them (other pragmatists in similar situations) are also buying the product. They do not wish to be pioneers, like the enthusiasts and visionaries of phase 1.

In Fig. 5.7, the Chasm at the beginning of phase 2 is the period in which adoption often stalls before sales occur in phase 2. Visionaries in phase 1 have adopted as much of the innovation as they need and are no longer interested in more of it. Pragmatists, with their stick-with-the-herd mentality, are not yet convinced that it is safe to adopt the innovation.

Building and Operating Routes to Phase 2 Customers

Geoffrey Moore pointed out that the only reliable way for the innovation to cross the chasm is to target a niche market composed of pragmatists who share a common problem for which there is no known solution. These pragmatists unite to adopt the innovation if, and only if, it is packaged as a whole solution to their problem. Moore recognized that there are multiple niche markets of pragmatists. In each niche market, the pragmatists wait until they are offered a whole solution tailored for their niche. Other niches need different whole solutions. Moore referred to the niches collectively as the "Bowling Alley." The vendor's goal in phase 2 is to knock down as many pins (market niches) in the bowling alley as possible.

Winning business in a niche is very attractive because the pragmatists in a niche collaborate to standardize on the same solution. This means that the vendor can win multiple orders in a short period of time if he can convince the pragmatists to standardize on his solution.

For phase 2, the vendor should segment the market based on how the offer can be used. There are several other dimensions on which markets can be segmented, such as company size for business-to-business (B2B) markets, income level for business-to-consumer (B2C) markets, geographic location, and loyalty. However, the most important dimension for market segmentation in phase 2 is usage, which is also referred to as "application" or "purpose." (Segmentation is discussed in Chap. 3).

Segmenting the market based on usage may be difficult for many vendors in phase 1 because their staff may not know very much about how customers can use the new offer. It was not important for the vendor to know that in phase 1.

The best sources for identifying uses for the offer in phase 2 are visionary customers and visionary solutions providers because they are adept at envisioning how they could use innovative offers to their advantage. The vendor should interview visionary customers and visionary solutions providers, whether they have actually bought the offer or are just evaluating it, to understand how they would use it, and also to understand whether there are other products or services, special skills or other resources (beyond the vendor's offer) that they will need in order to constitute a "whole solution" – the minimum set of products and services necessary for the target customer to completely satisfy his or her compelling reason to buy. (Whole solutions are discussed in Chap. 4).

In some cases, the interview with a visionary customer or a solutions provider can be conducted in an hour or less, but the more typical scenario requires multiple conversations with the same customers/providers over an extended period of time because their understanding of the innovative offer and the whole solution, will evolve as they gain more experience. Customers and solutions providers may experience "false starts" in which they thought that they would use the offer in a particular way, but then discovered that they had to use it in a different way, or that the biggest benefit was something different than what they originally expected.

For these reasons, phase 1 is a "learning experience" for the vendor as well as for customers and solutions providers. The key questions that the vendor should answer in phase 1 are the following:

- What will pragmatists use the new offer for? What can specialized retailers or solutions providers use the new offer for (such as entering a new market, or replacing a product line that has transitioned to broader distribution, or providing a new solution to sell to their existing customers)? Note that the answers for pragmatists will typically be different than the answers for specialized retailers and solutions providers.
- Which of these uses are situations in which the pragmatists or specialized retailers feel a lot of pain for which there is no other solution except for the new offer?
- Which of these uses are situations in which pragmatists, specialized retailers, or solutions providers have other alternatives? How do they describe the alternatives

and compare them to the vendor's new offer? If some of them have discarded the alternatives in favor of the vendor's new offer, why did they do that?

- What is needed for pragmatists, specialized retailers, and solutions providers to succeed with the new offer, such as other products or services, special skills, or other resources (beyond the vendor's offer)? These are the complementary products and services that constitute the whole solution discussed in Chap. 4. Which people or companies can provide these?
- What should the vendor do to form relationships with these people or companies in order to ensure the supply of the needed products or services, special skills, or other resources? (Alternative relationships include hiring, acquisition, joint venture, private label, resale, distribution, referral, and so on, with the vendor taking potentially different roles in each relationship).

The goal is not just to answer these questions, but to make and implement business decisions based on the answers. This can take months in even the most nimble of organizations, when you include time for the vendor to hire and/or train staff for this assignment, time for multiple third parties to evaluate the new offer, time to establish business relationships, time for the third parties to develop and roll-out the solutions, products, services, skills, and other resources related to the vendor's offer.

Answering these questions not only provides data for the business decisions, but it also educates the vendor's management and staff on the issues that they have to resolve in order to succeed in the remaining phases of the life cycle.

The ideal answers provide detailed information describing each type of usage, with qualitative and quantitative data on customers who have similar usage needs. The ideal answers document alternative ways for customers to obtain similar benefits or to achieve similar results. The ideal answers also define the vendor's go-to-market model for phase 2, and identify the people or companies that the vendor will partner with in the go-to-market model.

Usually, interviews with visionary customers identify several different uses for the offer in phase 2. Each use is normally a distinct market segment. Small vendors often feel a lot of pressure to choose one segment to pursue because they lack the resources to pursue multiple segments at the same time. New product groups in large vendors feel pressure to pursue multiple market segments in parallel in order to produce enough revenue from the new offer to meet corporate revenue objectives. However, both small and large vendors need to prioritize the segments they are going to focus on, in order to succeed.

What criteria should vendors use to prioritize the market segments for phase 2? Many different criteria may be considered, such as segment size, growth rate, cost of entry, and competition. However, Geoffrey Moore observed that the only reliable way to cross the chasm at the end of phase 1, is to target a niche market of pragmatists who are united by a common problem for which there is no known solution. The key criterion is the lack of alternative and competitive solutions for a problem that everyone in the market niche has. These "pragmatists in pain" are highly motivated to help the new product cross the chasm if, and only if, it is packaged as a complete solution to their problem.

The lack of competition makes the niche attractive from the profit perspective. But more important than the profit potential of this niche is the opportunity for the vendor to drive the transition from phase 1 to phase 2 for the entire market and thereby become the dominant vendor in a much larger market.

To create the whole solution needed by the "pragmatists in pain," vendors face a choice: do they have the knowledge, skill, and capacity to generate the whole solution by themselves for each attractive market niche, or should they partner with other companies to do that? The go-it-alone strategy may seem attractive because the vendor does not have to share revenue or control with other firms. The partner-with-others strategy, however, requires much less capital and is much more scalable and significantly less risky than the go-it-alone strategy. If the vendor sells a platform to which other companies can add their products and services, the best strategy is to partner. Platforms can be a computer, or a communications device, or software that can be customized for different uses, or a line of credit that be applied to different purposes, or a tool that can be put to different uses, and so on.

On the contrary, if the vendor sells something that is highly customized to a small number of customers, or cannot be enhanced by other companies because it is already complete by itself, then the best strategy is to go-it-alone because there is little room for others to add value. Products and services that fit these criteria include one-of-a-kind products and services (such as original artwork or highly customized computer programs), exclusive products whose value would be diminished by broader availability (such as luxury goods, high-end resort properties, or exclusive clubs), and specialized services for which there is a limited market (like a narrow medical specialization).

Many high-tech vendors find the partner-with-others strategy very attractive because each partner brings its own capital and know-how to the whole solution and broadens the market for their business. Their challenge in phase 2 is to shift the focus of marketing, sales, and customer service from their product or service (as they were focused in phase 1) to establish relationships with multiple third-party suppliers of products and services in order to create, market, and deliver whole solutions to customers in phase 2. This is an enormous change for many companies if they have no prior experience doing this.

Making this shift often requires a trial-and-error approach. If there are many qualified third parties, it will be difficult to know at the beginning which ones will be the most productive to work with. Neither the vendor nor the third parties will have enough information to know how much time and money they should put into building a particular whole solution, or which solutions will actually be viable. The best strategy is to pursue multiple solutions with multiple parties for the top priority market niches, and then put additional resources into the solutions that get the most traction with customers. In other words, the vendor should pay attention to customers' reactions to different whole solutions, when deciding which solutions to back.

Many products and services can be turned into different solutions for different market niches. For example, for a banking offer, there are many different "solutions." Loans are promoted differently to college students, people purchasing new cars, people purchasing homes, and so on. The solutions are distinguished by the marketing communications on the use of the loan funds, the terms and conditions of the loan agreement, and the distribution channels engaged to sell the loans. In the USA, loans to pay college tuition and living expenses are primarily provided through affiliation with college financial-aid offices. Auto dealerships are the principal channel for car loans and leases. Independent mortgage brokers are the largest channel for home loans. To succeed in these markets, banks must create a whole solution tailored to each market, and then recruit, train, and manage channel partners that fit that market.

Figure 5.8 shows the three different routes to customers that vendors typically use in phase 2.

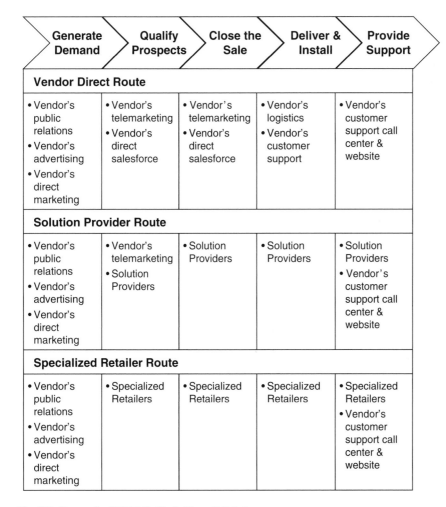

Generate Demand	Qualify Prospects	Close the Sale	Deliver & Install	Provide Support
Vendor Direct Route				
• Vendor's public relations • Vendor's advertising • Vendor's direct marketing	• Vendor's telemarketing • Vendor's direct salesforce	• Vendor's telemarketing • Vendor's direct salesforce	• Vendor's logistics • Vendor's customer support	• Vendor's customer support call center & website
Solution Provider Route				
• Vendor's public relations • Vendor's advertising • Vendor's direct marketing	• Vendor's telemarketing • Solution Providers	• Solution Providers	• Solution Providers	• Solution Providers • Vendor's customer support call center & website
Specialized Retailer Route				
• Vendor's public relations • Vendor's advertising • Vendor's direct marketing	• Specialized Retailers	• Specialized Retailers	• Specialized Retailers	• Specialized Retailers • Vendor's customer support call center & website

Fig. 5.8 Routes for RTM Life Cycle Phase 2 Solution

Note that vendors implement one of the following combinations of the routes for phase 2 that are shown in Fig. 5.8:

- Vendor Direct Route only (no other routes).
- Vendor Direct Route focused on expanding business within existing "house accounts" (or another "restricted territory"), plus the Solution Provider Route targeted to all other customers, typically for B2B products and services, not B2C.
- Solution Provider Route only (no other routes).
- Specialized Reseller Route only (no other routes).

To recruit and manage solutions providers or specialized retailers for phase 2 and subsequent phases, vendors implement a Partner Recruitment Route in phase 1, as shown in Fig. 5.9. This route does not sell the offer to customers. Instead, it

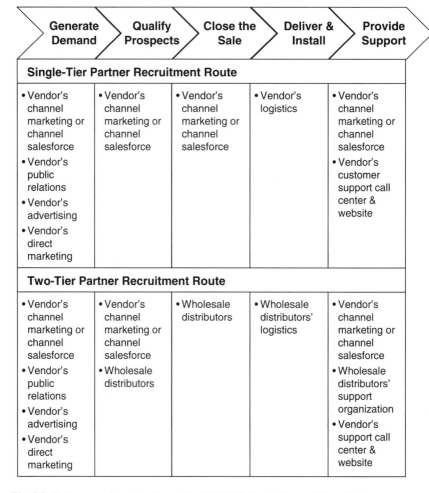

Generate Demand	Qualify Prospects	Close the Sale	Deliver & Install	Provide Support
Single-Tier Partner Recruitment Route				
• Vendor's channel marketing or channel salesforce • Vendor's public relations • Vendor's advertising • Vendor's direct marketing	• Vendor's channel marketing or channel salesforce	• Vendor's channel marketing or channel salesforce	• Vendor's logistics	• Vendor's channel marketing or channel salesforce • Vendor's customer support call center & website
Two-Tier Partner Recruitment Route				
• Vendor's channel marketing or channel salesforce • Vendor's public relations • Vendor's advertising • Vendor's direct marketing	• Vendor's channel marketing or channel salesforce • Wholesale distributors	• Wholesale distributors	• Wholesale distributors' logistics	• Vendor's channel marketing or channel salesforce • Wholesale distributors' support organization • Vendor's support call center & website

Fig. 5.9 Partner recruitment route used in RTM Life Cycle Phases 1 through 4

recruits, trains, incentivizes, and manages distribution partners that sell the vendor's offer to customers as part of a whole solution.

Distribution is usually single-tier in phase 2, so the vendor runs a Single-Tier Partner Recruitment Route in phase 1 to recruit partners for phase 2, starting as soon as the vendor can identify which partners should be recruited. Many vendors transition from single-tier distribution to two-tier at the end of phase 2, so we are presenting both routes in a single figure to make it easy to see the differences in the resources that are used.

The two distribution channel structures used in phase 2 are Direct Sales and Single-Tier Distribution, as shown in Fig. 5.10. Direct Sales corresponds to the Vendor Direct Route shown in Fig. 5.8. Single-Tier Distribution corresponds to the Solutions Provider Route and the Specialized Reseller Route, also shown in Fig. 5.8. For the vendor, it is critical to increase demand generation in phase 2. This is true for both B2B and B2C markets. Profits are good in phase 2. There is little presure on product prices.

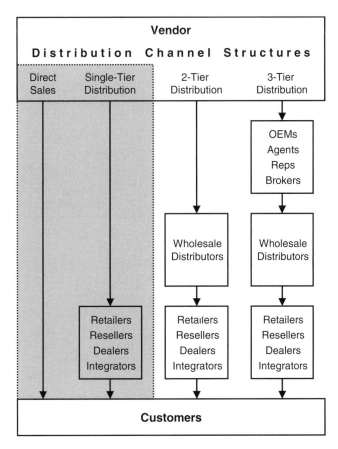

Fig. 5.10 Distribution channel structure for RTM Life Cycle Phase 2 Solution (highlighted in gray)

Preparing Routes for Phase 3

It is critical for the vendor to start preparing routes for phase 3 while the market is still in phase 2. Phase 3 routes differ from phase 2 in several ways: expanding distribution to cover all geographies and market niches not previously covered, adding a second tier of distribution to efficiently handle broader distribution, transferring channel partners that used to buy directly from the vendor to buy instead from wholesale distributors, and resolving channel conflicts which become much more numerous and significant in phase 3 compared to phase 2. These changes take time. The first vendor to make these changes successfully can grow faster than its competitors to become the market share leader, garnering not only the most revenue but also the highest profits and most defensible position in the market.

RTM Life Cycle Phase 3: Distribution

The primary job for phase 3 is to expand *distribution* as fast as possible, as shown in Fig. 5.11. This means building and operating high-volume routes to cover all of the pragmatists in the market, not just the ones in the market niches targeted in phase 2, and to cover the first conservatives to buy the vendor's product or service. The vendor's goal for phase 3 is to get big faster than competitors.

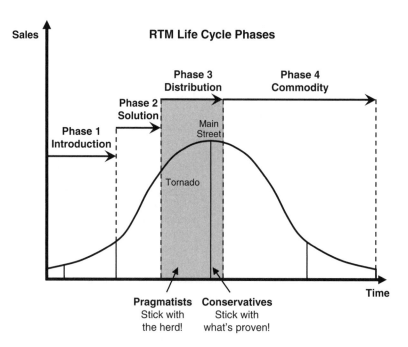

Fig. 5.11 RTM Life Cycle Phase 3 Distribution

At some point in phase 2, sales explode as the mass of pragmatists realizes that they do not want to be left behind while their fellow pragmatists buy whole solutions. Their "stick-with-the-herd" mentality compels them to buy the same solution as their peers within their market niche. When this happens in multiple market niches at the same time, a "Tornado" ensues, as described by Geoffrey Moore. The tornado is a period of hypergrowth caused when the remaining pragmatists adopt a new product en masse. Their behavior is reinforced by the large number of solutions providers and other vendors that have embraced the product or service as the market-leading choice, further validating its safety and effectiveness.

As the market matures through phase 3, sales growth slows and reaches a stable plateau, which Moore called "Main Street." The top vendors in the market continue to acquire new customers and get repeat business from existing customers, in proportion to their share of the market. Pragmatists expect regular improvements in the product or service. These improvements drive their additional purchases, along with their need to deploy the product or service more broadly within their companies (in B2B markets) or in their households (in B2C markets).

Conservatives: Stick with What Is Proven!

Phase 3 extends into the conservative segment of the population. Like pragmatists, conservatives buy products and services that reliably and predictably meet their specific needs. Conservatives do not buy products on the promise of competitive advantage, but they want to avoid being put at a competitive disadvantage. Conservatives are price and option sensitive and think that, by waiting for products to mature and become well-established, they can minimize the cost and risk of buying them.

Substantial revenue can be obtained by capturing conservative customers, but only the best-established vendor can capture that revenue because conservatives want to buy only the best-known and safest brand.

Building and Operating Routes to Phase 3 Customers

The first sign of a tornado is the signal that phase 2 is transitioning to phase 3. The rules of the game change again, as they did in the transition from phase 1 to phase 2.

From phase 2 to phase 3, there is a major transition from direct sales and a limited number of channel partners in phase 2, to broader distribution through two-tier distribution and many more channel partners in phase 3. To succeed in phase 3, the vendor must recruit, train, supply, and coordinate wholesale distributors, and transition existing channel partners to buying from wholesale distributors instead of directly from the vendor.

Channel Conflict

The more effective the coverage of the market is, the more likely there will be channel conflicts. Channel conflicts occur when two or more different sales organizations are simultaneously selling the same offer to the same prospective customer. The extreme channel conflict situation is one in which the principal competitor of the retailer is not another retailer offering a competing product, but the vendor's direct salesforce.

It is easy to be cynical by thinking that channel conflict is inevitable, or to establish territory assignments that allocate the most profitable customers to the vendor's direct salesforce and leave unprofitable customers with indirect channels. One way to do this is to declare large or "named" accounts as "house accounts" to be handled by direct sales, or to claim as direct accounts all prospects who request information or quotations from the vendor.

Some people think that channel conflicts are normal, even healthy. They believe that the absence of channel conflict would mean that the market was not sufficiently covered. This thinking indicates either ignorance of indirect routes or the lack of will to impose a clear sales policy on the direct salesforce.

A good partner is a partner in good financial health. Vendors can support the financial health of their partners by setting up good distribution policies and practices.

Vendors that fail to transition smoothly from direct sales to indirect channels in phase 2 cannot grow as fast as competitors that do, and typically become niche providers if they survive at all. Vendors that build profitable relationships with indirect channels in phase 2 are well positioned for phases 3 and 4, which are dominated by indirect channels and which together account for half of the customers in the life cycle. There are many reasons to avoid conflicts between direct and indirect channels in phase 3, but the smart way to avoid these conflicts is to put channel partners first.

The demand generation done by the vendor is carried out with the profit of its indirect channels in mind. Financial and operational discipline is essential. Profits are high in phase 3 because the high level of demand minimizes pressure on prices.

Figure 5.12 shows the two routes that are typical in phase 3: Two-Tier Solutions Provider Route and Two-Tier Volume Retailer Route.

Figure 5.13 shows the distribution channel structures that correspond to the routes for phase 3. Two-tier distribution becomes important for growing the market and keeping up with demand in phase 3.

Putting Phases 1, 2, and 3 Together: Baracoda's Experience

In 2002 Baracoda, a French start-up manufacturer of wireless data capture devices, introduced an innovative line of barcode scanners that used Bluetooth instead of physical wires to connect to data networks. Bluetooth is a standard for wireless communications between devices, widely used today to connect headsets wirelessly to mobile phones. Barcode scanners read barcodes printed on packages and

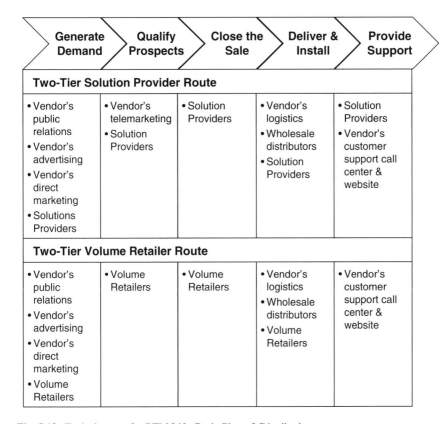

Generate Demand	Qualify Prospects	Close the Sale	Deliver & Install	Provide Support
Two-Tier Solution Provider Route				
• Vendor's public relations • Vendor's advertising • Vendor's direct marketing • Solutions Providers	• Vendor's telemarketing • Solution Providers	• Solution Providers	• Vendor's logistics • Wholesale distributors • Solution Providers	• Solution Providers • Vendor's customer support call center & website
Two-Tier Volume Retailer Route				
• Vendor's public relations • Vendor's advertising • Vendor's direct marketing • Volume Retailers	• Volume Retailers	• Volume Retailers	• Vendor's logistics • Wholesale distributors • Volume Retailers	• Vendor's customer support call center & website

Fig. 5.12 Typical routes for RTM Life Cycle Phase 3 Distribution

manufactured goods, for applications such as managing inventory in a warehouse. Baracoda's innovation was embedding Bluetooth technology in barcode scanners before the established barcode scanner manufacturers did that.

A few early customers bought Baracoda's Bluetooth scanners, but Baracoda's management was surprised that sales did not pick up as expected after they signed distribution agreements with barcode scanner distributors throughout Europe. Management thought that customers would buy Bluetooth scanners for their existing barcode projects because they were easier to use than scanners requiring wired connections. But the distributors were returning Baracoda's scanners one after the other because they could not sell them.

In 2003, interviews with Baracoda's early customers found that, instead of using Bluetooth scanners in traditional barcode applications, they were rolling out new applications which required data entry via barcode for mobile workers, such as field engineers recording part numbers when doing repairs, and delivery teams doing product replenishment. Baracoda's early customers were enthusiasts and visionaries in phase 1 who invested in developing their own software to make Baracoda's Bluetooth scanners work in their mobile environments. The reason that sales had

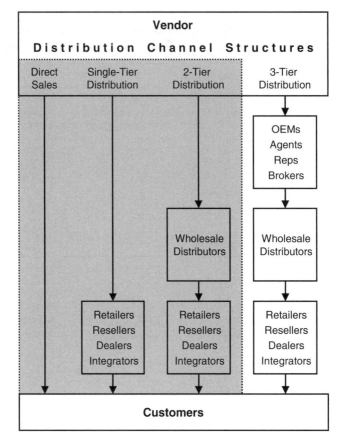

Fig. 5.13 Distribution channel structure for RTM Life Cycle 3 Distribution (highlighted in gray)

stalled was that pragmatic customers in phase 2 could not buy scanners without software for their specific needs. The customer interviews also revealed that customers who had bought wired barcode scanners did not see the business benefit for replacing their existing scanners with wireless units.

With those insights, Baracoda's approach changed radically. They started contacting independent software vendors who were developing solutions on mobile platforms, and gave them free scanners, technical training, support, and co-marketing help. Sales picked up as each software vendor completed development and their customers started buying Baracoda's scanners.

In 2004 Baracoda's US sales team closed a significant contract with Nextel (which later merged with Sprint) to distribute and support Baracoda's Bluetooth barcode scanners to Nextel's application partners, so that they could deploy mobile applications for Motorola and Blackberry handheld devices on the Nextel network. Nextel's application partners did not want to deal with multiple vendors of Bluetooth scanners because that would greatly complicate their deployments. Nextel chose

Baracoda and acted as a "value-added" distributor by providing an immediate physical point of presence across the US and access to all Nextel partners and customers. The result was a rapid increase in Baracoda's sales as Nextel partners sold Baracoda scanners combined with mobile applications software in several industries including construction, field services, professional services, and real estate.

Baracoda succeeded in navigating the transitions from phase 1 to phase 2, and from phase 2 to phrase 3. When management understood how phase 1 customers were actually using Baracoda's product, they realized that it met different customer needs than they had originally thought, and they changed their approach to exploit that opportunity, bringing Baracoda's product across the chasm. By showing Nextel management that they could accelerate the success of their applications partners by giving them a single, common product to deploy (instead of a variety of incompatible products), Baracoda drove the transition from phase 2 to phase 3 by triggering a tornado of orders.

Who Does Demand Generation?

Some people erroneously believe that distribution channels generate demand for the products and services that they distribute. They do have their own demand generation resources, but these are devoted to communicating the identity and capabilities of their own company, not generating demand for the products and services that they resell. Their marketing effort is focused on differentiating themselves from their competitors. The vendor must do all of the demand generation for his product or service.

However, it is important to distinguish between demand generation for a vendor's products or services, and other purposes that a distribution channel may have for promoting the vendor:

1. Some solution providers promote the vendor's product or service by specifically identifying it as part of the whole solution that they are selling. For example, companies that resell Oracle database software as part of their business applications, often promote the Oracle database software along with their applications products. Their objective is to associate the well-known Oracle brand and positive perception of Oracle products, with their company and products. This type of promotion does not generate demand for Oracle's products by themselves.
2. Some solution providers, retailers, resellers, and dealers promote the primary vendors that they sell, if their business model is to be a "specialist" in those vendors' products. Their objective is to be chosen over other resellers for the brands that they focus on. This type of promotion does not generate demand for those vendors' products by themselves.
3. Some solution providers, resellers, and dealers sell products or services to customers who already own a specific vendor's products. For example, many companies that offer training and support for specific vendor's product lines, such as Cognos' business intelligence software or Cisco's network routers, promote

those vendors in their advertising, direct mail and Web sites. In this situation, the distribution channels are targeting the installed base of the vendor, not generating demand for the vendor's products.

4. Some vendors pay their distribution partners to promote the vendors' products via Market Development Funds (MDF) or co-op programs. In this case, the cost of demand generation is paid by the vendor, not the distribution partner.

For obvious economic reasons a retailer serves requests rather than creating them. Wholesalers which supply retailers and do not deal with consumers or final customers, do not generate demand among final customers, nor among retailers. Many wholesalers provide ways for vendors to communicate with and train retailers, but they typically charge the vendor additional fees for providing these services, in addition to the margin they retain on the offer.

Preparing Routes for Phase 4

As in prior phases, vendors must use phase 3 to prepare routes for phase 4. The first challenge in making the transition from phase 3 to phase 4 is to repackage the product or service to fit the needs of conservative and skeptical customers by making the product as usable as possible without the involvement of support personnel, so that the price can be minimized while still providing an acceptable profit. The second challenge is to construct routes that maximize coverage of conservatives and skeptics. Solving one challenge often requires solving the other challenge.

RTM Life Cycle Phase 4: Commodity

The primary jobs for phase 4 are to maximize market coverage while maintaining the profit margin, and to hold back the forces *commoditizing* the product as long as possible. The customers in phase 4 are conservatives and skeptics, as shown in Fig. 5.14.

They are very price conscious. They try to avoid products that require extra-cost support, and prefer products that are usable without the involvement of support personnel. This means that vendors should repackage the product or service to simplify installation, learning, usage, and operation as much as possible. Another reason to do this, is that the low-price channels preferred by conservatives and skeptics provide little if any services to help customers make purchase decisions and utilize the vendor's product or service.

Skeptics: Just Say No!

"Just say no!" means that skeptics are the last group of people to adopt an innovation. Everyone else has adopted the innovation before them. To everyone except a skeptic, the innovative product or service is no longer innovative. Skeptics buy

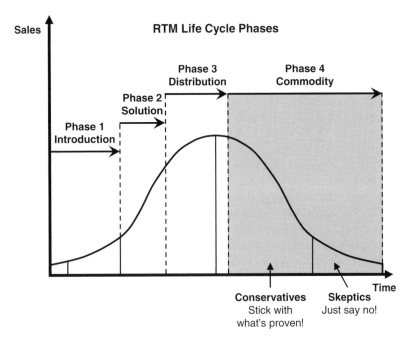

Fig. 5.14 RTM Life Cycle Phase 4 Commodity

products that are completely proven and risk free, products that they cannot live or work without, where they know that the cost of not having the product greatly exceeds the cost (and trauma) of buying it. The key to selling to skeptics is to emphasize the total absence of risk in buying the product or service.

Skeptics are 16% of the population, large enough to represent good revenue for vendors whose products have become so mainstream that everyone can buy them. Many vendors abandon markets as they progress from conservatives to skeptics in phase 4, in favor of other markets that are more attractive. This is one way to deal with commoditization.

Building and Operating Routes to Phase 4 Customers

Profit rates are lower in phase 4 than in phase 3 due to pricing pressure. Volumes are high but growth rates are low. It is necessary to adapt sales and distribution to reduce the cost of sales. Phase 4 customers already know something about the product or the category that the product is in. Demand generation campaigns do not try to make customers aware of the solution, because they already know that.

Marketing resources are reoriented towards exciting customers and enticing additional or incremental market segments to buy. Special promotions with discounted prices or bundled products are common.

In phase 4, the vendor's product development organization has stopped working on the product or makes only minor changes to support merchandising. Some of these changes are carried out by production without mobilizing the development resources, which have already been reallocated to other products.

Promotional campaigns can be orchestrated by each level of distribution, and possibly co-financed by the vendor. Prospects are qualified at the point of sale which can be in a store, warehouse, or over the phone or online.

Proximity to the customer becomes important, so packaging, merchandising, and physical product distribution becomes critical in many cases. This forces changes in the choice of distribution partners, emphasizing logistics capabilities and demand generation skills. Customer service is centralized and provided via Web sites and call centers, not at the point of sale

Distribution is expanded in phase 4 to include types of retailers and distributors that were not included in phase 3, but which serve conservatives and skeptics, such as mass market retailers, discount stores, catalog retailers, and distributors which cover geographies not previously covered by other channels.

The majority of mass-market products, such as television sets, automobiles, and personal loans, are in this phase. Retailers automatically track their campaigns, sales, and inventories weekly if not daily, and utilize computer networks to their vendors and distributors to optimize the flow of materials from sourcing to final sale.

Figure 5.15 shows the two routes that are typical in phase 4: Two-Tier Volume Retailer Route and Vendor Direct Volume Route.

The Volume Retailers Route shown in Fig. 5.15 employs two-tier and three-tier distribution and a broad range of volume retailers including mass merchants, "big box" retailers, superstores, etc. The vendor's internal organizations (marketing communications, direct sales, call centers, etc.) are involved only at steps 1 and 5 of the sales cycle.

The Vendor Direct Volume Route shown in Fig. 5.15 depicts the "direct" model used by Dell and other companies, where the vendor interacts directly with customers via call centers and the Internet. Making the "direct" model work impacts the entire company's business model, metrics, and performance. Few companies have built high-volume direct and indirect operations in the same product category or market. Choosing the "direct" model also impacts product decisions and market segment choices. As Dell found in 2006 and 2007, some products such as notebook computers sell better in independent stores where consumers can compare alternative brands hands-on and side-by-side.

Figure 5.16 shows the distribution channel structures that correspond to the routes for phase 4. Note that if Three-Tier Distribution is used, Original Equipment Manufacturers (OEMs) buy the vendor's product or service and embed it in their product or service, which they subsequently provide to their distribution channels. However, the other three types of firms (Agents, Reps, and Brokers) usually do not take title to the vendor's product or resell it, so they do not actually handle the product or distribute it physically.

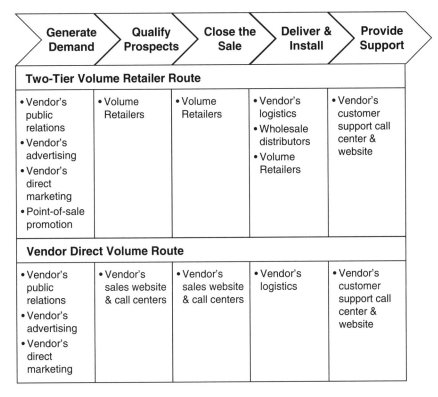

Fig. 5.15 Routes for RTM Life Cycle Phase 4

Dealing with Commoditization

Almost half of the market, in terms of the number of customers and total potential revenue, is in phase 4, but vendors are continually challenged by the forces that commoditize products, robbing them of differentiation and profit in phase 4. There are six strategies for dealing with the forces of commoditization. The next section outlines those strategies.

RTM Life Cycle and Commoditization

Innovative products and services start their life cycles in phase 1. The customers in phase 1 – enthusiasts and visionaries – are willing to pay high prices to get them. So margins are strong in phase 1. Sales growth is strongest in phase 2, where pragmatic customers buy in volume, and margins are comfortable. Margins are lower in phases 3 and 4 because conservatives and skeptics are only interested in mature products and will not pay premium prices.

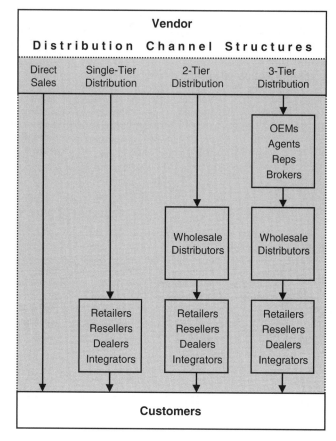

Fig. 5.16 Distribution channel structure for RTM Life Cycle Phase 4 Commodity (highlighted in gray)

A product or service becomes a commodity when it becomes indistinguishable from others like it, and customers choose among them based on price alone. As innovative products and services progress through their life cycles, they shift from being highly differentiated to selling in volume, and then to becoming commodities. Figure 5.17 summarizes this progression.

One contributor to commoditization is the pressure on competitors in mature markets to minimize investments to refresh their products. Without fresh differentiation, products from multiple competitors can become similar to each other as the competitors pursue the same set of conservative and skeptical customers.

A second contributor to commoditization is the assumption that all customers in phase 4 are the same. In reality, subsegments of phase 4 customers value differently each element of the product or service, and also each aspect of their experience with the vendor. Their attitudes about innovation may be the same, but their priorities on other issues can be very different.

RTM Life Cycle Phases – Commoditization

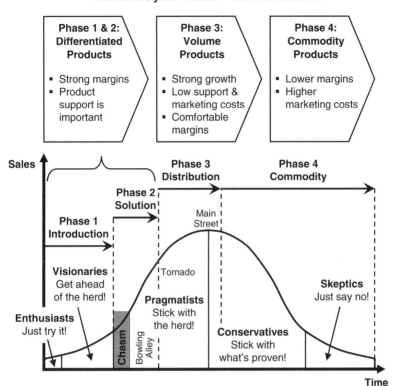

Fig. 5.17 RTM Life Cycle – commoditization

A third contributor is the challenge of innovating the product or service to reignite demand from customers in earlier phases of the life cycle. Incremental changes to mature products and services rarely excite enthusiasts, visionaries, and pragmatists to increase their purchases. Executives often consider making dramatic changes to established products and services as too risky because it can jeopardize a stable revenue stream with acceptable profits.

There are six basic ways for vendors to respond to the forces driving commoditization. Each of the contributors to commoditization are addressed by one or more of these six strategies:

1. Compete on something other than price.
2. Sell complementary products and services to grow within the installed base.
3. Transform products into services.
4. Innovate to generate new products and services that ignite new growth.
5. Acquire direct competitors to consolidate the market and reduce price competition.

6. Exit the market so that resources can be redeployed to pursue more attractive markets.

In each of these six responses to commoditization, RTM can help identify the commoditization problem and its causes, evaluate alternative solutions to the problem, and maximize the profitability of the solution selected by management.

Compete on Something Other than Price

It is very difficult to succeed by selling only on price. Only the largest vendors with efficient operations can succeed at this. Even within companies that are well-known for low prices, such as Wal-Mart, there are many different merchandising strategies (not just "low prices") being played out in parallel to maximize profits.

All conservatives are not the same, and all skeptics are not the same, even though each group is composed of people who share the same attitude about innovation. Although they prefer low prices, price is just one of many considerations for each person in these groups. Together, conservatives and skeptics account for half of the market opportunity. Within these two groups, there are many different subsegments that buy products and services based on factors other than price:

- Different subsegments buy different whole solutions that combine the vendor's product or service with other things they need or want. For example, phase 4 customers do not uniformly buy the least expensive personal computer on the market. Many phase 4 customers are drawn to promotions for low-cost PCs, but then opt for models that include additional features that configure the low-cost PC to fit their individual needs, such as a larger display, or a printer, additional software, and extended warranty. Creative bundles can be more appealing to many phase 4 customers than the basic lowest-price configuration, and also much more profitable for the vendor.
- Many phase 4 customers are drawn to vendors whose expertise, style, or values are attractive to them. Vendors with unique expertise in their product or its uses, or an engaging style for their brands, or a set of admirable values that they are following, should promote these. These dimensions are the sizzle that sells the steak to many phase 4 customers, who are much less interested in the product-centric sizzle that vendors promote to phase 1 and 2 customers. For example, attractive packaging that promotes a vendor's commitment to the environment can be more appealing than a long list of buzzwords about the product, when the customer believes that all products in the category are essentially the same.
- Many customers in every phase of the life cycle choose one vendor over another because of the shopping experience, not because of differences between their products. The shopping experience includes the customer's relationship with the vendor, the ease of doing business with the vendor, trust in the vendor, smooth functioning of the vendor's Web site and other communications vehi-

cles, high-quality assistance during and after purchase, product quality, and so on. These elements can be tuned to deliver a better shopping experience and even higher profit.

To compete successfully on something other than price, RTM can help identify the problem that is causing commoditization and prioritize the areas of differentiation to overcome the problem. Market research and experimentation are required to determine which customer subsegments should be targeted for different whole solutions, creative bundles, expertise, style, values, or shopping experience. Different combinations of these elements may have different costs. RTM can enable management to choose the lowest cost, highest impact approach, get everyone involved in implementing it aligned to a common plan, and monitor execution to keep it on track.

Sell Complementary Products and Services to the Installed Base

Customers who have bought one product or service from a vendor need complementary products and services. The vendor's customer base is a market that the vendor has already invested in. The vendor may be able to sell other relevant products and services to the same customers, especially if the vendor's existing routes to market can be used to do this.

An excellent example is the convergence of the telecommunications and television industries wherever they are unregulated enough to enable competition. In the USA, demand and margins for fixed or wireline telephone services are dropping rapidly in 2008, spurring telephone companies to sell their customers additional services such as broadband Internet access, which brings higher revenue and profits per customer than plain old telephone services. Like telephone companies, cable television companies broke out of their regulated industry by selling broadband Internet access delivered over their cable networks. Now both types of companies are invading each other's turf – telephone companies are starting to sell to their telephone customers TV services delivered via telephone lines, and cable TV companies are selling to their cable TV customers telephone services on their cable networks.

For many companies that have built a large customer base, but which now face commoditization pressures on their primary product, responding to these pressures by selling complementary products and services to existing customers is an excellent strategy. RTM can help by showing which complementary products and services can be sold successfully through the vendor's existing routes to market, and the cost to construct and operate different routes to market for them. RTM can also help at a tactical level in establishing budgets by function and department for each geographic team, tracking what works best, sharing that with other teams, and coordinating roll-outs for new offers. In this way, RTM can spread best practices across the company quickly.

Transform Products into Services

Many customers who would benefit from a product, lack the ability to adopt and use it because they lack skilled manpower. An example of transforming products into services is IBM's Global Services division, which combines professional services with computer hardware and software to solve customers' business problems that they would not have been able to address without IBM's expertise. There is a second way that products can be transformed into services: "rent" the product on a per-use basis instead of selling it. An example of the rental model is car rental company Hertz, which was owned by Ford from 1985 to 2005. Another example of the rental model is "software-as-a-service" company Salesforce.com, which provides Customer Relationship Management software via an online usage model, instead of shipping the software to customers for them to run on their own computers.

All of these examples of transforming products into services expand the market for the product to include customers who would not have bought the product by itself. But more importantly, they respond to commoditization by differentiating the product from competitors who do not offer it in a service model. They also generate additional, profitable revenue that would not have been available to the vendor if it had limited itself to selling just the product instead of selling services with the product.

RTM can help implement strategies to turn products into services in three ways. First, RTM can be used to diagnose the profitability of each service offer before launch, so that the vendor can focus on the most profitable service offers. For many service offers, the cost of services is easy to compute (as billable hours, or a usage rate, or for amortizing the cost of the service facilities), but the operating costs to market, sell, and deliver the services may be much harder to estimate, especially in a product company. RTM provides the framework to assemble all of the relevant costs and show how they impact profitability.

Second, RTM handles service offers the same way that it handles product offers. This enables the people using RTM to compare the routes for selling the service to the routes for selling the product, which enables better decision-making and also better implementation. Third, service businesses usually grow incrementally over time instead of in big but uneven sales spurts that happen in product businesses. RTM enables careful management of marketing and sales costs over time, avoiding the problem of overspending that threatens the profitability of slow-but-steady growth service offers.

Innovate to Generate New Products and Services

Note that the customers who dominate phase 4 – conservatives and skeptics – are not motivated to buy innovations, and therefore they are not the primary targets for innovative versions of established products. While a vendor sells an established product to phase 4 customers, it can bring out innovative products in the same product family, targeted to phase 1 and 2 customers in a new RTM life cycle that builds upon the existing life cycle.

The key to maximizing sales and profits from the new products is to understand which customers to target for each product in the product line. RTM excels at this because it explicitly links each product or service to a market segment. With RTM, vendors can optimize the launch of updated or innovative new products in the same market where they are already selling established products, and maximize growth and profitability for the entire product line.

Frequent innovation is not limited to technology products. It can also be done with consumer food products. Groupe Danone, the French food giant, has invested heavily in research to develop innovative products focused on health and nutrition. In 2006, it extended its Dannon yogurt product line in the USA by introducing a new yogurt product called Activia that contains live bacteria that aid regularity. According to *The New York Times*, sales of Activia soared well past the $100 million mark, a milestone that only a small percentage of new food products reach each year. *The Times* went on to note that the success of Groupe Danone's probiotic products such as Activia has helped boost its stock by more than 50% in the year since Activia's launch, and that Danone's growth was due in part to the introduction of innovative products in existing markets such as the USA.

Innovations that enhance existing products effectively extend the length of time that the product line remains in phase 3, thereby extending the time of stronger sales growth and more comfortable margins. The life cycle graph for each new product can be stacked on top of the life cycle graph for the previous product in the product line, producing the "S" shaped curve shown in Fig. 5.18.

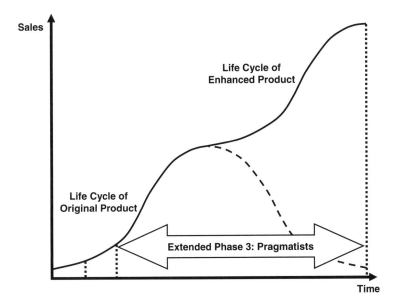

Fig. 5.18 Succession of RTM Life Cycles

Acquire Direct Competitors

To consolidate the market and reduce price competition, companies acquire their direct competitors. RTM is an excellent tool for assessing how well potential acquisitions fit the acquirer. For companies where marketing, sales, and customer service costs are 20% or more of revenue, these costs can be a significant factor to consider in making the acquisition and also in operating the combined company post acquisition. Incompatibilities between the routes to market for the acquirer and the acquisition candidate may require extra spending and time to smooth out, or force the acquirer to operate the acquisition as an independent division, delaying any integration benefits that may have been anticipated.

A classic example of this problem is Cisco's acquisitions of Linksys, Scientific Atlanta, and WebEx Communications, each of which has been run as an independent subsidiary of Cisco with its own operational model and routes to market since Cisco acquired them in 2003, 2006, and 2007, respectively. Incompatibilities between Cisco's routes to market and those of these three companies, combined with Cisco's executives' strong desire to avoid disrupting the success of those companies' businesses, have stopped Cisco from integrating them into Cisco's operations, despite the fact that Cisco paid a total of almost $11 billion to acquire them. In contrast to these three companies, Cisco has acquired and immediately absorbed over 70 other companies since it was founded in 1984, applying Cisco's routes to market to each acquisition. Cisco has learned to decide whether to take the acquisition's products through Cisco's routes to market, or to maintain the acquisition's routes to market, based on which would produce the best result.

Exit the Market

The last strategy for dealing with commoditization is to exit the market – the vendor abandons or sells off businesses whose products are locked in low-margin, low-differentiation industries. The classic example of this is Kimberly-Clark, whose story was told by Jim Collins in *Good to Great*. Kimberly-Clark had been a stodgy old paper company whose stock had fallen 36% behind the general market from 1951 to 1971. In 1971, the management team decided to exit Kimberly-Clark's traditional core business, manufacturing coated paper for industrial and other business markets, where the economics were poor, to focus exclusively on the consumer paper-products industry, where management thought the economics were much more attractive. From 1971 to 1991, the company transformed into the leading paper-based consumer products company in the world with the success of Kleenex tissues, Huggies diapers, and its other consumer brands. From 1971 to 1991, Kimberly-Clark's stock appreciated by 4.1 times the appreciation of the US stock market average, handily beating direct rivals Scott Paper and Procter & Gamble, and outperforming such successful companies as Coca-Cola, 3M, and General Electric.

RTM could have helped Kimberly-Clark's management realize earlier that their market was locked in a low-margin, low-differentiation model by examining their routes-to-market. They would have seen that none of their routes would be profitable enough to meet their goals because none of their routes could produce the desired revenue at a low enough cost. This is a situation where no finger-pointing is possible because everyone in marketing and sales can be doing their jobs perfectly and the net result is that the profit contribution from the routes is not sufficient.

RTM could have helped management evaluate alternative businesses to enter by projecting the revenue and profit for routes in different industries and markets, not in an abstract analysis, but for the specific economics of each industry and market. In hindsight, it is clear that the consumer paper-products industry was the right choice for Kimberly-Clark, but management would have been able to see this very clearly if they had compared the route costs for that industry to other choices.

Summary

The lifespan of products varies enormously from industry to industry. The lifetime of wireless phone models can be 12 months or less before they are superseded in the market by newer models, but some food products can be marketed for tens of years without any discernable change.

Phase 1 requires investment without significant income, but the opposite occurs in phases 2 and 3, where most of the product's lifetime profits will come. To maximize profits, it is necessary to resist pricing pressures and to find ways to extend phase 3 as long as possible.

Transitioning the routes to market for a product or service from one phase of the life cycle to another is critically important but also very difficult to accomplish. If a vendor's new routes to market are not in place for the next phase, competitors can leap ahead of the vendor and become dominant in the next phase of the market. Changing routes dynamically can drive market transitions. This can make the vendor the market leader and also maximize revenue and profit in each phase of the life cycle.

Chapter 6
Constructing a Route

In this chapter, we first explain how to construct a route, and then how to monitor its performance.

How to Construct a Route

Which resources are most effective for each of the five steps of the sales cycle, to get the best route to the customer? This is the key question to keep in mind when constructing a route. As we explained in Chap. 1, the sales cycle is the sequence of steps that vendors follow to connect with customers throughout their buying cycle, as shown in Fig. 6.1.

Several different resources are available for each step of the sales cycle. A route is constructed by selecting resources for each step and tasking them with performing specific activities to move customers in a target market segment from the beginning to the end of the sales cycle for a product or service.

In most companies, the marketing organization manages the resources selected for steps 1 and 2, and the sales organization is responsible for the resources in step 3. In some companies, some of the resources selected for step 2 are managed by marketing and others are managed by sales. The resources used in step 4 are often spread across sales, administration, logistics, indirect distribution channels, and customer services, depending on the characteristics of the product or service and on the mix of internal and external distribution channels. The customer service organization is typically responsible for step 5, but, as in step 4, external distribution channels may play an important role in step 5.

Progressing Through the Sales Cycle

Customers transition through different states of mind through the steps of the sales cycle. This is often described as the customer progressing from ignorance to awareness of the product or service, and then successively to interest, desire, conviction, and action (purchase and use).

P. Raulerson et al., *Building Routes to Customers*, DOI: 10.1007/978-0-387-79951-3_6,   103
© 2009 Peter Raulerson, Jean-Claude Malraison and Antoine Leboyer

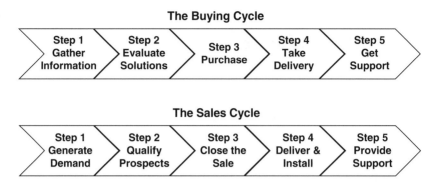

Fig. 6.1 The buying cycle and the sales cycle

The resources in step 1 of the route take customers from ignorance to awareness and then to interest, which is marked by customers requesting more information. The purpose of step 1 is to generate "leads" – customers who ask for more information. Leads are the output of step 1.

The resources in step 2 respond to the requests from the leads for more information. They take these customers from interest to desire. In addition to responding to the requests for more information, the purpose of step 2 is to "qualify" these prospects – to determine which of these customers meet pre-defined qualification criteria for being handed to the resources in step 3.

Normally, less than 50% of leads become "qualified leads" (the output of step 2), sometimes fewer than 10%. This ratio is called the "qualification rate" or "conversion rate."

By closing sales, the resources in step 3 move customers from desire to conviction and purchase. Typically, less than 30% of qualified leads become sales or "closed sales" (the output of step 3). This ratio is also called a conversion rate, but we refer to it as the "closing rate."

When measured on a cost-per-customer basis, the most expensive resource in steps 1 through 3 of a route is the salesforce that closes sales in step 3. Note that the salesforce can be internal (company employees) or external (a distribution channel). Both types of salesforces are so expensive to hire, train, manage, and motivate that they are given qualified leads, while less expensive resources (on cost-per-customer basis) are focused on unqualified leads in steps 1 and 2. Steps 1 and 2 generate and nurture sales opportunities and pass only the most attractive ones to step 3.

For example, a face-to-face sales call in a customer's office costs $200 or more, depending on travel time and cost. By comparison, sending a direct mail letter with a product brochure to a customer typically costs under $2 per customer, when done as part of a mass mailing campaign to thousands of customers. Handling an inbound telemarketing call from a customer costs about $20. For a budget of $200, only one customer can be contacted by a salesperson in step 3, but 100 customers can be contacted via a direct mail campaign in step 1, or ten customers handled by a call center in step 2.

Steps 4 and 5 take care of customers from initial delivery through their ongoing use of the product or service. For "off-the shelf" products that customers can use directly without any assistance, such as a replacement mouse for their computer or snack food they can consume from its package, customers can "install" the products themselves and need minimal ongoing support. On the other hand, families who are planning to build new "eco-friendly" homes, or airlines buying new airplanes to update their fleet, may need installation, integration, customization, maintenance, training, and operational support.

All sales cycle activities can be performed by external companies, which must be compensated to do this. Some types of external companies, such as marketing services firms (ad agencies, direct marketing firms, telemarketing firms, etc.), are usually compensated for their time, effort, and costs, whether or not the vendor's product is sold. Other types of external companies, such as retailers, resellers, and other distribution channels, are compensated on a "performance" basis – when a customer buys a product or service from them, they retain the difference between the customer's purchase price and the discounted price they paid for it. Vendors engage external distribution channels (also called indirect distribution channels) to take advantage of the customer coverage, economies of scale, and specialized facilities and skills they provide, and their variable-cost compensation model (compared to the fixed cost for the vendor's employees). It should be clear what activity the distribution channel is supposed to do to earn the vendor's compensation. The vendor's cost to recruit, train, and manage distribution channels is charged to route step 3 Close the Sale.

Building and managing routes-to-market that utilize the most productive and cost-effective resources at each step of the sales cycle, is critical for maximizing revenue and profitability.

Let us look at the route-to-market that Dell uses to sell PCs to small and mid-sized businesses, which is diagrammed in Fig. 6.2.

Dell generates demand in the small and mid-sized business (SMB) market segment through a combination of direct marketing, advertising, and public relations. These demand generation activities are directed at owners, executives, and managers of small and mid-sized businesses, and at publications that serve them. The public relations effort in particular is focused on getting Dell product evaluated and

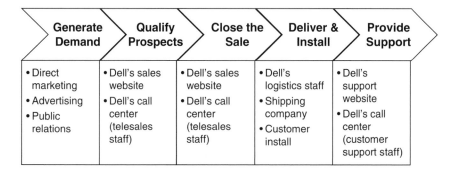

Fig. 6.2 Dell's route to small and mid-sized businesses

rated high in product comparison articles. The "call to action" in Dell's advertising and direct marketing is for the customer to go to Dell's sales Web site for special deals and additional information, or to call Dell's call center. The customer can order from either Dell's sales Web site or call center. Delivery is made by Dell's logistics department through a shipping company such as FedEx or UPS, which transports the product to the customer. The customer is responsible for installing it himself. Finally, support is handled by Dell's support Web site or call center.

The effectiveness and the profitability of a route depend on the performance and the coordination of the resources employed at each step of the sales cycle. Choosing resources which fit the customers' buying cycle is critical. A vendor that chooses the wrong resources is wasting money on them and missing opportunities to communicate and interact with the customer when they are gathering information about their needs and potential solutions, evaluating alternative solutions, and/or making purchase decisions.

Route Construction

There are three essential rules for constructing a successful route:

- Rule 1. Understand the business models, capabilities, and motivations of the internal and external resources available to you.
- Rule 2. Select resources for the route that best fit the roles or activities you need them to perform, within availability and cost constraints.
- Rule 3. Measure the effectiveness of the route by the revenue and profit contribution it produces, and by the performance of each resource on the route.

Different resources have different skills and capabilities, business models and objectives, motivations and incentives, effectiveness and efficiency, metrics and constraints.

Call centers that specialize in handling inbound calls from existing customers asking for support, do not do outbound calls to qualify prospective customers very well. Advertising firms do not create direct marketing campaigns. Promoting a company's brand is not the same as generating demand for the company's products. Retailers and distributors do not generate demand, no matter what they tell you. Their business model and capability is to fulfill demand.

Some marketing agencies offer a wide range of services, but may not perform each service equally well. You will get better results with an agency that specializes in the things that your route calls for.

There are several ways to select resources for a route. The most frequently followed approach is to simply choose the resources that your company has previously used for similar products in similar market segments. However, those resources might not be the best fit for the roles or activities required on this route, especially if one or more of the following is true:

- New Product: the product is new or significantly different from your company's other products.

- New Life Cycle Phase: the product has transitioned (or is expected to transition soon) to a new RTM life cycle phase, as discussed in Chap. 5.
- New Market: your company is a new entrant into the target market segment.

If your route fits any of these three conditions (New Product, New Life Cycle Phase, or New Market), then the resources your company has previously used are probably not good choices for your new route.

A better way to select resources in this situation is to first determine the activities that should be performed to move customers as quickly and efficiently as possible through steps 1 through 5 of the route. This can be done by interviewing target customers to understand their buying behavior by asking the following questions:

- What buying steps do the target customers typically go through?
- How do they make the transition from one step to the next in their buying cycle? What are the "gating items" for these transitions?
- Where do they turn for information about the type of need that our product meets, or for information about our type of product?
- Who influences the target customers?
- Where do they shop for our kind of product?
- What buying activities do they do, such as search the web, try out free samples, or do an ROI calculation, etc.?

Before and after interviewing target customers on these topics, it can help to discuss these issues with marketing, sales, and customer services people who have experience in the target market segment. They can usually provide examples from their experience for you to test in your research, and they can help interpret the data that you uncover.

With the answers to the questions above, your next step would be to resolve the following route design questions:

- Which resources have the capacity to handle the volume of activity (such as the number of the telesales calls, or the number of installations) that needs to be performed?
- Which combination of resources performs these activities best?
- Which combination of resources is most cost-effective?
- Which combination of resources is available for your route?
- Which combination of resources works well together?
- How much time and effort will be needed to recruit, hire (or engage), train, and manage these resources, if they are not already on staff or engaged by your company?

Constructing B2B Routes

As explained above, the first step in constructing a route is to determine the activities that should be performed to move customers through steps 1 through 5 of the sales cycle. This can be done by interviewing target customers to understand their buying behavior. Once the activities have been identified, the next step is to select the resources that can perform those activities best.

In this section, we present a case study of constructing a business-to-business (B2B) route by following the steps taken by BCSI, a hypothetical vendor of customized business computer systems for mid-sized and large companies. (This case study is based on the experience of the divisions responsible for customized business computer systems in Hewlett-Packard, Hitachi, IBM and Sun Microsystems – all of which use the RTM methodology.) To construct BCSI's routes, BCSI started by interviewing many customers in the target market (mid-sized and large companies) to understand how and why they bought products in BCSI's product category (customized business computer systems). Decision-makers, influencers, and other people in the customer ecosystem said that their buying cycles started with gathering information about the problems they were experiencing with their existing computer system, and information about their future needs. In the interviews, they talked about how, in subsequent steps of their buying cycles, they evaluated alternative solutions for their needs, purchased the products and services they selected, took delivery, and got support. They also identified where they turned for information at each step, which helped BCSI select the appropriate media and resources for each step.

Customers pointed out to BCSI that they wanted to learn about how other companies in their industry addressed similar needs. Based on this finding, BCSI's management concluded that they should provide case studies on how their customers solved their problems with BCSI's products. This, in turn, led to instituting a loyalty and growth program to get current customers to upgrade to BCSI's latest products and to increase their engagement with BCSI. Management thought that the loyalty and growth program would improve customer satisfaction and retention, and strengthen BCSI's position in the market.

BCSI's customer interviews also revealed the importance of doing the following activities in the sales cycle:

- Marketing related products and services in order to provide the "whole solution" for each customer's specific needs. This meant that BCSI needed to promote related products and services in step 1 of the buying cycle, include them in demonstrations and proposals in step 2, bundle them into the contract in step 3, take responsibility for installing them in phase 4, and provide support for them in step 5. Doing this would provide cross-selling and upselling opportunities, and increase BCSI's "share of wallet" and profit per sale. ("Share of wallet" refers to the percentage of the customer's total spending captured by the vendor.)
- Offering financing and leasing options in step 3 to speed up the sales cycle.
- Responding to customers' requests for support in step 5 in all of the ways that customers wanted to get support. BCSI expanded the self-service options on their support Web site to include features for searching BCSI's knowledgebase of support issues and solutions, and participating in discussion forums. BCSI also expanded the communications tools used by its customer support call centers to include text chat as well as telephone and e-mail.

We make a distinction in RTM between support services that are bundled with a product or service, and support services that are sold separately. If the support services are bundled with a product or service, then there is no additional charge for them, and they are provided in step 5 of the route-to-market for that product or service. If the support services are sold separately, then they are a separate offer with its own route-to-market.

Figure 6.3 summarizes the list of activities for BCSI's route for selling a complex B2B product (customized business computer systems) to mid-sized and large companies.

BCSI uses two different distribution channels:

1. BCSI's direct salesforce sells to large companies. BCSI's revenue goal for the large company segment in the upcoming fiscal year is $100 million.
2. An external, indirect channel of computer systems resellers sells to mid-sized companies. BCSI's revenue goal for the mid-sized company segment in the upcoming year is $330 million.

Resellers provide a variable-cost salesforce for BCSI because they are compensated by the margin they retain when they resell BCSI's products or services. The net effect of having two different sales channels is to divide the target market into two segments (large companies and mid-sized companies), and to split the route-to-market into two routes (a direct route for large companies, and an indirect route for mid-sized companies).

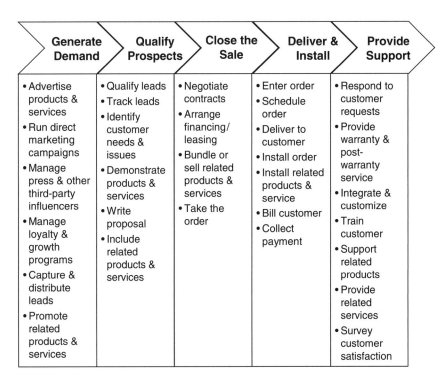

Generate Demand	Qualify Prospects	Close the Sale	Deliver & Install	Provide Support
• Advertise products & services • Run direct marketing campaigns • Manage press & other third-party influencers • Manage loyalty & growth programs • Capture & distribute leads • Promote related products & services	• Qualify leads • Track leads • Identify customer needs & issues • Demonstrate products & services • Write proposal • Include related products & services	• Negotiate contracts • Arrange financing/ leasing • Bundle or sell related products & services • Take the order	• Enter order • Schedule order • Deliver to customer • Install order • Install related products & service • Bill customer • Collect payment	• Respond to customer requests • Provide warranty & post-warranty service • Integrate & customize • Train customer • Support related products • Provide related services • Survey customer satisfaction

Fig. 6.3 BCSI's activities in the route for selling a complex B2B product to mid-sized and large companies

Figure 6.4 shows the direct route to the large company target market segment with the same list of activities from Fig. 6.3. The resources selected to perform these activities are *identified in italics* in Fig. 6.4. Figure 6.5 shows the indirect route to the mid-sized company segment, with its resources *identified in italics*.

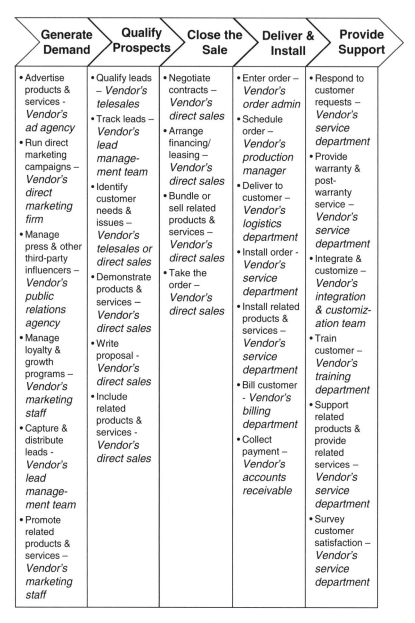

Generate Demand	Qualify Prospects	Close the Sale	Deliver & Install	Provide Support
• Advertise products & services - *Vendor's ad agency* • Run direct marketing campaigns – *Vendor's direct marketing firm* • Manage press & other third-party influencers – *Vendor's public relations agency* • Manage loyalty & growth programs – *Vendor's marketing staff* • Capture & distribute leads - *Vendor's lead management team* • Promote related products & services – *Vendor's marketing staff*	• Qualify leads – *Vendor's telesales* • Track leads – *Vendor's lead management team* • Identify customer needs & issues – *Vendor's telesales or direct sales* • Demonstrate products & services – *Vendor's direct sales* • Write proposal - *Vendor's direct sales* • Include related products & services - *Vendor's direct sales*	• Negotiate contracts – *Vendor's direct sales* • Arrange financing/leasing – *Vendor's direct sales* • Bundle or sell related products & services – *Vendor's direct sales* • Take the order – *Vendor's direct sales*	• Enter order – *Vendor's order admin* • Schedule order – *Vendor's production manager* • Deliver to customer – *Vendor's logistics department* • Install order - *Vendor's service department* • Install related products & services – *Vendor's service department* • Bill customer - *Vendor's billing department* • Collect payment – *Vendor's accounts receivable*	• Respond to customer requests – *Vendor's service department* • Provide warranty & post-warranty service – *Vendor's service department* • Integrate & customize – *Vendor's integration & customization team* • Train customer – *Vendor's training department* • Support related products & provide related services – *Vendor's service department* • Survey customer satisfaction – *Vendor's service department*

Fig. 6.4 BCSI's activities and resources for a direct route to the large company market segment for a complex B2B product

Generate Demand	Qualify Prospects	Close the Sale	Deliver & Install	Provide Support
• Advertise products & services - *Vendor's ad agency* • Run direct marketing campaigns - *Vendor's direct marketing firm* • Manage press & other third-party influencers - *Vendor's public relations agency* • Manage loyalty & growth programs - *Vendor's marketing staff* • Capture & distribute leads - *Vendor's lead management team* • Promote related products & services - *Vendor's marketing staff*	• Qualify leads – *Vendor's telesales* • Track leads - *Vendor's lead management team* • Identify customer needs & issues - *Vendor's telesales or reseller's sales* • Demonstrate products & services - *Reseller's sales* • Write proposal - *Reseller's sales* • Include related products & services - *Reseller's sales*	• Negotiate contracts - *Reseller's sales* • Arrange financing/ leasing - *Reseller's sales* • Bundle or sell related products & services - *Reseller's sales* • Take the order - *Reseller's sales*	• Enter order – *Reseller's order admin* • Schedule order – *Reseller's production manager* • Deliver to customer – *Reseller's logistics department* • Install order - *Reseller's service department* • Install related products & services – *Reseller's service department* • Bill customer - *Reseller's billing department* • Collect payment - *Reseller's accounts receivable*	• Respond to customer requests – *Vendor's & reseller's service departments* • Provide warranty & post-warranty service - *Vendor's service department* • Integrate & customize – *Reseller's integration & customiz-ation team* • Train customer - *Reseller's training department* • Support related products & provide related services - *Vendor's & reseller's service departments* • Survey customer satisfaction - *Reseller's service department*

Fig. 6.5 BCSI's activities and resources for an indirect route to the mid-sized company market segment for a complex B2B product

Figure 6.6 summarizes these two routes, <u>underlining</u> the resource differences and showing the annual expense budgets for each step in the sales cycle.

There are four important things to note about Figs. 6.4–6.6:

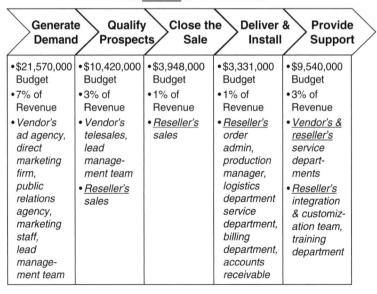

The <u>Direct</u> Route-to-Market

Generate Demand	Qualify Prospects	Close the Sale	Deliver & Install	Provide Support
•$7,190,000 Budget	•$7,920,000 Budget	•$8,520,000 Budget	•$3,570,000 Budget	•$5,010,000 Budget
•7% of Revenue	•8% of Revenue	•9% of Revenue	•4% of Revenue	•5% of Revenue
• *Vendor's ad agency, direct marketing firm, public relations agency, marketing staff, lead management team*	• *Vendor's telesales, lead management team* • *Vendor's direct sales*	• *Vendor's direct sales*	• *Vendor's order admin, production manager, logistics department service department, billing department, accounts receivable*	• *Vendor's service department, integration & customization team, training department, service department*

The <u>Indirect</u> Route-to-Market

Generate Demand	Qualify Prospects	Close the Sale	Deliver & Install	Provide Support
•$21,570,000 Budget	•$10,420,000 Budget	•$3,948,000 Budget	•$3,331,000 Budget	•$9,540,000 Budget
•7% of Revenue	•3% of Revenue	•1% of Revenue	•1% of Revenue	•3% of Revenue
• *Vendor's ad agency, direct marketing firm, public relations agency, marketing staff, lead management team*	• *Vendor's telesales, lead management team* • *Reseller's sales*	• *Reseller's sales*	• *Reseller's order admin, production manager, logistics department service department, billing department, accounts receivable*	• *Vendor's & reseller's service departments* • *Reseller's integration & customization team, training department*

Fig. 6.6 Comparison of BCSI's budgets and resources for direct and indirect routes for a complex B2B product

1. The resources in steps 1 and 2 are the same between the direct and indirect routes, except that qualified leads are distributed to resellers in the indirect route instead of to BCSI's direct salesforce. This means that the same resources can generate demand and qualify leads for both routes. The demand generation resources can use the same marketing messages, media, and direct marketing lists for both routes, or they can adjust the messages, media, and lists to fit each route specifically. For example, the messages, media, and lists could be tuned to match the market segments targeted by each route (large companies vs. mid-sized companies). The marketing messages for mid-sized companies could promote the resellers, either individually by name or collectively as members of BCSI's "authorized reseller" channel program. These refinements to the demand generation campaigns would make each route more productive, resulting in higher sales and profit contribution.

2. On the indirect route, the reseller's and BCSI's service departments must work together in step 5 to respond to customer requests, to provide warranty and post-warranty services, and to support related products and provide related services. One way to do this is for the reseller's service department to be the first point of contact for the customer, and to escalate to BCSI's service department only those problems that require BCSI's deeper knowledge or ultimate responsibility for repairing or replacing products under warranty.

3. Figure 6.5 does not show how the reseller obtains BCSI's product in order to deliver it to the customer in step 4. This is one of the functions of BCSI's distribution channel model discussed in the Choosing and Working with Distribution Channels section later in this chapter.

4. The budget data for the direct and indirect resources shown in Fig. 6.6 are a subset of the financial information for BCSI's operating plan (business plan). Figure 6.7 summarizes the vendor's Annual Operating Plan for its routes-to-market. The primary reason that companies engage indirect distribution channels is to expand market coverage and unit sales. In this case study, BCSI's indirect route will sell six times as many units as its direct route. BCSI's revenue per unit in the indirect route is 45% lower than the revenue per unit in the direct route, because the vendor's channel discount nets out to 45% off of its direct sales price. A channel discount of 45% is higher than the average discount of 30–35% to computer resellers, but can be appropriate when the unit volume and financials justify it. The cost of revenue per unit is the same for both routes, but it is much lower than it would be if BCSI sold only through the direct route because the higher volume of the indirect route enables BCSI to reduce its supply chain costs for both routes. The expense budgets for the direct and indirect routes are summarized in the RTM Expenses rows of Fig. 6.7. The Expense-to-Revenue (E/R) ratio for the direct route is 32%, 17 percentage points higher than the E/R ratio for the indirect route. This means that every dollar of revenue costs 17% more to obtain through the direct route than through the indirect route. The E/R ratio for indirect routes

	Direct Route	Indirect Route	Total	% of Total RTM Expenses	% of Revenue
Annual Operating Plan					
Unit Volume	400	2,400	2,800		
Revenue per Unit	$250	$138	$154		
Revenue	$100,000	$330,000	$430,000		100%
Cost of Revenue	20,000	120,000	140,000		33%
Gross Profit	80,000	210,000	290,000		67%
RTM Expenses					
Sales Cycle Step 1	7,190	21,570	28,760	35%	7%
Sales Cycle Step 2	7,920	10,420	18,340	23%	4%
Sales Cycle Step 3	8,520	3,948	12,468	15%	3%
Sales Cycle Step 4	3,570	3,331	6,901	9%	2%
Sales Cycle Step 5	5,010	9,540	14,550	18%	3%
Total RTM Expenses	32,210	48,809	81,019	100%	19%
Expense-to-Revenue Ratio	32%	15%	19%		
Contribution to Operating Income	47,790	161,191	208,981		49%
			All dollars are thousands ($000)		

Fig. 6.7 BCSI's annual operating plan including RTM expenses for example direct and indirect routes for a complex B2B product

is usually lower than for direct routes, and, consequently, the contribution to operating income is higher for indirect routes, assuming that the unit volumes are high enough to justify the channel discount. The bottom line is that BCSI's direct and indirect routes contribute to operating income almost the same percentage of the revenue they generate (48% and 49%, respectively), but the indirect route drives 77% of BCSI's total revenue and also 77% of BCSI's total contribution to operating income. More information on route costs is available at the book's Web site at www.RoutesToCustomers.com, along with example route calculation spreadsheets which can be downloaded at no charge.

Constructing B2C Routes

Business-to-consumer (B2C) routes should be constructed by following the approach described in detail in the Route Construction section earlier in this chapter:

1. Use resources that your company has previously used for similar products in similar market segments, unless your situation fits the New Product, New Life Cycle Phase, or New Market conditions.
2. If your situation fits any of the three "New" conditions, then survey target customers to understand their buying behavior, which will identify resource candidates for you to choose among based on how well they meet your needs.
3. Both types of routes – those based on previous experience and those based on deep research and analysis – should be tested, refined, and optimized, on an ongoing basis.

The number and diversity of resources for B2C routes is significantly greater than B2B routes. This makes selecting resources more complicated for B2C routes. Consumer spending is more than twice the level of business spending in most countries. There are about 1,000 times more consumers to sell to, than there are businesses to sell to – there are approximately 4 billion consumers in developed countries, compared to 4 million businesses, in very rough numbers, and the ratio does not change much when underdeveloped countries are included.

There are between 100 and 1,000 times more resources in touch with consumers (communicating with, selling to, or supporting), than the number of resources in touch with businesses. In March 2008, Mullen, a marketing agency headquartered near Boston, Massachusetts, distributed a poster titled "The New Marketing Ecosystem," which identified over 850 different types of resources for generating demand in B2C markets in the USA. They grouped these resources into nine major categories and nearly 60 subcategories as shown in Fig. 6.8.

Routes for Consumer Auto Insurance

GEICO, the fourth largest auto insurance company in the USA, owned by Warren Buffett's Berkshire Hathaway investment firm, sells auto insurance to consumers via a very different route-to-market than the number one and two auto insurance providers, State Farm and Allstate, as shown in Fig. 6.9.

All three companies advertise to generate demand, but GEICO spends approximately twice as much as State Farm on advertising, and more than Coca-Cola Inc. spends on Coke advertising. State Farm wrote $28.5 billion in auto insurance policies in 2006, while Allstate wrote $18.2 billion, and GEICO did $6.9 billion. But GEICO is the only one in the top four to achieve double-digit growth during the four years ending in 2006, at 13.1%. This compares to 5% growth for Allstate and essentially flat growth for State Farm.

Fig. 6.8 Mullen's list of resources for B2C demand generation

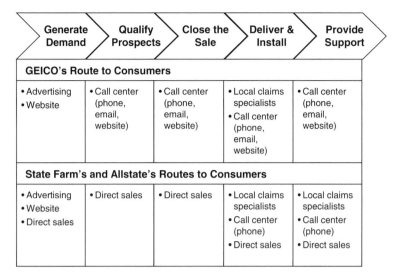

Generate Demand	Qualify Prospects	Close the Sale	Deliver & Install	Provide Support
GEICO's Route to Consumers				
• Advertising • Website	• Call center (phone, email, website)	• Call center (phone, email, website)	• Local claims specialists • Call center (phone, email, website)	• Call center (phone, email, website)
State Farm's and Allstate's Routes to Consumers				
• Advertising • Website • Direct sales	• Direct sales	• Direct sales	• Local claims specialists • Call center (phone) • Direct sales	• Local claims specialists • Call center (phone) • Direct sales

Fig. 6.9 GEICO's, State Farm's, and Allstate's routes for selling auto insurance to consumers

GEICO's extensive and clever advertising is widely viewed as the key driver of its double-digit growth rate, but it is the combination of GEICO's advertising with its efficient call centers and Web site that is outperforming State Farm's and Allstate's routes to customers. State Farm and Allstate have both increased their ad budgets recently, but their dependence on direct salesforces will continue to limit the performance and profitability of their routes-to-market.

GEICO is very profitable, says Buffett, without disclosing detailed numbers. Buffett told the *Wall Street Journal* in December 2006 that GEICO's ad spending is "sustainable as long as I am willing to write the checks [to pay for the ads], and I love writing them."

Choosing and Working with Marketing Agencies

Marketing agencies include communications (or marketing communications) firms, ad agencies, branding or naming firms, and press relations or public relations (PR) agencies. Each label implies a specialization, but many firms now include multiple specialties or partner with other firms to "do it all."

Marketing agencies are the key external resources for step 1. Their contribution can be limited to the design and execution of one demand generation campaign for a single product and market segment, or the campaign can be extended to several products and multiple market segments, up to the entire demand generation budget of the company. The same marketing agency can also be engaged in developing and executing brand promotion campaigns for the company. They may intertwine brand promotion campaigns with demand generation campaigns, which will require a little extra work to budget and track costs separately for promoting the company's brand versus route-to-market expenses.

Marketing communications agencies need to be managed well because they will show as much creativity as the available budget allows. That's their business model and motivation.

Having a healthy and productive relationship with a marketing agency requires focusing on the measurements that apply to step 1:

- the number and cost of contacting potential customers,
- the number and cost of the leads generated from these contacts,
- the conversion rate to qualified leads,
- the closing rate as a percent of the generated leads,
- and the revenue and profitability of the closed sales.

Marketing agencies are rarely paid based on the results they produce. Instead, they charge fees based on the number of staff they assign to the client and a percentage of the costs for materials and services they contract for. A more desirable relationship would be a true partnership between the vendor and its marketing agency in which they were both compensated for results measured in the same way.

It is important to work with agencies that know your product area and target market. This is particularly important for demand generation campaigns with modest budgets. Experience in generating demand for capital equipment in B2B (business-to-business) markets is not very useful for designing and running a campaign for luxury goods in B2C (business-to-consumer) markets. Few agencies recognize their limits, especially when competing for new projects in a tight economy.

There is an easy way to determine how much experience an agency really has in your field. Ask them to identify a campaign that they have done that they believe is relevant to your assignment, and ask them, how many and which customers in the target market for that campaign did they talk with to validate the campaign's messages before launching the campaign?

For B2B markets, their answers should be the names of companies and departments plus the job titles and responsibilities of the employees they talked with. For B2C markets, their answers should be demographic, lifestyle, and attitudinal profiles of the consumers they talked with. Either set of answers should include people from the same geographic regions where your campaign will be targeted. Even among the most famous marketing agencies, you will be surprised by the number of embarrassing answers.

A low-cost but "creative" demand generation campaign might look like a very good choice for step 1 of the sales cycle, but should it be selected if its impact on the entire route is unknown? An expensive campaign might generate many high-quality leads that cost less to qualify and close compared to the low-cost campaign. Choosing the more expensive campaign for step 1 may produce higher revenue and profitability if it enables the resources in steps 2 and 3 to be more productive. All resource choices should be evaluated on their impact on the entire route, as well as on their attractiveness for their specific assignments.

In our experience, marketing agencies propose demand generation campaigns without considering the entire route. Their pitches highlight the creativity of the proposed campaigns, without projections for the number or quality of the leads that would be produced, and without considering the costs for turning those leads into sales. Marketing firms provide many anecdotes about the high performance of their demand generation campaigns, but only fuzzy data on the number of leads produced and the conversion rate. Attempts to engage them in discussing these topics reveal that they have little information or experience with these issues, and are reluctant to work with clients on things that are beyond their responsibility.

Agencies often have more information on the results of brand promotion campaigns because they can measure changes in customers' brand perceptions via simple market surveys. Unfortunately, surveying customers' perceptions is not a substitute for tracking revenue and profit. Another reason why agencies have less information on the bottom-line results of demand generation campaigns is that those results depend on coordinating with other resources in the sales cycle, unlike branding campaigns, which are usually not connected to selling or tactical results.

It seems that most agencies prefer branding campaigns over demand generation work, if they do both, because branding work is more appealing to their creative staff. They also think branding has more visibility and importance to their clients, who are primarily marketing executives. If marketing executives measured the performance of their organizations on revenue production (like sales executives and general managers) and on profitability (like operations, finance, and chief executives), perhaps their agencies would have a more balanced view of the importance of demand generation to their clients' ultimate success.

Making Media Decisions

Traditional advertising and direct marketing have been characterized as "interruption marketing" because they "interrupt" the entertainment or information that the audience is watching on TV, reading in a magazine, listening to on the radio, or retrieving from their mailbox. People are now bombarded by more than 3,000 unrequested messages per day from ads and direct marketing. They cannot assimilate, remember, and act on that many messages, no matter how creative the ads may be. Advertisers are losing the battle for people's attention.

Seth Godin identified the interruptive nature of traditional advertising and direct mail, and characterized an alternative approach in his 1999 book, *Permission Marketing*. Godin declared that marketers must first gain permission from their customers to communicate with them, then build a relationship via those communications, and eventually sell them something based on that relationship.

Godin's ideas fit the "new media" created with the growth of the Internet, including blogs (web logs), wikis (collaborative Web sites), online communities, social networks, online multiplayer video games, and virtual worlds. These new media have enabled hundreds of millions of people to form online relationships that influence their attitudes about many things including what products and services to buy. These relationships, sometimes called "personal networks," are based on a high level of trust and permission. Bloggers and the people who read their blogs have a back-and-forth dialog on topics of mutual interest, just as participants in online communities and social networks share their thoughts and emotions and provide feedback. All of these communications, collectively called "user-generated content," now get more attention and are more influential than traditional media and marketing communications from vendors.

For example, a November 2007 survey of 4,400 information technology (IT) decision-makers found that they spend an average of 3.5 hours per week participating in online social networks, more than they spend reading IT magazines and vendor-provided content such as direct marketing brochures and white papers. The survey also found that topic-based networks and personal networks are the most important sources of information to these customers through all steps of their buying process for IT products and services.

The study was sponsored by and conducted among the members of ITtoolbox, an online community for IT professionals with more than 1.1 million members. ITtoolbox was founded in 1998 and acquired in July 2007 by the Corporate Executive Board (CEB), a provider of best practices research, decision support tools, and executive education. CEB had annual revenue of $533 million in 2007. CEB is using the ITtoolbox platform to build communities for professionals in other domain areas such as finance, operations, procurement, human resources (personnel), and sales and marketing.

SAP, the leading provider of business automation software, has changed the way that it markets to IT managers as a result of the growing importance of customer communities such as ITtoolbox. Previously, SAP communicated extensively "to" its customers, providing many brochures, white papers, and other media detailing the features and benefits of SAP products and services. SAP has augmented that with stepped up participation in community Web sites where SAP people can "listen" to customers and join conversations selectively. For example, as of March 2008, there were nearly 10,000 different group discussions in progress regarding SAP products and services on ITtoolbox, of which about 8,400 (84%) were initiated by customers, not SAP. Most of these discussions began with requests for advice on buying or using SAP products, and almost all of the replies were from customers, not SAP employees. SAP has changed its communication style to accommodate the dynamics of the customer community.

Online communities and user-generated content are changing marketing communications across a wide range of industries. Consider the following:

- Trying to decide which camera to buy? Read independent reviews and user-to-user advice at Photo.net, the oldest and largest online community of photographers.
- Do you need a repairman to fix a plumbing or electrical problem at home? Check an online directory of service providers rated by their customers at Angie's List, instead of scanning ads in the yellow pages.
- Trying to decide where to stay or shop while traveling on business or vacation? Use Google Maps to see not only the roads you will be traveling but also hotels and shops along your route, along with customer comments from their visits to these establishments. This type of information changes the dynamics of the travel, dining, retail, and entertainment industries.

- Need a contract manufacturer to build parts for a new product that your company is developing? Post your specs and a request for quotation online at MFG.com, a B2B marketplace for sourcing manufactured parts from all over the world, currently handling over $50 million worth of quotations per day.

If you market cameras, home repair services, resorts, contract manufacturing, or any other product or service where blogs, online customer communities, and social networks are becoming important, you should include them on the list of resources for brand promotion and demand generation. Keep in mind that they do not work in the same way that traditional media, advertising, and direct marketing works.

To get the most benefit from these "new media" resources, you should join them, participate in the online discussions in your product area, and respond to questions or comments about your company, products, and services. Your goal is to establish yourself as a credible and trustworthy "face" for your company. Use a genuine and conversational tone of voice, not "corporate speak," in your communications in these communities. Make friends with the other members. Provide straight answers to their questions (as a friend would answer, not as a press agent), helpful information not easily found on your corporate Web site, and other things that the other members would accept as a fair trade for taking time to read your messages, such as free samples, a contest, or a survey of their opinions (unless prohibited by the community's rules).

For both brand promotion and demand generation campaigns, choosing the right media requires a solid understanding of the target market. The right media is the media preferred by the target market.

Marketing to Small and Mid-Sized Businesses

Many marketing campaigns target Small and Mid-sized Businesses (SMBs), companies below the size of the Fortune 1,000. In many product and service categories, SMBs in aggregate account for more than 50% of the total market opportunity. Many marketers dream of reaching SMBs, but it can be like catching a mirage – you can see it, but you cannot grasp it.

Reaching all of the SMBs in a geographic region can be very expensive. SMB decision-makers do not read the same publications or go to the same trade shows. They think differently about many issues, such as corporate strategy (grow rapidly vs. maintain current size vs. other strategies). Lead qualification and closing rates vary significantly between different groups of SMBs, making it difficult to control spending for steps 2 and 3 of the sales cycle. This is why it is so difficult to grow sales profitably in the SMB market.

For these reasons, it makes sense to divide your SMB target market segment into multiple subsegments. Each subsegment should be homogenous – every customer in the subsegment buys for the same reasons, buys from the same distribution channels, and responds in the same way throughout the sales cycle. It should be easy to determine which subsegment a customer belongs to, based on information already known about the customer or by asking the customer a few simple questions.

Vendors have divided their SMB target markets into multiple subsegments on one or more of the following dimensions: vertical industry, company size, business model, trading partners, corporate strategy, affinity with the same small-business accountants, chambers of commerce, professional or trade associations, etc.

The best way to determine which criteria are relevant in your segmentation of the SMB market is to survey SMB decision-makers with questions on their needs, their purchase plans, and the media they prefer, along with their profiles on the potential subsegmentation criteria. Using an Internet-based survey tool makes this quick and easy.

One convenient by-product of this approach is that your route-to-market resources can quickly determine if an SMB prospect is inside a prioritized subsegment by simply asking the same questions that were used on your survey to divide the SMB market into subsegments. Usually, only one or two such questions are needed, making it very inexpensive to boost qualification and closing rates significantly.

We have used this technique very successfully at IBM, Cisco, Microsoft, and other companies, including small private companies, to inexpensively separate and prioritize SMB customers by subsegment. The net result has been predictable, high profitability for their SMB routes-to-market.

Based on this example of the SMB market, the same reasoning applies to the large company market or to the consumer market. We will not develop it further here, since the goal for this chapter is to explain how to select resources when constructing a route.

Customer Database

The customer database is a collection of data about your customers and prospects that enables you to understand them and to communicate with them based on that understanding. The customer database can be used at every step of the sales cycle, from demand generation through post-sales customer support, by both internal and external resources.

With a customer database, you can target communications directly to specific customers, selecting them based on information about them previously captured in the database. You can also create or continue an ongoing dialog with them.

Customer Relationship Management (CRM) systems are based on a customer database. Without the database, CRM would not function at all. Whether you have a CRM system or not, you should build and maintain a customer database. It is one of the most important tools for optimizing marketing, sales, distribution, and customer service. The customer database enables all go-to-market resources to focus on the customers with the highest returns, and to share their knowledge of the customer with other resources on the route.

For example, if you are planning to use direct mail to reach potential customers in a demand generation campaign, the customer database would be not only the source of the customers' names and addresses for the mailing, but also the repository where each response to the mailing is recorded. Every item returned by the postal service as "undeliverable" or "refused" should trigger an update to those customers' records in the database to flag this problem. Perhaps these customers are important enough to justify a second attempt, or a phone call, to identify their correct address. Or maybe the appropriate action is to mark their records "do not mail" to reduce the cost of the next mailing. Either action improves the performance of your demand generation resource for the next campaign to this market segment.

You can get three times as many responses from a mailing if you put the person's name on the address, not just their title (in a B2B campaign) or "Resident" (in B2C). You are five times more likely to reach prospects on the phone if you ask for them by name instead of by department or position. The higher productivity justifies the extra time and money to add people's names to a customer database and keep it current.

Many contact lists are available for rent or purchase. They provide basic contact information that you should consider to be only a "start" for building your customer database. Some of these lists are only available for one-time use – you can keep only those contact records for customers that respond to your mailing. Sources for contact lists include list brokers, magazines, and companies that compile directories or provide high-volume direct marketing services. Contact lists of consumers, businesses, government, and educational organizations are available. Before spending the money to rent or buy a complete list, use a sample of it to test how well it works for you.

Another way to start building your customer database would be to capture contact information from every customer who registers for a newsletter, requests literature, stops at your booth at a trade show, etc. You need to make these exchanges a "win–win" for the customer and your company – the customer must get something of value in exchange for providing his or her contact information.

Customer contact information can also be acquired by offering discount coupons or rebates for registering a recent purchase – this works well for product manufacturers that sell through retailers. An alternative would be running contests – customers provide their contact information so they can be notified if they win. The contest prizes should be relevant to your target market, but do not have to be your products. Some companies offer T-shirts, caps with the company's logo, consumer electronics products (such as Apple iPods), or other "cool" merchandise.

These techniques can be used to update your customer database for about $1 per contact record per year. The cost to acquire a new contact, however, is about $25. These are order of magnitude costs, but they highlight the importance of updating customer data instead of buying new data each time you need it.

The customer database is a strategic tool. Its quality depends on accuracy and completeness. Keeping it up to date is critical. Getting the most value from it requires specialized skills and appropriate tools. Without those skills and tools, you should have a specialized external resource, such as a direct marketing agency, customer contact center operator, or database marketing consultant, maintain your customer database.

Plantronics used a customer database in a creative campaign to raise the visibility of its headset products to the "C-suite" of its target customers. The goal was to remove the image of telephone headsets as only for call center staff, who were typically tied to their computer workstations and were not mobile during their work shifts. Instead, Plantronics wanted executives to realize that headsets could also be used by regular office staff (who need to walk around their offices during the work day) and by employees who travel on business in their automobiles. In addition to the wireless, "hands-free" feature of Plantronics' Bluetooth headsets, these headsets could be used with mobile as well as office phones, and included noise cancellation circuitry to make sure the user's communication was as clear and understandable as possible.

Plantronics' marketing managers realized that it would be impossible to get appointments with CEOs and their direct reports to explain headset features and benefits to them. So they decided to send each executive something valuable that would get their attention and convey the image and idea they wanted to communicate to these executives.

Plantronics' marketing managers compiled a database of the top executives of companies in their target market, which in this case were large public companies. They bought a contact list with the names, positions, and addresses of these people from a public source. They coordinated with Plantronics' salesforce to make sure that they included the top executives from every active sales opportunity.

Plantronics' marketing agency designed a large box to attractively present a sample of Plantronics' different headset models. The presentation was designed to encourage the recipient to try on different headsets to get a sense of their comfort, sound quality, and mobility. By seeing the value in using these headsets themselves, they would also see the value for their people.

A presentation box was Fedexed as a gift to each executive in the contact database. By addressing the shipment to each executive personally, and shipping it via Fedex, the headsets were certain to be delivered directly to the executives or their personal secretaries. The size of the box and the high-quality presentation of the headsets ensured that the secretaries would not throw the box away or fail to mention it to their bosses.

Shipping the boxes to arrive simultaneously for all of the executives at each company made it likely that they would talk about Plantronics' headsets at their next meeting. The campaign was very successful in achieving its objectives, more than justifying the cost.

Choosing and Working with Distribution Channels

This section is a quick overview of distribution channels for people who are not familiar with them. This section does not cover channel management.

To use distribution channels productively, it is important to understand their business models, capabilities, and motivations. This is especially true of indirect distribution channels because they are independent businesses, not employees of the vendor. The primary motivator for indirect distribution channels is profitable market opportunities.

There are three generic channel maps for B2B and B2C markets: direct, single-tier, and two-tier. Figure 6.10 shows a direct channel – the vendor sells directly to customers through its own internal resources, which could be face-to-face salespeople, telesales, online, or catalog (mail order).

Figure 6.11 shows a single-tier indirect channel – the vendor sells its products or services at a discount to retailers, resellers, or dealers, who resell the products or services to customers at a mark up to their cost. A retailer operates a store where customers visit and buy. The store can be online or bricks-and-mortar or both. Retailers usually stock a limited level of inventory. Resellers and dealers sell directly to customers without a storefront. They typically carry no inventory and fulfill orders from vendors and/or wholesale distributors.

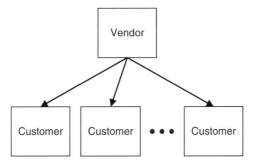

Fig. 6.10 Direct channel map

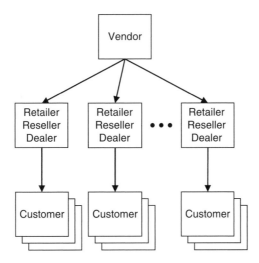

Fig. 6.11 Single-tier indirect channel map

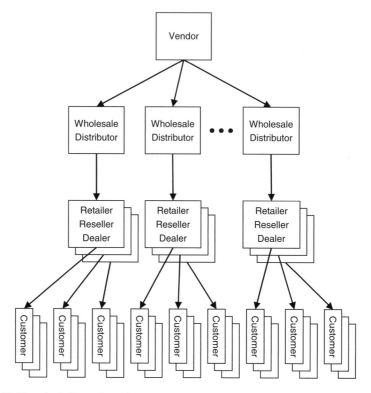

Fig. 6.12   Two-tier indirect channel map

Figure 6.12 shows a two-tier indirect channel map – the vendor sells it products or services to wholesale distributors at a discount, who then resell to retailers, resellers, or dealers at a lesser discount (so that the distributor can retain a margin); the retailers, resellers, or dealers resell to customers at a mark up to their cost. Wholesale distributors buy products in bulk from vendors, stock the products in warehouses, take orders from and provide credit to retailers/dealers/resellers, and ship small quantities to them or directly to users (called "drop shipping"). Distributors often combine products from multiple vendors into a single shipment for a retailer/reseller.

In Figures 6.11 and 6.12, the arrows from the vendor to its distribution channel partners represent the flow of marketing communications, support, and compensation as well as product distribution. Unfortunately, the real world is not perfect like these black-and-white diagrams. In the real world, distributors compete with each other to sell the same product to a retailer/reseller/dealer. Retailers compete with each other to sell the same product to a customer. Sometimes a vendor's direct salesforce competes with its indirect distribution channel to sell products to the same customer. The real world is gray and full of overlap and channel conflict. But these are not topics for this book.

In addition to the three generic channel maps depicted above, some industries have additional types of firms that can be included in the flow of marketing communications, support, compensation, and/or product distribution from the vendor to customers. For example, in B2B markets, vendors can engage independent manufacturers representatives (also called "manufacturer's reps" or "rep firms") to sell their products or services to distributors, retailers/resellers/dealers, or customers. They act as sales agents and provide the vendor with local market coverage on a variable-cost, commission basis, but unlike distributors they do not take title to or resell products or services. In B2C markets, brokers or agents perform the same function as manufacturers reps by selling a vendor's products or services to wholesale distributors or to retailers.

In some B2B markets, vendors sell to industrial distributors which resell directly to customers in a variation of the wholesale distributor business model. For example, industrial distributors in the construction industry sell building materials to building owners, and also to construction contractors who resell them to building owners along with their services.

In addition to the channel maps in Figs. 6.10–6.12, vendors sell their products or services to other vendors on an "OEM" (Original Equipment Manufacturer) or "private label" basis – the selling vendor's product or service is embedded in the buying vendor's product or service. Many electronic components are sold on an OEM basis – most customers who buy computers or digital music players do not know or care about the component parts, until there is news about a product recall. The same is true for ingredients in prepared foods or individual stocks in a mutual fund.

The cost of market coverage is the primary criterion for a vendor to consider when deciding whether to sell through a direct, single-tier, or two-tier distribution channel. Optimizing the costs for recruiting, managing, communicating with, handling orders from, and providing products to channel partners will have a big impact on the total cost and profit contribution of a route. The easiest way to see this will be in the Expense-to-Revenue ratio. For example, Fig. 6.7 summarizes a plan for a direct route with an E/R ratio of 32% to sell 400 units of a complex B2B product to generate $100,000,000 in revenue, and an indirect route with an E/R ratio of 15% to sell 2,400 units to produce $330,000,000 in revenue. The indirect route yields a higher Contribution to Operating Income in Fig. 6.7 due to the significantly higher unit volume and the 17 percentage point difference in the E/R ratio. The higher unit volume also reduces the Cost of Revenue (Cost of Goods Sold), which in this example boosts the profitability of the direct route as well as the indirect route because both routes sell the same product. The RTM methodology makes it easy to see the financial impact of choosing one type of distribution channel versus another. This enables management to optimize the company's channel mix.

We assume that the vendor knows the cost for the administrative and logistical activities of communicating with and handling orders, billings, and collections from channel partners. These costs are as follows:

- The cost to maintain an administrative relationship with a retailer, reseller, or dealer
- The cost to accept and process an order
- The cost for a line on an order
- The cost for scheduling delivery
- The cost for a line on a delivery form

- The cost for preparing an invoice
- The cost for a line on an invoice
- The cost for collecting an invoice
- The cost per line for collection
- The cost for storing an SKU (Stock Keeping Unit).

Each alternative channel model will have a different total cost for administration and logistics that can be calculated by multiplying the costs listed above by the appropriate number of items in each category. For example:

- If a wholesale distributor will manage 100 retailers, resellers, or dealers, then you can divide the cost to maintain administrative relationships with them by 100.
- Assuming that a wholesale distributor will manage 100 retailers, resellers, or dealers, you can divide the total number of orders by 200, the total number of lines on orders by 1,000, the number of invoices by 200, the number of deliveries by 300.

The total cost for administration and logistics after engaging wholesale distributors should be a very tiny percentage (under 1%) of the cost of dealing with retailers, resellers, or dealers directly. Consolidating country-based distribution to a regional or continental level should reduce the cost even further.

The cost differences between direct, single-tier, and two-tier distribution can be calculated easily when the specific costs for administrative, logistical, and other activities are known, and when the performance of each type of channel partner is understood. The cost differences can be substantial. For example, the Expense-to-Revenue ratios shown for the indirect route in Fig. 6.5 included a 45% discount from the vendor to the indirect channel. This is high enough to support a two-tier distribution channel in the computer industry. This means that the indirect route in Fig. 6.5 could be constructed as either single-tier or two-tier. Either way, it would be 17 percentage points less expensive than the direct route.

Choosing and Working with Resources for Step 5 Provide Support

Many customers buy products and services primarily to consume, use, or experience them. They think that steps 1 through 4 of the sales cycle are necessary only so that they can consume what they are buying. For example, shopping for groceries is a chore that precedes cooking and eating a meal (step 5). Getting a customized business computer system is a painful exercise that precedes the benefit of using it to better run a business (step 5). Buying an insurance policy is a confusing and costly effort that precedes the time during which the insurance policy provides peace of mind by protecting the customer from financial loss (step 5).

Other customers focus on the shopping experience more than consumption. For them, the primary objective of their buying process is the shopping experience itself. However, for all customers, the shopping experience clearly has a big impact on customer purchases, whether the customer's primary goal is to shop or to consume.

For complex B2B products, the activities that must be performed in step 5 include responding to customer requests for support, repairing, and maintaining the product, and training the customer how to use the product. For consumer packaged goods such as food, beverages, footwear, apparel, home furniture, and cleaning products, customers may not need any step 5 support except repair or replacement of defective goods.

The resources available for performing these activities may include the same resources that delivered and installed the product or service in step 4, such as the vendor's or reseller's service department or service companies contracted by the vendor. These service organizations can use telephone, e-mail, and Web sites to communicate with customers. The vendor's or reseller's logistics and administrative organizations may need to be involved to pack and ship replacement parts. Many B2C retailers will replace defective goods at no charge to the customer as long as the vendor will accept the return and replenish the retailer's stock.

As pointed out earlier in this chapter, support is provided in step 5 at no additional charge because it is bundled with the product or service. This means that the manufacturer or original source of the product or service is ultimately responsible for support, regardless of which resource closed the sale. However, if support is sold separately, then it is a separate offer with its own route-to-market.

How much should a vendor budget for the costs of step 5? Historical data on the incidence and cost for support, replacement parts, shipping, etc., can help answer this question. If there is no historical data, then the budgeting task is much more complicated. In this case, the vendor should start with a small test market or ramp up sales slowly while tracking the costs for step 5, before expanding the route to cover the entire market. In many cases, the vendor's product development, manufacturing, and service organizations can reduce support costs over time by improving product quality, reliability, availability, maintainability, and/or serviceability.

There is a significant benefit to the vendor for having direct contact with customers in step 5: it enables the vendor to assess and improve customer satisfaction and loyalty, and to maximize the customer's lifetime value. For this reason, most vendors should continue to spend money to contact customers in step 5 for customer satisfaction surveys and loyalty programs, even if support costs have been driven to zero. The cost to sell products to existing, satisfied customers is substantially less than to new customers. In many industries, acquiring new customers is profitable only after they become repeat buyers.

How to Monitor the Performance of a Route

Demand Generation Campaigns

The success of a demand generation campaign is measured by the following:

1. The number of people contacted or "touched," and the average cost to contact them.
2. The number and average cost of the leads generated.

3. How many of the generated leads become qualified (the conversion rate).
4. How many of the generated leads become sales (the closing rate as a percentage of all generated leads).
5. The revenue and profit contribution of those sales.

If any of these measurements is absent, the campaign may not be very effective:

- If the campaign generates many leads but these leads have a low qualification rate, then the campaign may be eye-catching but few respondents understand what is being offered. Many campaign respondents are disappointed that they do not meet the qualification criteria. The cost of qualification is high because so many leads are not qualified. If you measured the campaign only on the number of leads it generated, you would be delighted. But you would be disappointed by the lower revenue and profitability of the few sales that result from the campaign.
- A low volume of sales compared to the number of qualified leads means that there is a problem somewhere along the route. A call center can be very proud of its high rate for converting raw leads into qualifying leads, but if few of those leads turn into sales, the overall performance of the route will be low. The problem could be in the call center – the qualification script might need to be tightened. Or the problem could be in step 3 of the sales cycle, Close the Sale – the salesforce might need more training or more people to cover the large number of leads before they grow stale (lose interest or buy from the competition). The problem could be pricing – the product may be overpriced. Follow-up conversations with qualified leads who did not become customers should enable you to identify the problem, so you can fix it and get performance back on track.
- If customers return more products after delivery than expected, or if surveys of customer satisfaction are lower than expected, then you are not meeting customers' expectations. This can result from one or more problems along the route, such as the demand generation piece sets customers' expectations higher than the product can meet, or customers are not happy with their experience with the vendor or distribution channels at any point in the sales cycle.

We exclude from a route all activities that do not promote a specific product or product family. Promoting the company's brand is important, but it is not part of a route-to-market for a product or service. The stronger a company's image is, the more effective will be the routes for the company's products.

Compare Expense-to-Revenue Ratios to Select the Best Resources

As explained in Chap. 8, dividing the total revenue from a route by the total cost for the route yields the expense-to-revenue ratio, sometimes written as E:R or E/R. Expense-to-revenue ratios are very useful in evaluating alternative resources when constructing a route because they let you compare the impact on the revenue and profit contribution of the route for different resource choices.

For example, a demand generation campaign manager could choose between renting a carefully screened contact list that costs 17 times as much as an unscreened list. Which list will produce more revenue?

The E/R ratio can answer that question. The campaign manager can run an A/B test of a sample of both lists, keeping all other elements of the route the same. To do this, he would rent a limited number of contacts from each list, run them through the entire route from step 1 through step 5, and track carefully all route expenses. He would then calculate the E/R ratio for the two tests. The list with the lower E/R ratio is the better choice financially because it costs less to produce each dollar of revenue.

Marketing Optimization

A/B tests can be run to compare any two differences between one route and another, and multiple differences can be tested at the same time. All online resources, such as e-mail, e-commerce, digital download, and online support, can be tested online. Multiple combinations of online resources can be tested online every day or every week (depending on the amount of traffic the Web site receives per day).

Many important elements of a route – marketing messages, visuals, information flow, pricing, terms and conditions, delivery, and support options – can be tested, refined, and optimized online. Testing requires standard analytic tools for Web site optimization, process optimization, data mining, and business intelligence.

Routes that involve physical resources, such as in-person meetings or providing samples of physical products for hands-on evaluation, can be prototyped and tested in an online form with the physical resource treated as off-line components in the workflow. This means that almost all routes (physical and online) can be tested, refined, and optimized online. The buzzword for this is "marketing optimization" but it goes beyond marketing to include all of the marketing, sales, distribution, and customer service resources on a route.

Managing a Route Like a Factory Production Line

If a factory received an order for 1,000 units of one of its high-end products, the factory manager and his or her staff would develop a plan to meet the order's requirements for quantity, quality, and delivery date as profitably as possible. They would work backwards from that goal to establish the following:

- the sequence of steps that must be done
- the amount of raw material and components needed
- a schedule for the workers and production lines that took into account their capacity, throughput, and constraints.

Then they would supervise the production effort to make sure that everyone followed the plan.

Let us apply this approach to managing a route-to-market. In this case, the goal is to get 1,000 sales next quarter. First, they need to get qualified leads. But only 20–30% of the qualified leads will buy. So 3,000–5,000 qualified leads will be needed in order to get 1,000 sales.

To get 3,000–5,000 qualified leads, they will need about 9,000–15,000 responses from customers (requests for more information), because about 33% of leads convert.

Not everyone will respond to the demand generation campaign. Typical response rates are 2–3%. This means that at least 750,000 people need to be contacted by the campaign. A smaller contact list might not yield enough leads to produce 1,000 sales.

In this example, the closing rate (20–30%), conversion rate (33%), and response rate (2–3%) were presented because they are typical of computer industry sales of established products from leading manufacturers. Your company's actual experience with prior demand generation campaigns should be the source for these numbers in your calculations. Market conditions change over time, and other factors can impact results, so it is best to track these three rates over time and use your best judgment when choosing the rates used in these calculations. We have found it best to be conservative because getting more responses, conversions, or orders than expected is usually preferred to getting fewer than expected.

Now, let us look at the staffing level needed to get these 1,000 sales next quarter. Let us say that the demand generation campaign is prepared ahead of time and mailed on the first day of the quarter. Also, the call center staff are trained and ready to start qualifying leads, and the sales people are ready to follow up with the qualified leads to close them. Then the schedule for the route would be as follows:

- Week 1: direct mail in transit to 750,000 people in the target market segment.
- Weeks 2–3: approximately 15,000 or 2% of these 750,000 people respond to the direct mail by contacting the call center for more information. The call center staff qualifies about 5,000 or 33% of these 15,000 callers. If a call center agent can handle 4 callers per hour, then about 50–100 agents will be needed to handle the calls, depending on peak load, shift length, queue depth, and other factors. If a call center agent can handle 10 calls per hour, then only 20–35 agents may be needed. In general, if the number of agents is limited, then the demand generation should be spread out over time in order to avoid the problem of callers waiting on hold too long.
- Weeks 3–13: about 5,000 qualified leads are contacted by the salesforce, of which 1,000 sales are closed. If 100 salespeople are dedicated to this, and each salesperson closes 1 sale per week, they will produce 1,000 sales in 10 weeks.
- Weeks 4–13: as each order is closed, it is shipped from the warehouse or factory, and invoiced at that time. The date on the invoice must be before the end of the quarter in order to count towards the 1,000 sales.

The staffing levels in the call center and salesforce have a big impact on achieving the goal for the quarter. All of the numbers and the schedules must "line up" because, otherwise, the sales goal cannot be achieved:

- The number of people "touched" by the demand generation piece (750,000), including when that occurs (at the beginning of the quarter, not later in the quarter).
- The number of responses produced by the demand generation piece (15,000), and the number of call center agents available to handle them when they call (20–100 depending on call center loading).
- The number of qualified leads (5,000) turned over to the salesforce, and the number of sales people following up on those leads (100 depending on how many they can handle at the same time).

It is best to know before launching a campaign that will touch only 10,000 contacts that a "miracle" will be needed for it to sell 1,000 units. This is simple reasoning, but few people apply it systematically.

Summary

To construct a successful route, the product or service vendor must engage the combination of resources that best fit the roles or activities that must be performed. The resources must meet several constraints including availability, capacity, cooperation (vs. competition), cost-effectiveness, and (most importantly) presence with or access to customers in their buying cycle. The best way to determine which resources to use is to start by interviewing target customers to understand their buying behavior, then identify activities and resources that fit the customers' buying behavior, and then choose among those resources based on their availability, capacity, cooperation, and cost-effectiveness.

Demand generation campaigns should be measured on the number of people "touched," the number and average cost of leads, the conversion rate to qualified leads, the closing rate, and the revenue and profit contribution of the resulting sales. Each of these measurements, and the ratios between them, can indicate potential performance problems.

Comparing expense-to-revenue ratios for different resources or routes is a very useful way to evaluate alternatives.

All online resources and many off-line or physical resources, including marketing messages, visuals, information flow, pricing, and many other elements of the five Ps (product, positioning, price, promotion and place) can be optimized via online testing. This applies to all of the marketing, sales, distribution, and customer service resources on a route, although the buzzword for this is "marketing optimization." This is a very powerful approach to improving performance, and RTM makes full use of it.

Thinking of a route as a factory production line, is a good way to break down a route into discreet steps on a timeline. Calculating how many workers and other resources will be required to handle the work at each step, can help to identify potential bottlenecks and deadlines. This is another powerful approach for improving performance and predictability.

Chapter 7
Go-to-Market Performance Assessment

There are two different ways to assess a company's go-to-market performance. One way is to use the Routes-to-Market methodology to analyze the company's go-to-market costs to identify spending that can be optimized to make marketing, sales, and customer service more effective and efficient. This type of analysis is a real eye-opener for executives because it is usually the first time that they will see how the budgets for these organizations are connected and can be adjusted to drive more revenue and profit. This is discussed in the first section, "Analyzing and Optimizing Go-to-Market Costs."

The second way to assess a company's go-to-market performance is to compare the company's practices to the best practices of competitors or other relevant companies. This is discussed in the second section, "Comparing the Company's Go-to-Market Performance to Best Practices."

Analyzing and Optimizing Go-to-Market Costs

If a company has not used the Routes-to-Market methodology, it has implicit routes composed of the resources that perform marketing, selling, and customer support activities. We can analyze the revenues and expenditures for the company's implicit routes to evaluate the company's go-to-market performance.

The expense categories on many companies' income statements include Cost of Sales, Cost of Goods Sold, or Cost of Services; Selling, General, and Administrative Expenses; Research and Development Expenses; and other expense categories such as Interest Expense and Income Tax Expense. Unfortunately, these figures are not broken down into the specific categories that we need in order to use RTM to evaluate the company's go-to-market performance.

To use RTM for performance assessment, we need the company's marketing, sales, distribution, and customer service expenses. These numbers typically come from the budgets for these resources, whether they are internal departments or external contractors. Ideally, these numbers will be broken down by product and market segment. But the first assessment can be done with expenses broken down by product or product family. A second assessment can be done later with the expense numbers broken down by market segment.

P. Raulerson et al., *Building Routes to Customers*, DOI: 10.1007/978-0-387-79951-3_7,   135
© 2009 Peter Raulerson, Jean-Claude Malraison and Antoine Leboyer

In all RTM performance evaluations, the expense numbers must be assigned to the appropriate steps of the sales cycle. That will reveal how much of the total go-to-market costs are spent in each step. Seeing these relative percentages can be a real eye-opener for executives because it can highlight areas where money is being spent unproductively or where a larger investment could significantly boost revenue and profit.

Let us go through the departmental budgets and identify which steps of the sales cycle their costs should be mapped to. In the following sections, whenever we refer to a budget, we mean the costs actually incurred, not simply the amount budgeted.

Marketing Budget

By "marketing budget" we mean all costs for marketing communications, public relations, advertising, direct marketing, product marketing, etc. This includes costs for both internal resources (employees who perform these functions) and external resources (agencies, contractors, media buys, and so on).

However, we must separate the costs for promoting the company and its brand in general, from the costs for generating demand for the company's products and services. Costs for PR and marketing communications that provide general information about the company or that promote the company's brand image, should be assigned to marketing overhead because they do not serve a specific product or service.

Costs for marketing campaigns that promote products or services, or that generate leads, should be assigned to the routes for those products or services, not overhead. This is especially true if a campaign's leads are going to be contacted for qualification or follow up, because, in that case, the demand generation campaign is clearly part of the sales cycle for those products or services.

The ratio of the marketing overhead cost compared to the total cost of the routes shows the balance between resources devoted to promoting the company's image versus selling products and services. If this ratio exceeds 20–30%, the extra spending on marketing overhead may be unproductive.

There is an optimum budget for any activity. Spending more than the optimum amount produces less value for every extra dollar spent. It would make more sense to spend those extra dollars on other productive activities. If the budget for promoting the company and its brand is more than 20–30% of total route costs, then the overage should be redirected to demand generation for products and services, or to other resources such as sales, distribution, or customer support.

The overage could simply be saved (not spent on anything), in which case it becomes profit. It should be clear that profitability can be maximized by spending the optimum amount (not more, not less) for each go-to-market activity. Determining how much the company is spending today is a good first step in optimizing future spending.

Marketing overhead costs are not broken down by products or product families. But all other marketing costs must be. All go-to-market costs must be assigned to specific products or product families.

Channel Management Budget

Channel partners are the companies in the vendor's distribution channel. They can be retailers, resellers, dealers, systems integrators, or other firms that resell the vendor's product or service to the final customer. They can also be distributors, manufacturers' reps, agents, brokers, or other firms that sell to retailers or dealers. For example, many manufacturers of electronic components for PCs sell their components to distributors or brokers who sell them to PC manufacturers; these distributors and brokers are channel partners for the component manufacturers.

Channel partners can also be product providers and professional services firms that do not resell the vendor's product, but provide products or services that complement the vendor's product, such as software developers, consultants, or facilities engineers (for computer room wiring, cooling, physical security, etc.). Financial and legal advisers are channel partners for investment products such as annuities and mutual funds; sometimes they are paid commissions by the mutual fund company, and sometimes they are paid a consulting fee by the customer. Another example would be physicians who are channel partners for prescription drug companies because they prescribe drugs to patients; they usually do not resell the drugs.

Channel partners become members of the vendor's channel program. The channel program is usually run by channel marketing. In some companies, channel marketing is separate from channel sales. Channel marketing costs are part of the marketing budget, but channel sales costs are in the sales budget. Channel sales people recruit, train, manage, and support channel partners. In some cases, they make joint sales calls on the final customer with channel partners, to help close sales.

In the RTM model, all channel management costs (channel marketing, channel sales, channel support, etc.) are charged to the Close the Sale step after they are broken down by product or product family. This includes costs for recruiting, developing, training, managing, supporting, and communicating with distribution channels, along with channel incentive payments such as MDF (market development funds) and SPIFs (sales promotion incentive funds).

However, cooperative marketing funds and other expenditures for co-marketing with channel partners are charged to the Generate Demand step after breakdown by product or service, provided that the basic rules for demand generation campaigns are met (leads are contacted for qualification or follow up, and tracked to closure).

If it is not possible to break down channel costs by product or product family, then they cannot be included in the route costs, just as marketing overhead is excluded from route costs.

Channel discounts are typically applied before the company invoices the channel partner, so that the discount is taken before the company records the sale. Therefore, channel discounts do not show up in the company's income statement and are not typically tracked as an expense on the company's books. RTM leaves them out as well.

Channel rebates are sometimes captured as adjustments to net revenue, in which case RTM leaves them out. However, if channel rebates are treated as incentive payments (not as revenue adjustments), they should be charged to the Close the Sale step after they are broken down by product or product family, just like other channel incentive payments.

Sales Budget

There are two questions that come up when breaking down the sales budget for RTM:

1. In most companies, the salesforce sells multiple products or services to multiple customers. Often, the customers are in different market segments. How much of the sales budget should be charged to the route for each offer and market segment?
2. When one considers the wide range of activities performed by sales organizations in different industries, it is clear that, in aggregate, salespeople do things that fit each of the five steps of the sales cycle, Generate Demand, Qualify Prospects, Close the Sale, Deliver, and Provide Support. The sales budget is not typically split into budgets for these steps. How should the sales budget be broken down into the five steps of the sales cycle?

The answer to these questions is to break down the salesforce's time in three different ways: (1) by product or service, (2) by customer (market segment), and (3) by activity. The intersection of the first two ways, by product/service and market segment, provides the percentage of the salesforce's time that is dedicated to each route. The third way, by activity, is used to distribute that percentage across the steps of the sales cycle.

Table 7.1 shows a breakdown of the salesforce's time by steps of the sales cycle for a hypothetical software-as-a-service company that provides two online services, Customer Relationship Management (CRM) and Service Management (SM), to two market segments, Large Companies, and Small/Mid-sized Companies.

Referring to Table 7.1 as an example, the percentage in each of the five steps of the sales cycle would be multiplied times the total sales budget for the company to calculate the sales cost for that step. This calculation would be done for each route.

The example in Table 7.1 shows that the hypothetical company's salesforce spends just over half of its budget closing CRM deals in Large Companies and qualifying Large Companies for CRM, with its remaining budget distributed in small amounts across other steps of the sales cycle and other routes. The data in Table 7.1 suggest that management should check to see if the company's CRM service is selling very well to Large Companies, because 64% of the salesforce's time is devoted to this route. Another take away is that the other three routes are getting very little sales attention. How can more sales time be focused on these routes? Are they even worth pursuing?

Breaking Down the Salesforce's Time

There are two ways to break down the salesforce's time:

1. Implement Activity-Based Costing (ABC). This is the most comprehensive and accurate solution. ABC is a method for assigning costs based on tracking the time and resources each worker spends on individual products, customers, and

Table 7.1 Breakdown of the salesforce's time for a hypothetical software-as-a-service company

Route	Service	Market Segment	Generate Demand	Qualify Prospects	Close the Sale	Deliver & Install	Provide Support	Total
1	Customer Relationship Management	Large companies	3%	20%	32%	6%	3%	64%
2	Customer Relationship Management	Small, mid-sized companies	0%	4%	6%	1%	0%	11%
3	Service Management	Large companies	3%	5%	9%	1%	0%	18%
4	Service Management	Small, mid-sized companies	0%	4%	3%	0%	0%	7%
Total			6%	33%	50%	8%	3%	100%

activities. With ABC, work time is tracked on an ongoing basis using automated tools, and can be analyzed periodically.

2. Conduct a quick survey of a subset of the salesforce, and extrapolate the survey results to the entire salesforce. This is much quicker and less disruptive than implementing ABC, but not as accurate. The survey must be repeated when there are major changes in the size or composition of the salesforce, or in the activities, products, or customers that the salesforce works with.

ABC is very similar in concept to tracking workers' time in service industries such as healthcare, law, and consulting. The resulting time records are used to bill the customer for the workers' time. For example, a law firm typically bills customers for the time lawyers actually work on their cases. Time records identify the activity or procedure being performed, which enables the law firm to bill specific rates for different activities as opposed to a flat rate for all of a worker's time. The time records can also be used to analyze the law firm's total work time by activity, which is helpful for firm-wide productivity improvement, or to provide additional training to workers who take longer to perform a standard procedure than the average.

Most salespeople, however, have never tracked their time. Activity-Based Costing has been done with very few sales organizations.

Instead of implementing ABC, a quick survey of the salesforce could be done to break down their time by product, customer, and activity:

1. First, identify the products, customers, and activities that the salesforce typically spends time on. The products can be grouped to simplify the survey. Customers must be identified by market segment. Activities should be listed with descriptions, so that salespeople will choose the proper activity code. (A test run can

help improve this.) The product groupings, market segments, and activities should match the company's RTM model.

2. Design a form or spreadsheet for the salespeople to fill in throughout the work day. Time tracking software or an online service can be used instead of a paper form or spreadsheet. Data collection needs to be as fast and easy as possible to maximize participation and accuracy, and to minimize the time taken from selling to perform this administrative chore.

3. Ask a representative subset of the salesforce to track their time using the form or software for a fixed period of time, such as a day or a week (long enough to smooth out the variation in their daily activities). If only a small percentage of the salesforce has the same workload, it may be necessary to do a census instead of a survey – every salesperson tracks his or her time for a day or a week or longer.

4. Analyze the results. The survey needs to provide a valid breakdown of the entire salesforce's time for at least a quarter, and ideally a year. The survey should be repeated if there are major changes in the size or composition of the salesforce, or in the activities, products, or customers that salesforce works with.

To map sales activities to the appropriate step in the sales cycle, consider the following:

- Sales time spent searching for prospective customers should be focused on finding prospects for the products or services in that market segment. Promoting the company and its brand in general is an auxiliary task better done by marketing.

- Sales time spent contacting leads from demand generation campaigns should be focused initially on qualifying these prospects. That time goes into the Qualify Prospects step. Additional time spent with these prospects may go into the Qualify Prospects step or the Close the Sale step. The traditional sales progression is to qualify a prospect on need, authority, budget, and time frame (which activities are all in the Qualify Prospects step) before investing time to prepare a specific proposal (which is in the Close the Sale step). However, the salesperson and the prospect may engage in other activities, such as needs analysis, demos, performance tests, benchmark runs, pilot projects, or visits to the vendor's installed customers or home office. One criterion for determining whether a sale is in the Qualify Prospects or Close the Sale step, is whether the prospect has transitioned from evaluating alternative vendors (still in the Qualify Prospects step) to making a selection among a short list of finalists (in the Close the Sale step). This distinction is meaningful to the customer as well as the potential vendors in large, complex procurements, because it signals a milestone in the procurement process and, depending on the context, may impose legal and financial obligations on both parties for completing the procurement process. Less formal purchasing processes may zigzag between evaluating alternative vendors and selecting from a short list of vendors. Activities in the Qualify Prospects step are focused on helping the prospect evaluate the vendor's product or service. Activities in the Close the Sale step are focused on finalizing a proposal, getting selected as the winner, and negotiating the contract. It is important to define carefully which activities are performed in each of these two steps because that makes it possible to create high-performing teams of lower-cost inside sales (telesales) resources combined with higher-cost direct sales (field sales) resources to do these two steps. This distinction is also useful in determining whether a potential sale qualifies for special treatment or scarce resources such as help from a centralized "bid desk" or "proposal team" to help the salesperson prepare a proposal, sales calls by senior management, special pricing or financing to beat the competition, delivery priority, or other "deal sweeteners."

- Deal registration has become very important over the last few years for companies with value-oriented indirect sales channels. Motivating channel partners to engage in their own lead generation activities and having them share details of these opportunities with the vendor has proven difficult for many vendors. Too many partners still harbor a sense of distrust and secrecy with their pipeline information out of fear that sharing these details could result in the vendor's direct sales team (or even another partner) swooping in and stealing the deal. Vendors have set up deal registration systems to help their partners build profitable businesses while getting insight into the partners' pipelines. The reseller "registers" a potential sale to a prospective customer via an online deal registration system on the vendor's Web site. This "protects" the opportunity from being closed by the vendor's direct salesforce and competing resellers, assuming that the registering reseller meets the vendor's requirements. To minimize the possibility that a reseller would register deals that he was not actually pursuing, it is important that the vendor's requirements establish clearly how far along the prospect is in the sales cycle. Aligning these requirements with RTM makes it possible to leverage both.

- Sales time spent after the sale has been closed goes into either the Deliver step or the Provide Support step. If the salesperson is involved in delivering, installing, or customizing the product or service, then that time should be charged to the Deliver step. But the more typical situation is that the salesperson's role in the Deliver step would at most be to let the customer know when his or her order will be delivered, or to introduce to the customer the person who will handle delivery, installation, and customization. Of course, it is in the salesperson's best interest to follow up with the customer during delivery, installation, and customization to make sure these go smoothly. However, the salesperson should put more time into the Provide Support step than the Deliver step because it is during the ongoing Provide Support step that most customers reorder supplies and buy additional, related products and services. This is the "lifetime value" period during which repeat business with the customer greatly magnifies the customer's value to the vendor. It is also during this period that any turnover in the customer's staff, change in the customer's corporate strategy or business situation, or dissatisfaction with the vendor's product or service can provide opportunities for competitors to win the follow-on orders and displace the initial vendor. From a risk/reward perspective, following up with the customer during the Provide Support step has very high value for the salesperson.

Call Center Budget

Call centers generally have a profusion of statistics that can simplify the cost analysis. The costs that are eligible for being assigned to routes are the call center's operating expenses: costs for personnel, data base management, campaign management, infrastructure, and telecommunications.

All costs must be broken down by product or product group. Costs are assigned to different steps of the sales cycle as follows:

- Data base management, campaign management, and outbound calls and e-mails to contact prospective customers "blind" (i.e., when those customers are not in a sales cycle with the vendor) are charged to the Generate Demand step.
- Contacting prospects to qualify them is charged to the Qualify Prospects step.
- Telesales costs are assigned to the Close the Sale step. Note that "telesales" means selling the customer, getting a purchase decision and order over the phone, not just generating demand or responding to a request for information.
- Unsolicited incoming calls, e-mails, text chats, and other communications, whatever their nature, including support calls from customers and channel partners, are charged to the Provide Support step after breakdown by product or product family.

Administrative Budget

Costs for all activities related to delivery, installation, or customization, including order taking, logistics, storage, and invoicing are charged to the Delivery step. However, costs for general administrative services, facilities, and other overhead are not charged to the routes.

Expense-to-Revenue Ratios

At this point, we can add up the costs for each step of the sales cycle to compute the total route or go-to-market cost for the product or product family. Dividing the total route cost by the total revenue for the product or product family yields the expense-to-revenue ratio, sometimes written as E:R or E/R.

An expense-to-revenue ratio lower than 5% is exceptional for a manufacturer. It is more typical of a wholesale distributor or retailer with efficient logistics, little added value, and very little demand generation.

An E/R ratio from 5% to 10% is characteristic of products in RTM Life Cycle phase 4 Commodity, where the customers are conservatives and skeptics. These products are well known to the market and therefore demand generation is usually very efficient. Low-cost two-tier distribution keeps the route costs low.

An E/R ratio from 10% to 15% is typical of products in phase 2 Solution and phase 3 Distribution, where the customers are predominantly pragmatists. Volumes are growing rapidly, the transition from single-tier value-added channels to two-tier volume channels is coming or already underway, and margins allow sufficient demand generation to expand the market and grow faster than competitors.

Expense-to-revenue ratios higher than 15% are indicative of products in phase 1 Introduction, where the customers are enthusiasts and visionaries. The products are just getting into the market, revenues are very low, and marketing and sales costs are very high. People talk about "investing" to create the market for the product.

Example Routes (Tables 7.2–7.5)

Each industry has its own set of go-to-market models. There is no single optimal Route-to-Market for products because products evolve through the life cycle, requiring changes in the route. However, some general comparisons are valuable.

- All routes must have a good balance between demand generation and prospect qualification to make demand generation campaigns effective. As the product evolves through its life cycle, it becomes better known and more widely accepted, so demand generation produces better leads and prospect qualification becomes easier. In this situation, it costs less to qualify the same number of prospects as at an earlier phase of the market. This is why the ratio of the expense for Qualify Prospects divided by the expense for Generate Demand

Table 7.2 Route A: Strong demand generation for a product in RTM Life Cycle phase 2 Solution

			Unit Volume: 40,000			
			Revenue: $50.0M			
Route A			Expenses: $12.5M			
			Expense-to-Revenue Ratio: 25%			
	Generate Demand	Qualify Prospects	Close the Sale	Deliver & Install	Provide Support	Total
Expenses	$2.5M	$1.5M	$2.0M	$4.0M	$2.5M	$12.5M
% of Total	20%	12%	16%	32%	20%	100%

Table 7.3 Route B: Rapid sales growth for a product in RTM Life Cycle phase 3 Distribution

			Unit Volume: 100,000			
			Revenue: $100.0M			
Route B			Expenses: $15.0M			
			Expense-to-Revenue Ratio: 15%			
	Generate Demand	Qualify Prospects	Close the Sale	Deliver & Install	Provide Support	Total
Expenses	$3.5M	$2.0M	$3.5M	$4.0M	$2.0M	$15.0M
% of Total	23%	13%	23%	27%	13%	100%

Table 7.4 Route C: Low margin and high volume for a product in RTM Life Cycle phase 4 Commodity

					Unit Volume:	130,000
					Revenue:	$100.0M
	Route C				Expenses:	$9.0M
			Expense-to-Revenue Ratio:	9%		
	Generate Demand	Qualify Prospects	Close the Sale	Deliver & Install	Provide Support	Total
Expenses	$2.0M	$0.5M	$2.0M	$3.0M	$1.5M	$9.0M
% of Total	22%	6%	22%	33%	17%	100%

Table 7.5 Summary of Tables 7.2–7.4

	Route A		Route B		Route C	
Product in RTM Life Cycle	Phase 2		Phase 3		Phase 4	
Unit Volume	40,000		100,000		130,000	
Revenue	$	50.0M	$	100.0M	$	100.0M
Total Route Expenses	$	12.5M	$	15.0M	$	9.0M
Expense-to-Revenue (E/R) Ratio	25%		20%		15%	
Route Expenses						
Generate Demand	$	2.5M	$	3.5M	$	2.0M
Qualify Prospects	$	1.5M	$	2.0M	$	0.5M
Close the Sale	$	2.0M	$	3.5M	$	2.0M
Deliver & Install	$	4.0M	$	4.0M	$	3.0M
Provide Support	$	2.5M	$	2.0M	$	1.5M
Total	$	12.5M	$	15.0M	$	9.0M
Route Expenses per unit sold						
Generate Demand	$	62.50	$	35.00	$	15.38
Qualify Prospects	$	37.50	$	20.00	$	3.85
Close the Sale	$	50.00	$	35.00	$	15.38
Deliver & Install	$	100.00	$	40.00	$	23.08
Provide Support	$	62.50	$	20.00	$	11.54
Total	$	312.50	$	150.00	$	69.23
Ratio: Qualify Prospects / Generate Demand	60%		57%		25%	
Average unit price of the product	$	1,250.00	$	1,000.00	$	769.23

drops from 60% in phase 2 (Route A) to 57% in phase 3 (Route B) to 25% in phase 4 (Route C) in the example above.

- The expense-to-revenue ratio decreases as revenue increases. In the example above, the E/R ratio falls from 25% to 20% to 15%.
- In the example, total route expenses drop in absolute terms from $15M in phase 3 (Route B) to $9M in phase 4 (Route C), as the product becomes a commodity and its average sales price falls. The $6M decrease in route expenses (from Route B to Route C) flows directly to the bottom line for the product.
- As volumes increase, the per unit cost for the Deliver step decreases from $100 in phase 2 (Route A) to $40 in phase 3 (Route B) to $23.08 in phase 4 (Route C) in our example.
- As volumes increase, the per unit cost for the Close the Sale step falls from $50 in phase 2 (Route A) to $35 in phase 3 (Route B) to $15.38 in phase 4 (Route C). This means that the distribution channel becomes more efficient.
- As volumes increase, the per unit cost for the Provide Support step falls dramatically from $62.50 to $20 to $11.54 per unit.

After evaluating the company's go-to-market performance by product, more insight can be gained by breaking down the numbers by market segment, if the data are available.

Comparing the Company's Go-to-Market Performance to Best Practices

By definition, a "best practice" is the most efficient and effective way of accomplishing a task. Using a best practice does not commit a company to an inflexible, unchanging way to do something. Instead, the adoption of best practices is a philosophical approach based on continuous learning and continual improvement. Comparing a company's current practices to best practices can stimulate discussions about better ways to accomplish the company's goals, which usually go well beyond a numeric quota for sales to include objectives such as market share, customer satisfaction, profitability, and contribution to the community.

This section explains the second way to assess go-to-market performance, using F5 Networks as an example.

F5 Networks

Today, F5 Networks, Inc., is the global leader in Application Delivery Networking. F5 provides equipment and software that make network applications secure, fast, and available, helping organizations get the most out of their investment in servers, networks, and applications software. By adding intelligence and manageability into the network to off-load applications, F5 optimizes applications and allows them to work faster and consume fewer resources.

Seven of the Fortune 10 companies, and nine of the top ten financial firms rely on F5's products and services. Microsoft, Oracle, BEA, and SAP all recommend F5 to their customers. Over 16,000 organizations and service providers worldwide trust F5 to keep their applications running. The company is headquartered in Seattle, Washington and has offices and distribution channels worldwide. F5's sales in 2007 totaled $526 million with net profit of $77 million.

The first half of F5's story is its growth during the "dot com" boom of the late 1990s and its turnaround during the dot com bust from 2000 to 2002. All of this happened before F5 used RTM. The second half of the story begins at the end of 2002 when the executive team decided to drive 100% of F5's business through indirect distribution channels, and the company began using RTM.

F5 in the dot com Boom and Bust

F5 was founded in Seattle in 1996 by Jeffrey S. Hussey, an investment banker who had identified a market opportunity for Internet traffic management products. Hussey served as F5's first president, CEO, and chairman.

F5 introduced its first product, named the BIG/IP Controller, in July 1997. By using BIG/IP Controllers to manage their Internet traffic automatically and intelligently, customers could run their existing servers more efficiently instead of adding additional and costly servers. This is a substantial benefit for companies with large or rapidly growing Web sites, where good traffic management can be worth millions of dollars in cost savings and in customer satisfaction with the Web sites' performance.

F5's sales started slowly, with only $229,000 in revenue in 1997. The dot com boom propelled sales to $4.9 million in 1998, $27.8 million in 1999, and $109 million in 2000, F5's first profitable year. Along the way, F5 broadened its product line with related products and services, and expanded sales and distribution to Europe and Asia. F5 raised a total of $56 million in an IPO in June 1999 and a second public offering later that year.

Optimism about the new Internet economy drove F5's stock price to an all-time high of $160 per share in November 1999, up from the IPO price of $10 just 5 months earlier.

To manage the company's rapid growth, F5's board brought in John McAdam as president and CEO in July 2000. McAdam was previously general manager of the web server sales business at IBM, and, before that, president and COO of Sequent Computer Systems, Inc., a manufacturer of high-end server systems, which IBM acquired in September 1999.

Soon after joining F5, McAdam realized that his challenge was not managing growth, but dealing with the bursting of the dot com bubble. Eighty percent of F5's revenue had come from Internet start-ups, but many of them were now retrenching or going out of business.

Interviewed by Jeff Meisner of the *Puget Sound Business Journal* in December 2001, McAdam said, "When I came on board [in July 2000], our business model was broken. It was a real problem. Expenses were out of control. We had to take some quick action. We moved really fast."

F5's Turnaround

McAdam quickly refocused F5 on Fortune 1,000 companies, reduced staff by 15%, and subleased office space in the company's newly built headquarters. Over the next two years, 2001–2002, McAdam streamlined F5's product line to make it more appealing to large companies, and signed distribution agreements with Nokia Corporation and Dell Computer Corporation to resell F5's products to their Fortune 1,000 customers. McAdam also signed a wholesale distribution agreement with Ingram Micro Inc., the world's largest technology distributor. These distribution agreements helped shift the profile of F5's customer base from small, unstable dot coms to large, established enterprises. Nokia also invested $35 million in F5 for a 9.9% stake.

Remarkably, McAdam's turnaround efforts maintained revenue at $107 million in 2001 and $108 million in 2002, almost equal to F5's revenue of $109 million in 2000. Net profit fell from $14 million in 2000 to losses of $31 million in 2001 and $9 million in 2002, as McAdam cut product and overhead costs while continuing to invest in marketing, sales, and product development to stay ahead of competitors.

Cisco Systems and Nortel Networks – two giants of the computer networking industry – had each bought a traffic management competitor to F5 in 2000, and were pushing those products through their much-larger salesforces and broader distribution channels. By the end of 2001, it was a three-horse race for control of the $385 million traffic management market. Cisco had 47% share of the market. Nortel had 17%. F5 was a very close third with 16%.

"It's a definite turnaround for this company," said Brent Bracelin, an analyst with investment bank Pacific Crest Securities of Portland, Oregon, in December 2001. "You have to give credit to McAdam and his team. F5 went from being 80 percent reliant on dot com customers to 90 percent reliant on large enterprises."

Changing F5's Go-to-Market Process and Strategy

At the end of 2002, McAdam and his management team decided to drive 100% of F5's business through the channel to grow the company faster and more profitably. He engaged Peter Raulerson, one of the authors, and his consulting firm, The PARA Marketing Group, to analyze and recommend improvements for F5's existing go-to-market process and strategy. A cross-functional team was formed for the project, with managers from F5 sales, channels, marketing, customer services, product management, and finance organizations.

During their first meeting, the cross-functional compared F5's current go-to-market efforts with industry best practices that Raulerson had compiled from previous research with IBM, Cisco, Nortel, Microsoft, Symantec, Adobe, and other industry leaders. The team concluded that F5 was using basic or better practices in every performance category except Optimized Routes-to-Market, as shown in Fig. 7.1.

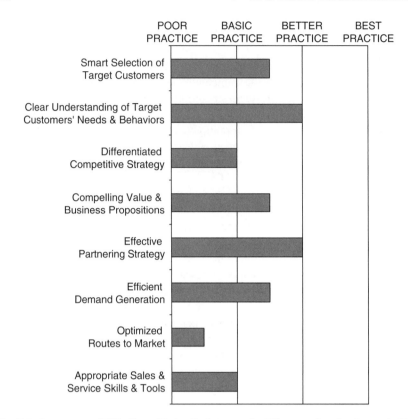

Fig. 7.1 Assessment of F5's Go-to-Market Performance by F5's cross-functional team in 2002. (See The Eight Dimensions of Go-to-Market Performance below for more information.)

In the next step of the project, F5 staff were trained in RTM. This was followed by steps to analyze competitors' programs and processes, test channel business propositions and program changes, and develop plans for driving 100% of F5's business through channels. To close the performance gap between F5's current approach for Optimized Routes-to-Market and industry best practices, the F5 channel marketing manager used the RTM methodology to reevaluate F5's channel structure and spending with support from the finance department. Over the next few months, budgets for marketing and sales were adjusted, F5's salesforce got better at leveraging partners to qualify prospects and close sales, and the channel program was tweaked to reduce F5's costs for recruiting, training, and supporting channel partners. F5's score on the Optimized Routes-to-Market dimension more than doubled.

In retrospect, the recommendation with the biggest benefit was to integrate the channel into F5's management processes, metrics, and reporting, making channels an integral part of the company's day-to-day operations.

For example, before F5 management had been exposed to RTM, product plans and launch plans did not involve channels. After using RTM, F5 incorporated channels into every aspect of product and launch plans, including strategy, tactics, and deliverables.

Before RTM, F5's sales grew from zero to $108 million over 6 years, but only one year was profitable. F5 went public during this period, but its stock price climbed from $10 to $160 during the dot com boom and then fell to $3.75 in April 2001 in the dot com bust, just before the company's turnaround started to show results.

After RTM, one of F5's biggest innovations was DevCentral, an online community of tens of thousands of customers, channels and developers collaborating to enhance and extend F5's application delivery management software, and to support each other with tips from their real-world experience managing the widest range of network applications anywhere. Microsoft, Oracle, BEA, and SAP are active participants in DevCentral. None of F5's competitors have anything like DevCentral.

After RTM, F5's sales increased at a compound annual rate of 37% to $526 million in 5 years, net profit increased almost 19 times, to $77 million. An investment of $10,000 made in F5's common stock at the start of this five-year period would have grown to $98,500, compared to only $23,000 for the NASDAQ Composite. (F5 stock is traded on NASDAQ.)

The Eight Dimensions of Go-to-Market Performance

This section explains the assessment model shown in Fig. 7.1. Typically, a cross-functional team discusses how their company performs each of eight go-to-market dimensions or categories, with the goal of assigning a numeric score for the company's performance on each dimension. The score can range from 0 (the company is doing nothing on this dimension, or its practice is poor) to 3 (the company is following a best practice on this dimension). The scores can have fractional steps like ½ or ¼, whatever is the consensus of the team.

One goal for assessing the company's go-to-market performance as a team is to stimulate discussions about better ways to accomplish the company's goals. Many people have no prior experience in thinking about best practices. They may know different ways to do things, depending on their experience in different jobs or different companies. But they often do not know which way works better, or which factors might impact that. For these reasons, it can be very helpful to take time to draw each person on the team into the discussion of how their company's performance on each dimension compares to basic, better, and best practices.

This model was developed by analyzing how several leading companies go-to-market, across a wide variety of products and services. It became clear that there are eight relatively independent dimensions or categories of information and activities that are important for success. Analyzing start-ups and companies that were number 2 or number 3 (or number 14) in their markets was even more illuminating because it showed the impact on go-to-market performance for competitors with different resources, market positions, partner communities, technologies, etc.

1. Smart Selection of Target Customers

   - Poor Practice (score 0): No prioritized targets; sell to anyone/everyone
   - Basic Practice (score 1): Market segmented by demographics only; segments selected by size; no prioritization of customers within segments
   - Better Practice (score 2): Market segmented by demographics and psychographics; segments selected by multiple internal criteria; customers prioritized opportunistically
   - Best Practice (score 3): Market micro-segmented by demographics and psychographics and value chain; segments selected and customers prioritized by weighted fit to vendor and customer criteria

2. Clear Understanding of Target Customers' Needs and Behaviors

   - Poor Practice (score 0): No understanding; keep pitching until someone buys
   - Basic Practice (score 1): Know features and benefits customers need today
   - Better Practice (score 2): Understand features and benefits customers need and want and customers' buying behavior today
   - Best Practice (score 3): Understand features and benefits customers need and want and customers' buying behavior and how these are evolving

3. Differentiated Competitive Strategy

   - Poor Practice (score 0): No idea how company stacks up versus competitors or how differentiated
   - Basic Practice (score 1): Vendor-centric sales-oriented comparison to competitors' features and benefits
   - Better Practice (score 2): Detailed customer- and partner-centric strategy to differentiate from competitors' features, benefits, and business practices
   - Best Practice (score 3): Detailed customer- and partner-centric leadership strategy to differentiate from competitors' features, benefits, and business practices

4. Compelling Value and Business Propositions ("value propositions" are for customers, "business propositions" are for business partners and channel partners)

   - Poor Practice (score 0): Untested value and business propositions for vendor's product or service
   - Basic Practice (score 1): Validated value propositions for vendor's product or service; business proposition = margin
   - Better Practice (score 2): Compelling value propositions for solutions based on vendor's product or service; business propositions = margin + leverage
   - Best Practice (score 3): Compelling value propositions for solutions based on vendor's product/service and relationship; business propositions = margin + leverage + relationship

5. Effective Partnering Strategy

- Poor Practice (score 0): Work with partners that approach the vendor; no coordinated plan
- Basic Practice (score 1): Formal channel program with a silo sales model; partners prioritized by volume; some recruitment and technical enablement
- Better Practice (score 2): Multi-track channel program with a hybrid sales model; partners prioritized by volume and coverage; periodic recruitment and technical enablement
- Best Practice (score 3): Multi-track channel program with a hybrid sales model, tuned to different partners' needs; partners prioritized by multiple criteria; ongoing recruitment, technical, and business enablement

6. Efficient Demand Generation

- Poor Practice (score 0): Untracked, haphazard demand generation
- Basic Practice (score 1): Marketing mix determined by budgeting demand generation functions independently (advertising, direct mail, telesales, etc.)
- Better Practice (score 2): Marketing mix optimized by evaluating trade-offs across demand generation functions (advertising, direct mail, telesales, etc.); results tracked and analyzed
- Best Practice (score 3): Marketing mix used in prior campaigns extensively analyzed and combined with data mining of CRM database to maximize lifetime customer value

7. Optimized Routes to Market

- Poor Practice (score 0): No integration of demand generation, direct and channel sales, and customer service
- Basic Practice (score 1): De facto routes; leads segmented and passed to direct sales or channels; service is different for customers and partners
- Better Practice (score 2): Formal route planning with defined roles in the sales cycle for different players; timing of demand generation synchronized with partner enablement
- Best Practice (score 3): Routes optimized by integrating demand generation and CRM data mining with partner management to accelerate sales cycles and maximize ROI

8. Appropriate Sales and Service Skills and Tools

- Poor Practice (score 0): Each direct sales and service person creates their own tools; no tools for channels; skill levels not tracked
- Basic Practice (score 1): Sales and service people are trained in standard sales processes and tools, but the only monitoring is on their results
- Better Practice (score 2): Skills development and career tracking, with a technical certification program; each step of sales and service processes is monitored
- Best Practice (score 3): Balanced scorecard approach with activity-based management; extensive skills development and career tracking; continuous process and tool improvement

Summary

This chapter provides two ways to assess go-to-market performance. One is based on the expense-to-revenue ratio (E/R), which is simply the total cost of a route divided by the total revenue for the route. There are a range of values for this metric that are "normal" for different market situations. Comparing the E/R for a route to normal values, and to the E/R for other routes, can highlight expenses that may be too high or too low. The E/R also provides a measure of cost efficiency – the RTM team that is operating a route should expect to improve its E/R over time. It is a very useful tool.

The second way discussed in this chapter to assess go-to-market performance is to compare a company's practices to the best practices of other successful companies in the same or relevant industries. This can highlight gaps in the company's strategies, tactics, tools, skills, programs, market coverage, etc. By closing these gaps, the company can boost performance quickly. This helped F5 Networks' management and staff make changes that significantly improved their business. After adopting RTM, F5 achieved spectacular growth in revenue, profits, and market value.

Chapter 8
Connecting RTM with Corporate Strategy

Up to this point in the book, Routes-to-Market (RTM) has been presented as a methodology used by executives responsible for marketing, sales, distribution, and customer services in field organizations. This chapter shows how RTM can also be used in product management and corporate strategy at headquarters. The following case study of Adobe Systems Incorporated provides an example.

Adobe Adapts Its Go-to-Market Strategy with RTM

A key player in the desktop publishing revolution of the 1980s, Adobe became a leading provider of graphic design, publishing, and imaging software for web and print production during the 1990s. Adobe's customers were collectively called "creative professionals" because they designed or created visual content for print publications, advertising, electronic documents, and Web sites. By 1999, Adobe's software was running on 70% of the desktop computers used by creative professionals.

Milestone

In 1999, Adobe's revenue exceeded $1 billion for the first time in the company's history, and net income (net profit) reached a record level of $238 million. Industry analysts projected that its market segments would expand at a compound annual growth rate (CAGR) of 27% for the next several years. The company was on a roll and the future looked very bright.

But there were storm clouds on the horizon. Disruptive forces were putting pressure on the publishing workflow of Adobe's corporate accounts. The Internet had become the "information superhighway" for delivering all types of content including advertising and electronic documents, changing the way that creative professionals designed and published content. The rapid growth of smart phones and other handheld devices was starting to cause creative professionals to rethink

P. Raulerson et al., *Building Routes to Customers*, DOI: 10.1007/978-0-387-79951-3_8,   153
© 2009 Peter Raulerson, Jean-Claude Malraison and Antoine Leboyer

content design and distribution for a second time. Both forces were disrupting the way that Adobe's customers created, managed, and distributed documents and other media. Industry analysts projected that publishing executives would retool their creative and production environments to meet the growing demand for content 24/7, anytime, anywhere. Change on this scale would give competitors new opportunities to make inroads into Adobe's customer base.

Network Publishing

In 2000, Kyle Mashima, Adobe's VP of Strategic Development, summed up the projections by telling Adobe's management team and board of directors that over the next few years, change would sweep through the publishing value chain, driving Adobe's corporate customers to seek better integration across a wide range of media and consumer devices, streamlined and automated production and delivery processes, and new roles and business models. They decided to create and sell products to meet these new needs. They named the emerging Internet-centered publishing model "Network Publishing," which they described as "harnessing the power of the Internet for the creation, management, and distribution of visually compelling, interactive and personalized digital content reliably on any device."

Before Adobe publicly announced its Network Publishing strategy in November 2000, Adobe product managers and software engineers had started to develop several new products that fit the Network Publishing model. These products were intended to augment Adobe's existing product line by streamlining production workflows, facilitating collaboration, customizing content dynamically, and delivering it to multiple devices automatically. The new products were designed to run on server computers instead of running on desktop computers, as almost all of Adobe's products operated at the time. Over 90% of Adobe's 1999 revenue came from desktop software.

Adobe product and marketing managers expected that server software products would leverage sales of desktop software in some situations. They saw market opportunities with the US Internal Revenue Service, other government agencies, and large financial institutions where many more employees would need Adobe desktop software if the organization standardized on the new all-electronic workflow enabled by Adobe server software. This would actually reduce the organization's cost to serve their customers, so the result would be a "win–win" for the customer and Adobe.

Coming out with server software products would be a radical change for a desktop software company like Adobe, but the company did not yet realize the extent of the change. Almost every department in the company would be impacted, including product development (software engineering), product testing, maintenance, manufacturing (product packaging), finance, marketing, sales, distribution, and customer service.

Ready to Go to Market

Part way through the development process for the new products, preannouncement customers started to ask questions about Adobe's plans to help them integrate the new software into their environments and provide an ongoing account management relationship for their IT managers. Their questions highlighted the fact that server software is more complex to operate than desktop software. Unlike desktop software, managing an installation of server software often requires coordinating multiple vendors of hardware, software, and network products. How was Adobe planning to help customers do that?

As the customers' questions filtered up to Adobe's executives, it became clear that there was a broader problem: Adobe was not ready to market, sell, and support server software. Mashima concluded that Adobe's switch from desktop software to server software required changes in Adobe's go-to-market strategy, skill sets, and routes to market, in addition to changes in product development.

Mashima engaged Peter Raulerson, one of the authors, and his consulting firm, The PARA Marketing Group, to help Adobe figure out the gaps in its current go-to-market strategy and capabilities, how to fill them, and how to prepare products better to go to market in the future. A cross-functional Adobe task force was quickly formed for the project. The task force used the RTM methodology to evaluate the go-to-market plans for Adobe's server products to identify gaps that Adobe needed to fill. They also profiled several companies in the server software business to understand how their capabilities compared to Adobe's, and analyzed the financials of 27 leading software companies to forecast the impact on Adobe's financials for closing these gaps.

Working with the product and marketing managers for the new products, the task force segmented the markets for Adobe's server software to understand the target customers' needs beyond the product features that had already been analyzed. The task force focused on understanding the whole solution for each market segment. Introduced in Chap. 1 and discussed in detail in Chap. 4, a "whole solution" is the minimum set of products and services necessary for the target customer to completely satisfy his or her compelling reason to buy. For each server software product, the task force used RTM to design routes to the selected target market segments, and developed budgets for the marketing, sales, and customer services resources for each route.

Gap Analysis

The task force uncovered gaps in product plans, value propositions, and go-to-market strategies for the server products. One gap, previously highlighted in the questions from preannouncement customers, was that the whole solution for server software was much more complex than for desktop software, as shown in Fig. 8.1.

Whole Solution = the minimum set of products and services necessary for the target customer to completely satisfy his or her compelling reason to buy.

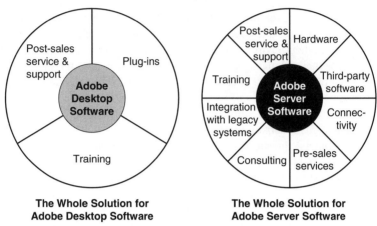

**The Whole Solution for
Adobe Desktop Software**

**The Whole Solution for
Adobe Server Software**

Fig. 8.1 Whole solutions for Adobe desktop and server software

To close this gap, Adobe would have to do more work to provide the products and services needed to complete the whole solution for server software.

The second gap was that different people were involved in the customers' eco-systems for server software than for desktop software. As we discussed in Chap. 4, a customer's ecosystem is the people who participate in, contribute to, and influence purchase decisions. The ecosystem gap meant that Adobe needed to communicate with different people in the market than they traditionally reached, both inside the customers' companies and in organizations that influenced the customer. (Customer ecosystems are discussed in detail in Chap. 4.)

The third gap was the most dramatic: Adobe's server software would enter the market at a much earlier phase of the RTM Life Cycle than Adobe's desktop software was currently selling, as shown in Fig. 8.2. In December 2000, Adobe's desktop products were in phase 4 of the RTM Life Cycle where the customers are primarily conservatives and skeptics. They buy mature, standardized products requiring minimal customization and cost, from mass market retailers, discount stores, catalog retailers, and other high-volume channels. (See Chap. 5 for a complete explanation of the RTM Life Cycle.)

In contrast to Adobe's desktop software products, the task force concluded that Adobe's server products would enter the market in late phase 1 or early in phase 2 of the RTM Life Cycle, where customers are primarily visionaries and pragmatists. Visionaries buy immature, innovative products directly from the manufacturer or developer, and then customize them to their specific needs. Pragmatists buy innovative products, but only after they have been packaged with other products and services as a whole solution to completely satisfy their needs. Pragmatists buy from solutions providers such as value-added resellers (VARs) and systems integrators (SIs). (Whole solutions are explained in Chap. 4.)

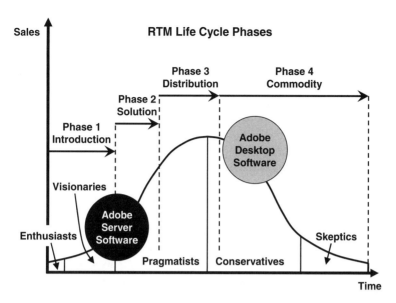

Fig. 8.2 RTM Life Cycle for Adobe's server software and desktop software products, December 2000

The impact of the difference between the life cycle phases for Adobe's desktop and server products was huge: Adobe's server products would require very different routes to market than Adobe's desktop products. Adobe's desktop software had been in phase 4 for several years prior to December 2000. All of Adobe's marketing communications were focused on phase 4 customers. Adobe's primary distribution partners were high-volume distribution channels that served phase 4 customers; those channels would not have the skills or the motivation to serve phase 1 and phase 2 customers who need a lot of support. Adobe had outsourced customer service to a call center company that looked up predefined answers to customers' questions in a database; this would not work for customers in phases 1 and 2 because predefined answers would not fit very many of their customized or packaged implementations.

Adobe had very few of the sales resources they would need for phase 1 and 2 customers, such as direct sales people, VARs, and SIs. Their marketing and customer service resources for phase 1 and 2 customers were also very limited. The task force realized that the difference between the RTM Life Cycle phases for desktop and server software was going to significantly impact Adobe's entire go-to-market strategy and also Adobe's marketing, sales, and customer service organizations.

New Routes to Market

Using RTM, the task force designed new routes to market for each of Adobe's server products. This included a detailed analysis of the go-to-market activities that needed to be performed to move customers from beginning to the end of the sales cycle. The task force focused on the gaps between the activities that Adobe was already doing to take desktop software to market, and the activities that they now realized would be needed for server software. Some of these gaps were things that Adobe needed to do differently for server products, but had already been doing for desktop products. Other gaps were things that Adobe had never done before, but which had proven to be very productive for other server software companies.

The task force also used RTM to develop itemized expense budgets for the new routes, and profit margin projections for each server product. This was the first time that Adobe executives had seen projections for go-to-market costs while a product was still in the early stages of the development process. At most companies, go-to-market costs are not estimated until development is nearly complete, when the product's launch is being planned just before public announcement. By that time, the entire development budget has been spent.

Adobe's executives realized that by using RTM, product managers could forecast go-to-market costs for new products before money is committed and spent to complete development and well before product launch. This would enable product managers, business unit general managers, and executives to make much more timely and informed decisions about Adobe's product investments.

The RTM methodology includes a spreadsheet-based Route Calculator that can be used to evaluate the performance and costs for alternative go-to-market activities for each step of the sales cycle. When a cross-functional team of marketing, sales, and customer services people use the Route Calculator, they can optimize the mix of activities to achieve their business goals, and they can optimize the budget for each activity. The Route Calculator generates profit margin estimates and useful ratios such as the Expense-to-Revenue (E/R) ratio discussed in Chaps. 6 and 7. (The Route Calculator spreadsheet can be downloaded at no charge from the book's Web site, www.RoutesToCustomers.com.)

The Route Calculator also provides detailed metrics for measuring the performance of each budgeted activity. This makes it especially valuable as a tool for improving go-to-market performance over time, as the team repeats the Route Calculator analysis quarterly or annually, comparing actual performance to prior projections and adjusting budgets accordingly.

AlterCast Route Calculations

AlterCast was the first product Adobe announced for which they used the Route Calculator to develop revenue and cost projections. Adobe CEO Bruce Chizen described AlterCast in an interview published by CNET's News.com on January 2, 2002, just before the first version of AlterCast was released to customers. He said that AlterCast "generates images or graphics dynamically. It's really taking variable data and generating the image or graphic on the fly …. Those organizations that do a lot of images and a lot of graphics and a lot of variation of the same image or graphic will enjoy this product … [such as] retailers that do catalogs for electronic or paper [publication]."

Before using the Route Calculator, the AlterCast product manager and marketing manager segmented the market for AlterCast and decided to target companies with graphically dense Web sites and more than 100 employees. They thought that the decision-maker for AlterCast would be the Director of Creative Services, Web site Production Manager, or Director of Web site Development, and, in companies with a more complex workflow, the Marketing Director and/or IT Manager (CIO or CTO). They also determined that the industry verticals to target were retail, financial services, professional services, publishing, entertainment, and manufacturing.

The product manager and marketing manager set $8.3 million for the first-year revenue goal for AlterCast based on analyzing the market opportunity and competition. Senior management approved the revenue goal.

The product manager broke down the cost of revenue (cost of goods sold) for AlterCast as follows: (1) costs for software that Adobe had licensed from other sources and embedded in AlterCast, and (2) the packaging costs for AlterCast. These two components totaled 10% of AlterCast's revenue, approximately the same at the 9% cost of revenue that Adobe averaged across all of its products from 2001 through 2007. (Note that the cost of revenue for many software companies is in the range of 8% to 15% of revenue.)

The task force identified two routes to market for AlterCast:

1. A "direct" route in which Adobe direct salespeople would perform the Close the Sale step of the sales cycle. The Delivery and Installation and Provide Support steps would be done by Adobe's service staff. These sales and service personnel would be specially trained on AlterCast. They would be dedicated to AlterCast or AlterCast would be a priority for them. The task force expected the direct route to produce 95% of Adobe's first-year revenue for AlterCast, based on the logic that new technologies are best sold by the vendor's direct salesforce in phase 1 of the RTM Life Cycle.
2. A "VAR" route in which Adobe would provide qualified leads to independent VARs and SIs who would Close the Sale. The VARs and SIs would provide front-line support to the customer in the Delivery and Installation and Provide Support steps, with backup support from Adobe. The task force expected that these VARs and SIs would already be familiar with the publishing workflows and software in use in the target market segment. They expected the VAR route to produce only 5% of AlterCast's first-year revenue, but more in subsequent years.

Using the Route Calculator, the task force determined how many qualified leads would be needed to achieve first-year revenue of $8.3 million. This calculation divided the revenue goal of $8.3 million by the expected average revenue per deal, which was $10,000 for direct sales and $5,000 for sales through VARs (after a 50% VAR discount). The result was that 874 deals had to be closed. To close 874 deals, a much larger number of qualified leads would be needed. The task force thought that a "closing rate" of 35% was appropriate, given input from preannouncement customers and Adobe's sales management. The "closing rate" is the percentage of qualified leads that actually purchase the product. Dividing the target number of

874 closed deals by the expected closing rate of 35% for AlterCast, resulted in 2,842 qualified leads that would be needed.

What would be the most productive and cost effective way to generate 2,842 qualified leads for AlterCast? The task force used the Route Calculator to evaluate alternative ways to generate qualified leads, considering all of the demand generation resources typically used for marketing server software to business customers, including advertising, public relations (PR), editorial coverage, direct marketing, outbound telemarketing, solution seminars, trade shows, trade associations, and tie-ins with other products and communication vehicles (such as educational programs).

The Route Calculator models the way that each of these resources generates qualified leads. The model takes into account the differences between these resources on key parameters such as cost per touch, audience size, response rate, and qualification rate. For every possible marketing mix, the Route Calculator shows the number of qualified leads that will be generated and the cost for each resource in the mix. The Route Calculator enabled the task force to optimize the total demand generation budget and the budget for each resource. Using the Route Calculator, the task force decided that, to generate the required number of 2,842 qualified leads, the optimal budget for the Generate Demand step of the sales cycle would be $1,063,763. They also decided to allocate that budget 65% to direct marketing, 32% to outbound telesales, 2% to trade shows, and 1% to PR/editorial coverage.

Following a similar decision-making process, the task force used the Route Calculator to choose among alternative resources and activities for steps 2 through 5 of the sales cycle, and to optimize the budgets for these resources. Figure 8.3 summarizes the combined resources the task force selected for the two AlterCast routes. The resources are listed in priority order by share of that step's budget. Table 8.1 shows the breakdown of the $3.7 million total budget they requested for the routes. Table 8.2 shows the forecast for AlterCast's first year revenue and contribution to Adobe's operating income for the two routes.

The itemized budgets developed by the task force included an incremental $1.1 million in year 1 to close the gap between Adobe's existing resources and the resources needed to sell and support server software products. This drove up the E/R ratio for the combined AlterCast route to 45% (=$3.7 million/$8.3 million), much higher than the E/R ratio of 32% that Adobe averaged for its other products.

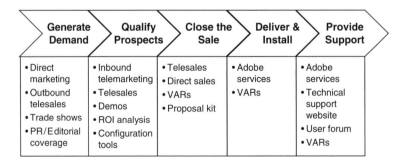

Fig. 8.3 Resources for AlterCast's two routes

Table 8.1 Budget for AlterCast's two routes

	Generate demand	Qualify prospects	Close the sale	Deliver and install	Provide support	Total budget
Program expenses	$709,763	$125,000	$5,000	$–	$135,000	$974,763
Head count expenses	$354,000	$879,527	$719,613	$242,100	$564,900	$2,760,140
Total	$1,063,763	$1,004,527	$724,613	$242,100	$699,900	$3,734,903
% of Total budget	28%	27%	19%	6%	19%	100%
% of Product revenue	13%	12%	9%	3%	8%	45%

Table 8.2 Forecast of AlterCast revenue and contribution to operating income

	AlterCast direct route	AlterCast VAR route	Total for both routes	% of Total revenue
Revenue	$7,880,000	$430,000	$8,310,000	100%
Cost of revenue	$788,000	$43,000	$831,000	10%
Gross profit	$7,092,000	$387,000	$7,479,000	90%
Route expenses	$3,153,173	$581,729	$3,734,903	45%
Contribution to operating income	$3,938,827	$(194,729)	$3,744,098	45%

The incremental $1.1 million would enable Adobe to build a larger installed base and to do a better job of recruiting and supporting VARs in year 1. This would boost revenue in year 2 above the previous projection, and more than cover the incremental investment in year 1. The net result would be that the E/R ratio for year 2 would be in-line with Adobe's average, and the revenue and profit for years 1 and 2 combined would be higher than previously planned, without increasing development costs or impacting time-to-market. The executives were excited about this insight and quickly approved the incremental investment.

The task force recommended that Adobe adopt the RTM methodology company-wide and integrate it with Adobe's existing Product Life Cycle (PLC) process. PLC is a standard stage-gate product management process, similar to those used in other high-tech product companies. All Adobe product managers had been using PLC to develop product plans and manage products throughout their life cycles, without being able to determine what kind of routes and go-to-market budgets would be needed to take their products to market. Integrating RTM with PLC would solve that.

Adobe's executives accepted the task force's recommendations. Adobe adopted RTM corporate-wide and integrated it with PLC in 2001. AlterCast, Adobe's first server software product, was announced in 2001 and starting shipping to customers in January 2002.

Between 2001 and 2007, Adobe brought on board executives and staff with experience in server and enterprise software. Adobe acquired software companies with server software products along with sales and support personnel with this expertise. Adobe also established significant partnering arrangements for its server software with SAP and IBM. SAP, the largest provider of business applications software, standardized on Adobe's document creation and management software for print output from its business management applications. IBM partnered with Adobe to integrate Adobe's server software with IBM's server software. The total revenue to Adobe from the SAP and IBM partnerships totaled several millions of dollars annually.

Impact on Adobe's Performance

After integrating RTM with Adobe's product life cycle management process, Adobe's management found that the cost and performance parameters for every go-to-market resource in the Route Calculator could be updated to reflect Adobe's actual cost and performance for those resources on an ongoing basis. This meant that decisions on which resources to use, and how much to spend, could be based on detailed data on how well those resources performed last week, last month, or last quarter. This kind of "feedback loop" enabled Adobe managers to make better decisions over time to optimize the performance and costs of the company's routes to market.

Adobe's annual revenue grew 17% per year from $1.2 billion in 2001 (when Adobe adopted RTM) to $3.2 billion in 2007. Net profit grew 23% per year, significantly faster than revenue, from $206 million in 2001 to $724 million in 2007.

Adobe's revenue from server software grew 65% per year to over $200 million in 2007, and the profit from server software grew even faster. In addition, every dollar of Adobe server software sales is estimated to leverage $3 in sales of Adobe desktop software. The net impact is that server software drove approximately 25% of Adobe's total revenue and more than 25% of profit in 2007.

From 2001 through 2007, Adobe's stock price increased 179%, more than five times the gain in the NASDAQ Composite Index and more than six times the gain in the S&P 500 Index. Adobe's total return was almost seven times the total return on Microsoft and more than two times the total return on Oracle and SAP. Microsoft is widely regarded as Adobe's primary competitor. Oracle and SAP are two of the leading vendors in the server software business. All three companies were included in the task force's financial analysis to forecast the impact on Adobe's financials for closing the gaps between Adobe's original go-to-market strategy for server software and the strategy that the task force developed with RTM.

Classic Management Pitfalls Revealed by RTM

Management often encounters unforeseen problems when the real world turns out differently than expected. Many of the unforeseen problems were there all along. No one saw these hidden problems or pitfalls, and consequently, the company's plans did not take them into consideration.

RTM is a "spotlight" or "crystal ball" that management can use to reveal several different kinds of hidden problems and fix them.

The Average Cost Pitfall

Management decides to develop a new product based on a revenue estimate, the estimated development cost, and an average or typical cost for taking products to market. Everything goes according to plan except that the actual costs for marketing, selling, and supporting the product are much higher than expected, robbing profitability. The true go-to-market cost for the product could have been determined early on, before most of the product development funds were spent and well before the product was announced, by using the RTM methodology including the Route Calculator.

Management could make better and earlier "go/no-go" decisions if all of the product costs, including go-to-market costs, were really known, not just assumed to be an average of go-to-market costs for other products or markets. It makes sense to use average costs when all of the decision parameters are in-line with the averages and nothing is new or different. First-line and middle managers can and should handle those decisions.

Decisions that have an aura of "rolling the dice," "betting the company," "doing something we haven't done before" are obviously the domain of top management. RTM can be used as a diagnostic tool to check assumptions about a product's marketability, or to evaluate the profitability of entering a new market, or to think through corporate strategies for taking the company into fields where marketing, sales, distribution, or customer service could be different than where the company has been before.

It is better to use RTM to look before you leap into new areas.

The "New Product, Same Old Channel" Problem

Companies develop truly new products, not just updated versions of existing product, by putting a lot of intellectual effort into research and development, both to create the product and to ensure that it can be manufactured efficiently and cost-effectively. The coordination between R&D and manufacturing is excellent at most companies. High but secondary priority is given to understanding customers' needs, competitors' products, industry trends, and other factors that impact the market. The target customers are well in sight.

However, very little or no effort is invested in analyzing who should sell, install, and support the new product. Instead, assumptions are made implicitly, but never documented or discussed, about the routes to market for the new product.

If companies put any serious effort into exploring alternative routes to market for their product concepts and new products under development, they would develop them differently. One difference is in deciding which components of the whole solution should be provided by the company versus by partners. Many products leave little room for partners to profit by adding value, so the manufacturer must pay them a large discount and other financial incentives to sell the product. The manufacturer could make more money by creating opportunities for partners to enhance or extend the product instead of only distributing it.

Another difference would result from thinking of the new product as an opportunity to build a new channel or expand the current one – how can your company design and manufacture the product so that it is more successful for channel partners that currently serve the target market for the product? This type of approach is especially important when those channel partners influence customer preferences and decisions, or when it could take a lot of time and money to recruit and make them productive with your company.

Channel programs are usually designed long after the decisions have been made on product features and target markets. What would happen if channel programs were being debated at the same time that product features and target markets were being resolved – would this help your company find and exploit competitive advantages ignored by your competitors, or ways to change the dynamics of your industry?

The Lack of Alignment Trap

Many companies struggle with alignment issues. There are many symptoms. Initiatives are kicked off but do not accomplish much and then die out. Different employees talk to the same customer but say different things and seem to be unaware of the other conversations. Customers see frequent delays and cost overruns, but there is never any news about the company achieving a milestone ahead of schedule or at a lower cost than expected. Management talks about breaking down silos that separate the organization into uncoordinated departments, but nothing changes.

RTM enables management to align resources to a common strategy and plan of action. RTM is more than a go-to-market strategy. It is a way to bring together all of the customer-facing organizations in the company (and the departments that support them, such as order administration, logistics, and legal) to work as a team to accomplish the company's goals. RTM can do this at many levels:

- With front-line workers in field organizations and also in product management and product marketing
- With managers of different functions, where improvements in tactical coordination often boost productivity significantly
- With general managers and senior executives, where complex strategy decisions and execution can make or break opportunities for the company
- Between the company and its business or distribution partners, where finding common priorities and coordinating resources to pursue them is the true definition of "partnering."

The Mistake of Ignoring the Life Cycle

Many executives want to drive market adoption of their products as fast as possible to the point of highest product volume and maximum distribution. They assume that signing a wholesale distributor will boost unit volume, and that the higher unit volume will result in higher profits and more market share. So they try to skip earlier phases of the life cycle. They are unwilling to do the hard work of winning business with visionaries, or crossing the chasm with pragmatic customers, or growing their volumes with specialty or regional distributors to get the company and its market ready for high-volume mass distribution.

The reality is that understanding the current phase of the life cycle for your product or service is the same thing as coming to grips with your current reality. You cannot succeed if you are out of touch with reality. You cannot change your reality by wishful thinking.

Succeeding in the current phase of the life cycle is absolutely critical for survival. Otherwise, your product and your company will not be around for the next phase of the life cycle. Each phase of the life cycle calls for different marketing, sales, and customer support activities. Doing the wrong activities for the current phase of the life cycle, or not switching to activities that are more appropriate when the life cycle shifts, will definitely sub-optimize the company's performance.

RTM can help you figure out what phase you are in and what to do to succeed in that phase. RTM can also improve your ability to transition quickly to the activities that will be successful in the next phase. In both cases, RTM can help you minimize costs and maximize profits, so that your company gets stronger as it progresses through the life cycle. This is the smart way to drive market adoption.

The Stockholm Syndrome Hazard

The Stockholm syndrome is a psychological response sometimes seen in an abducted hostage, in which the hostage shows signs of loyalty to the hostage-taker, regardless of the danger in which the hostage has been placed. The hostage confuses the hostage-taker with friends who are genuinely interested in the hostage's welfare.

Many companies think of their channel partners as customers. They ask their existing channel partners about how or whether to sell their products to different markets. They confuse their current channel partners with customers.

The reality is that there are many roles in every industry – raw materials source, original equipment manufacturer, contract assembler, technology combiner, physical product distributor, adviser or influencer, consumer (in the sense of consuming the product or being the user of the product), and so on.

It makes little sense to ask someone who plays one role to represent people playing other roles. The first step in using RTM is to talk to potential customers for your product or service, so that you can understand their needs, wants, and behaviors, and decide which segments of them you are going to pursue. One of the most important behaviors to ask customers about is where they would buy your product. Getting the facts straight about your customers and potential customers is absolutely critical. Filtering the truth through channel partners is not a viable substitute.

You should definitely talk to your current and potential channel partners about their needs, wants, and behaviors, including how they connect with specific customers or customer segments. But do not mistake those conversations for talking with customers directly. Triangulation takes three data points – the customer, the channel, and your own company. Do not use a proxy for the customer because you will get a false reading for your triangulation. Then you will not hit the target at all.

The Product Distribution Problem

The costs for order administration, logistics, and product delivery can kill your go-to-market plan. If you try to sell a product to consumers through retailers without putting the product in a retail package, you will fail. The first IBM PCs sold through retail had multiple components packed into one large box so that there would be a single barcode for the cashier to scan. Unfortunately, the box was too heavy for consumers to lift onto the cashier's counter.

Many companies offer discounts for orders at higher quantities, such as a 10% discount for ordering 100 units. Unfortunately, as we observed in Chap. 3, a company will make more profit if quantity discounts are based on the company's actual cost savings, not just on a round number like 100 units. For example, shipping costs for a full pallet are normally less per unit than shipping costs for smaller quantities, so profits will be higher if the threshhold for a quantity discount is a full pallet, and that might not be 100 units. The hidden problem is the need for communication and coordination among all of the organizations involved in product distribution.

The underlying problem is that the things that impact profit are distributed throughout the company, and it is very difficult to identify them and to make decisions that maximize total profit. It is too easy to change something in one department that benefits their operation but negatively impacts another department. Profit is elusive and transitory. Finding and holding on to profit is very difficult. You have to get everyone collaborating to maximize profit. RTM can help you do this.

Summary

RTM can be used to develop go-to-market plans before or during a product's development phase. This enables management to see the cost for marketing and selling the product before the entire development budget has been committed and spent, which leads to better investment decisions. This also enables management to identify long before product launch any additional resources that will be needed to launch the product. This helps deal with situations where there is a long lead time to recruit, train, and ramp up those resources.

Many companies run into the same situation that Adobe's executives faced: a new, soon-to-be-introduced product is sufficiently different from their company's existing products that it will require different marketing, sales, and customer service than their company normally provides. Products like this usually fail in the market because the company did not apply the right resources to sell and support it. RTM can help recognize and solve this problem.

Management often encounters unforeseen problems when the real world turns out differently than expected. RTM is a "spotlight" or "crystal ball" that management can use to reveal several different kinds of hidden problems and fix them. These problems include the following:

- *The Average Cost Pitfall.* RTM can help to diagnose marketability problems and profitability challenges when a company is planning to develop new products, enter new markets, and/or build new channels. These are situations where the company's historical or average costs understate the true cost for succeeding with the new product, new market, or new channel.
- *The "New Product, Same Old Channel" Problem.* Most new products are distributed through a company's existing channels without analyzing alternatives to find the optimal channel. RTM can solve this problem quickly and easily. More importantly, it can turn the company's distribution channel into a significant competitive advantage.
- *The Lack of Alignment Trap.* Many companies struggle with alignment issues that sap energy, limit productivity, and rob the company of profits. RTM enables everyone, from front-line workers in marketing, sales, and customer service, to the heads of those organizations, and also general managers, to align to a common strategy and plan of action. RTM also helps align the company with its business or distribution partners.
- *The Mistake of Ignoring the Life Cycle.* Succeeding in a product's current phase of its life cycle is absolutely critical for survival. If it fails in the current phase,

it will probably be discontinued. Transitioning successfully to the next phase of the life cycle is also critical to success. RTM can help to understand the current phase and enable a quick transition to the next phase.

- *The Stockholm Syndrome Hazard.* The customer, the channel, and the vendor's own organization are the three constituents that every product or service must satisfy. RTM brings together their perspectives without confusing one constituent for another. Triangulating to hit the vendor's objectives requires these three different data points.
- *The Product Distribution Problem.* Finding and holding on to profit is very difficult. It is too easy for decisions made in one department to drive up the costs in another. RTM helps to identify and fix these kinds of problems by bringing together everyone involved in taking a product to market, so their cost structures can be included in the RTM profit-maximizing model.

Chapter 9
Implementing RTM Company-Wide

Up to this point in the book, the Routes-to-Market (RTM) methodology has been explained by showing how it applies to selling a single product or service to one market segment. Obviously, few companies live with only one product or only one market segment. This chapter shows how RTM can be applied to all of a multiproduct company's products and markets.

Using RTM for all of a company's products and markets may initially appear risky to the CEO because RTM changes the way companies allocate marketing, sales, and customer service resources. Most companies prepare operating plans (or business plans) that set goals and allocate resources for the coming quarter or year. Changing the methodology for allocating resources is a scary proposition to anyone who is responsible for the performance of those resources.

However, it is easy to start using RTM for a single product or market. When this proves successful, the scope for RTM can be expanded incrementally to other products or markets. At some point in the "organic" growth of RTM within a company, senior management gets enough evidence of RTM's success to switch the entire company to using RTM. Integrating RTM into a company's planning and management processes is described in the next few sections.

RTM optimizes the performance of marketing, sales, and customer service for each product and market segment to which it is applied. However, the benefit of embracing RTM throughout a company is greater than the sum of these optimizations. RTM also enhances the company's agility, the ability to adjust quickly to changing market conditions and to pursue new opportunities. RTM improves cross-functional coordination and teamwork, reduces time-to-market, and strengthens relationships with channel partners and customers.

Route Consolidation

When we talk about "route consolidation," we mean adding up the expenses and revenues for all of the company's routes. By definition, a route consists of resources that perform activities to take customers in a market segment through the steps of the sales cycle for a product or service. Therefore, a route is defined by the following items:

P. Raulerson et al., *Building Routes to Customers*, DOI: 10.1007/978-0-387-79951-3_9,
© 2009 Peter Raulerson, Jean-Claude Malraison and Antoine Leboyer

1. The product or service to be sold, along with the unit volume goal and/or revenue goal for the route, normally broken down by fiscal quarters.
2. The targeted market segment. (Selling a product to two different market segments requires two different routes.)
3. The activities to be performed at each step of the sales cycle, along with the dates and times that the activities will be performed. (Sometimes the messages or content communicated by the activity are included in the route definition, and sometimes it is assumed that the company's current messages or content will be communicated, without specifying them.)
4. The output of performing each activity, such as number of leads generated by advertising, or the number of qualified leads provided to the salesforce by telemarketing. (Each activity has inputs and outputs, like any business process.)
5. The resources that will perform those activities.
6. The amount budgeted to compensate the resources for performing those activities, including the costs to engage, train, and manage those resources.

For each route there is a quarterly projection for the expenses for these resources, subtotaled at each of the five steps of the sales cycle. There is also a quarterly projection of the revenue for the route. As shown in Fig. 9.1, the expenses and revenue

RTM Expenses by Route and Sales Cycle Step – 4th Quarter
RTM Expenses by Route and Sales Cycle Step – 3rd Quarter
RTM Expenses by Route and Sales Cycle Step – 2nd Quarter
RTM Expenses by Route and Sales Cycle Step – 1st Quarter
RTM Expenses by Route and Sales Cycle Step – Total for Year

	Route A	Route B	Total	% of Total RTM Expenses	% of Revenue
Revenue	$100,000	$330,000	$430,000		100%
Cost of Revenue	20,000	120,000	140,000		33%
Gross Profit	80,000	210,000	290,000		67%
RTM Expenses					
Sales Cycle Step 1	7,190	21,570	28,760	35%	7%
Sales Cycle Step 2	7,920	10,420	18,340	23%	4%
Sales Cycle Step 3	8,520	3,948	12,468	15%	3%
Sales Cycle Step 4	3,570	3,331	6,901	9%	2%
Sales Cycle Step 5	5,010	9,540	14,550	18%	3%
Total RTM Expenses	32,210	48,809	81,019	100%	19%
Expense-to-Revenue Ratio	32%	15%	19%		
Contribution to Operating Income	47,790	161,191	208,981		49%

All dollars are thousands ($000)

Fig. 9.1 Example of route consolidation

for all routes can be consolidated in tables for each quarter and totaled in an annual table. If the cost of revenue (cost of goods sold) is included, then each route's contribution to operating income can also be projected.

More information on route consolidation is available at the book's Web site at RoutesToCustomers.com, along with example route calculation spreadsheets which can be downloaded at no charge. Figure 9.1 repeats the data from the example of a company selling a complex B2B product in Chap. 6. Route A in Fig. 9.1 is the Direct Route, which consists of the vendor's marketing, sales, and customer service organizations selling customized computer systems to large companies. Route B is the Indirect Route, which consists of computer systems resellers working with the vendor's marketing and customer service organizations to resell customized computer systems (the same product as in Route A) to mid-sized companies (a different market segment than the market segment in Route A).

Evaluating the Company's Go-to-Market Model

The route consolidation provides valuable information for evaluating the company's go-to-market model. Let us look at the information in Fig. 9.1 in more detail:

- The company is planning to spend 35% of total route expenses on step 1 demand generation and 23% on step 2 prospect qualification, which totals 58%. Is this the best allocation of the funds available for marketing, selling, and providing customer support for these products?
- Only 15% of the budget will be spent on the salesforce and distribution channels in step 3, which is one-fourth of the spending on marketing resources in steps 1 and 2. Will this result in overloading the salesforce or distribution channels with more leads than they can handle? Should the capacity of the distribution channels be evaluated before executing this plan?
- On the other hand, if a demand generation campaign is cut from the plan in order to reduce costs, or lower-cost marketing resources are substituted, would there be a corresponding drop in revenue?
- Is the projected Expense-to-Revenue (E/R) ratio of 19% acceptable across all of the routes? To evaluate this, one must understand the company's other operating expenses – research and development expenses, general and administrative expenses, and brand communications expenses (which are not included in route costs if they promote the company's brand and not its products or services). These other operating expenses, added to route costs, determine operating income. Figure 9.1 shows that, before including these other operating expenses, the contribution to operating income is 49% of the company's total projected revenue. If brand communications costs are budgeted at 4% of revenue (30% of total RTM expenses), research and development at 15% of revenue, general and administrative expenses at 6% of revenue, then operating income would be 22% of revenue. This kind of analysis connects budget allocations for marketing, sales, and customer service, with the company's profitability goals. This enables management to allocate budgets that optimize profitability.

• If any expense does not increase revenue and profit, is it really necessary? This can be a very useful question to ask regarding each route expense, especially when marketing, sales, and customer service operate as cost centers or are measured on revenue but not profitability.

The purpose of Fig. 9.1 is to show how the relevant figures fit together, not to recommend specific percentages for companies to adopt.

Budgeting Costs by Department

Most companies develop operating plans and establish budgets by department, such as marketing, sales, or logistics. Traditionally, the budgets for the next year are based on the budgets for the previous year. Departments that are considered more strategic for the next year receive budget increases that are higher in percentage terms than the planned increase in the company's total operating expenses.

The next step in the traditional budgeting process is for department heads (or the people in charge of different functions within a department) to negotiate with general managers and product managers on the tasks that their budgets will be used for. For example, the manager of direct marketing may tell product managers that the budget for direct marketing cannot accommodate all of their demand generation requirements, so at least one product will get less. Often, the decision on which products get more or less of the direct marketing budget is unrelated to business priorities and to the funding for other resources that would be needed to follow up on the leads from direct marketing.

In some companies, major initiatives driven by top executives are intended to focus resources on new priorities. Many departments and functions view these initiatives as potential sources of funding for their work, so they try to position their organizations as the best resources for accomplishing the goals of those initiatives. Politics and personal connections often trump logic in these environments.

After the traditional budgeting process runs its course, senior management rarely has any visibility into how the budgets at the departmental and functional levels relate to each other or to the company's revenue, profitability, and market share goals. The net result is lack of alignment, wasted resources, poor performance, failure to achieve the company's key business goals, and employees who focus on internal issues instead of customers.

With the RTM methodology, the routes are planned by cross-functional teams responsible for executing those plans. Alignment comes naturally during the planning process as the team determines which activities must be performed to move customers through the sales cycle quickly and efficiently, selects the best resources for these activities, and allocates budgets that will optimize performance.

When the routes are consolidated, it is easy to view the budget for each selected resource. Figure 9.2 shows the same RTM expense budgets shown in Fig. 9.1 broken down by resource and by market segment. The Large Company Segment in Fig. 9.2 is targeted by Route A, and the Mid-sized Company Segment is targeted by Route B. Example route calculation spreadsheets can be downloaded at no charge

RTM Expenses by Resource and Market Segment – 4th Quarter					
RTM Expenses by Resource and Market Segment – 3rd Quarter					
RTM Expenses by Resource and Market Segment – 2nd Quarter					
RTM Expenses by Resource and Market Segment – 1st Quarter					
RTM Expenses by Resource and Market Segment – Total for Year					
Resource	Large Company Segment	Mid-size Company Segment	Total	% of Total RTM Expenses	% of Revenue
Advertising	$ 2,157	$ 6,471	$ 8,628	11%	2%
Direct Marketing	3,595	10,785	14,380	18%	3%
Public Relations	719	2,157	2,876	4%	1%
Marketing Staff	2,303	4,241	6,544	9%	2%
Telesales	3,168	8,336	11,504	14%	3%
Direct Sales	11,688	0	11,688	14%	3%
Channel Sales	0	3,948	3,948	5%	1%
Admin Staff	357	333	690	1%	0%
Delivery & Install	3,213	2,998	6,211	8%	1%
Service Dept	5,010	9,540	14,550	18%	3%
Total RTM Expenses	32,210	48,809	81,019	100%	19%

All dollars are thousands ($000)

Fig. 9.2 A different view of the example route consolidation

at the book's Web site, RoutesToCustomers.com. They provide the views shown in Figs. 9.1 and 9.2 plus other views by product or service, geography, department, activity, or time period. Having multiple views of the same data makes it easy to connect RTM expenses with the company's financial data, and to track performance and make adjustments over time.

RTM expenses include all marketing, sales, and customer service costs that can be identified with specific products or services. Brand communications expenses that promote the company's brand and not its products or services, are excluded from RTM expenses. However, the example route calculation spreadsheets available at the book's Web site, RoutesToCustomers.com, provide cells for entering brand communication expenses, so these expenses can be included in calculating and viewing the total marketing budget.

Allocating Costs

There are several ways that a company's finance department can allocate fixed costs and indirect costs for overhead and shared resources, such as facilities, administration, and logistics. These costs can be allocated to different organizations based on the number of people in each organization, or based on the revenue or unit volume of each business unit or division. Activity-Based Costing (ABC) is another way to allocate these costs. ABC is based on the type and amount of activity performed by each worker, or each machine, or each facility.

These allocation methods may be valid from a financial analysis perspective, but they can mask inefficiencies and distort actual costs, making it difficult to understand the effective contribution to operating profit for each product or market segment.

For example, the difference in cost between delivering a pallet loaded with 1,000 units to a wholesale distributor who will ship smaller quantities to individual retailers, versus the manufacturer taking orders directly from the retailers and fulfilling them from the factory, can be as high as a factor of 400 – the lowest cost delivery approach can be as little as 0.25% (one quarter of 1%) of the highest cost approach. But if the shipping budget is set at a fixed percentage of revenue or unit volume, it will be very difficult to identify the lowest cost approach and follow it, because the budget allocation method masked the inefficiencies of the highest cost approach.

To decide which approach will be most profitable, you need to see the actual cost of each approach. We have found that it is best to work with actual costs, uncorrected by any allocation mechanism, when developing plans with the RTM methodology. This avoids the distortions that allocation mechanisms can introduce. Profit is very difficult to achieve and even harder to hold onto, because there are so many ways for profit to be dissipated or dribbled away when costs are masked or distorted by allocation formulas.

How to Launch a Shared Resource

Internal call centers are resources that are shared by multiple product and marketing managers who engage them to handle different tasks, campaigns, or assignments. Generally, these engagements involve a scope of work with objectives, budgets, schedules, and performance metrics. How do companies launch internal call centers or other kinds of shared resources such as direct marketing centers, market research groups, and marketing analytics teams?

The challenge is twofold. First, it may be difficult to secure funding to hire or transfer staff into the shared resource, equip and train them, and build up capacity in advance of the demand for their services. Many companies have an internal investment process for starting up new products, new factories, new businesses, but not for starting up internal shared resource organizations. Marketing and sales are normally operated as cost centers without access to investment funding.

The second challenge is in getting product, marketing, and sales managers to use the shared resource. They may be blocked by a lack of familiarity or experience in using the services performed by the shared resources, such as telemarketing, telesales, and Internet-based communications (e-mail and text chat).

Managers may also be blocked by the chicken-and-egg funding problem. To pay for starting up the shared resource, they may have to forgo spending on other marketing and sales resources. It can be difficult for a new shared resource to get the "critical mass" of work assignments needed to cover their operating costs. Without seed money and a minimum level of commitments from their clients (product, marketing, and sales managers), they cannot get off the ground.

IBM found one solution to this problem when it started up its internal call centers in the 1990s. IBM management simply charged the product and marketing managers for the call centers whether they used them or not. This kind of "tax" or "automatic deduction" motivated the product and marketing managers to put call centers into their routes to market. Within a few months, IBM had their call centers up and running in each geography, serving the needs of multiple product and marketing managers. After the start-up period, planning and contracting between the call centers and their clients (product and marketing managers) kept things in balance. Cooperation and coordination between call center managers and their clients progressed so well that IBM dropped the automatic charging at the start of the next fiscal year.

Adopting the RTM Methodology

The prospect of using a new planning or management methodology can trigger negative reactions. Many employees will complain about a bureaucratic exercise, useless paperwork, or time taken away from doing productive work. They would prefer that administrative staff be tasked with the planning work, instead of them. But the company's routes to market are too strategic to be relegated to administrative formalities.

Nothing is more frustrating than to spend time and effort to report data that people think are useless. On the other hand, most people are energized by participating in a dialogue with their coworkers and management on the vision, objectives, and approaches for achieving their goals.

Planning routes to market for the next fiscal period requires discussion, negotiation, and the give-and-take necessary to reach agreement. This is an excellent opportunity to create new initiatives and to establish consensus on goals, priorities, tactics, assignments, and budget allocations.

The RTM methodology is an excellent platform for communication, synchronization, and optimization. Each cross-functional team can develop and implement coordinated plans that are focused on achieving the team's objectives. The emphasis is on execution. Planning is a step in the process, not the result.

Launching RTM in Ten Steps

Figure 9.3 provides a flow chart view of the ten steps for launching RTM in a company.

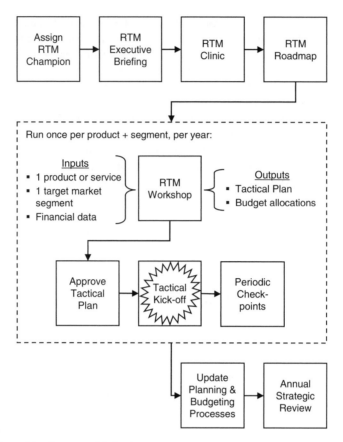

Fig. 9.3 Launching Routes-to-Market in ten steps

Steps 1 through 4 are run when the company first implements RTM.

1. *Assign RTM Champion*: appoint a highly visible, cross-functional senior manager or executive who will become the RTM guru (expert). He or she will own the roadmap for introducing RTM into the company. Good motivational and support skills are needed to get other managers and employees on board.

2. *RTM Executive Briefing*: hold an executive briefing to get commitment to using RTM as a strategic tool for achieving an ongoing objective such as revenue growth, profit optimization, resource allocation, market coverage, and launching new products or services. In other words, align RTM with an important company objective that RTM can help accomplish. RTM is not an objective in itself. It is a means to an end.

3. *RTM Clinic*: Run a short project, called the RTM Clinic, to analyze the company's current go-to-market model, identifying the resources currently used and costs for each step of the sales cycle, by product family and market segment. Finance involvement is mandatory. Use existing internal data. Benchmark

resources used by competitors but not by your company, to understand alternative go-to-market models. The RTM Clinic serves multiple purposes. First, the clinic educates people on the RTM methodology without the pressure to become instant experts. Second, it establishes the company's baseline for marketing, sales, and customer service – what the company currently spends in each area along with the performance that it achieves. This enables top management to see their company in a new way and to prioritize where RTM should be introduced first. Third, it provides an opportunity to investigate alternative go-to-market models, including how competitors use resources. This is almost always an eye-opener because it reveals new ideas in a framework that shows what can be accomplished with them.

4. *RTM Roadmap*: Develop a high-level roadmap for implementing RTM. Start by sharing the RTM Clinic's findings with management across the company. Prioritize objectives and agree on the sequence for rolling out RTM (roadmap). Top management should play an active role in prioritizing objectives and approving the roadmap, but it is equally important to use the RTM Clinic's findings to sell middle and first-level managers on using RTM.

Steps 5 through 8 are run once for each selected product or service and market segment during the company's business planning cycle (typically annually).

5. *RTM Workshop*: Run a cross-functional RTM Workshop (a few hours) for each selected product or service and market segment. The goal of the RTM Workshop is to develop new routes (or recommend changes to existing routes) to take the selected product or service to the selected market segment, including budget allocations for the routes' resources. The RTM Workshop should be led by the manager or executive responsible for the revenue and expenses of the selected product or service and market segment, with the RTM Champion's help. Include in the Workshop the managers (or employees representing the managers) of marketing campaigns, marketing communications, call centers, channel management, direct sales, product management, product marketing, logistics, customer support, and finance. In companies where marketing agency personnel participate in the vendor's decision-making on tactics or budgets (as opposed to recommending them), they should participate in the RTM Workshop. Assemble the following data in advance as inputs to the workshop: description and planned evolution of the product or service (including its maturity on the RTM Life Cycle and competitive data), needs and buying behavior for one target market for the product or service (including market sizing and ecosystem), and relevant financial data (including costs and performance for the resources on existing routes). As in most business decision-making sessions, it is important to know the business objectives, current issues and problems with the product, service, market segment, and resources. Most companies already have all these inputs, but in some cases it may be necessary to define the product, segment the market, and analyze costs before conducting the RTM Workshop. The outputs of the RTM Workshop are a Tactical Plan which includes a complete specification of the routes for taking the product or service to the target market segment, and

budget allocations. Note that the RTM Workshop is normally run for the combination of one product + one target segment, or one service + one target segment. If a company sells 3 different products to 4 distinct market segments, then the RTM Workshop would be run 12 (=3 × 4) times.

6. *Approve Tactical Plan*: get management approval for the Tactical Plan developed in the RTM Workshop, including commitments by each functional group to implement the new (or changes to) routes and resource allocations.

7. *Tactical Kick-off*: The executive responsible for the revenue and profit of the product or service runs a cross-functional tactical kick-off meeting to get everyone on the extended team committed to executing the new routes and excited about working together with a common objective and plan. By "extended team" we mean people who participated in the RTM Workshop and those who were represented by others in the RTM Workshop, but who have personal responsibility for making the Tactical Plan successful, such as account managers at the company's marketing agency, field marketing or sales managers, executives of alliance partners, or key distribution partners. During the Tactical Kick-off meeting, each participant makes a personal commitment to make their piece of the plan happen. This approach breaks down the barriers that typically prevent functional areas from cooperating, and also energizes people by giving them personal responsibility and visibility for their function's role in the success of the route. Without this type of Tactical Kick-off, the RTM Workshop in step 5 would be only a staff exercise that prescribed actions for functional groups, but did not engage them in deciding what actions were the most appropriate and also feasible (given their other obligations). At the end of a year in which the team achieves the goals in the Tactical Plan, the executive responsible for the revenue and profit of the product or service should hold a celebratory dinner for the team and recognize each person's contribution. Like the Tactical Kick-off, this type of event builds teamwork.

8. *Periodic Checkpoints*: run periodic meetings of the participants in the RTM Workshop to solve execution issues. These could be weekly, monthly, or quarterly, depending on the frequency or complexity of the execution issues.

Step 9 is normally done once, after steps 1 through 8 have been completed. Step 10 is an annual event.

9. *Update the Company's Planning and Budgeting Processes* to include RTM methodology. This integrates RTM into future planning and budgeting cycles. It also integrates the output of the RTM methodology with the company's management systems, including scorecards, dashboards, performance indicators, performance reviews, etc.

10. *Annual Strategic Review*: once or twice a year, run an executive session to assess and evolve the company's go-to-market model. Once RTM is in place, a wide range of strategic considerations become possible that were not visible before. For example, the strategic review could consider opportunities to develop new products for the company's existing distribution channels, which would leverage the company's investment in developing those channels and

strengthen the company's position in those channels. Another example would be using marketing analytics to improve end-to-end route performance, not just the performance of the marketing department; this could have a significant impact on the way that sales and customer service operate.

Summary

Route consolidation is adding up the expenses and revenues for all of the company's routes. It provides valuable information for evaluating the company's go-to-market model. RTM changes the company's traditional budgeting process from a top–down, department-centric approach, to a bottom–up approach conducted product by product, market by market. Route consolidation shows the total budget for each resource and department, making it easy to connect resource budgets in RTM with the company's existing management information systems. RTM can be integrated easily with the company's other planning and operational processes.

RTM can be launched company-wide in ten steps. Four of those steps are repeated for each product or service and each market segment annually on the company's planning cycle, or more often when needed.

Adopting RTM company-wide enhances the company's productivity, teamwork, and agility. It reduces time-to-market and strengthens relationships with channel partners and customers. Most importantly, it drives profitable growth.

References and Resources

The facts and data mentioned in this book come from multiple sources, including our work with companies which have used the Routes-to-Market methodology and the following books, articles, and other public sources. Also included below are items for further reading.

Prologue

- The story of Bob Wilson, National Software Corporation, Skyline Software, and the other characters and events in the Prologue is fiction. Any resemblance to persons living or dead, or to actual companies and events, is purely coincidental.

Chapter 1. What Is Routes-to-Market?

- IBM had lost $16 billion on declining sales over three years. Source: IBM Corporation's SEC 10-K filings (annual financial reports) for 1991, 1992, and 1993, available on the US Securities and Exchange Commission EDGAR website at http://www.sec.gov/edgar.shtml.
- This reduced SG&A by 25%, $5.3 billion. Source: private communication with IBM executives.
- Michael Hammer, author of *Re-engineering the Corporation,* said in 2005 that IBM's turnaround was "the single greatest turnaround in modern business history." Source: CNN interview with Michael Hammer on December 8, 2005, http://edition.cnn.com/2005/BUSINESS/12/08/go.ibmgerstner/index.html.
- Adobe's revenue and net profit growth, stock price gain, and comparison to indices and Microsoft's total return. Source: the authors' spreadsheet analysis of Adobe Systems Incorporated's SEC 10-K filings (annual financial reports) for 2001 through 2007, available on the US Securities and Exchange Commission EDGAR website at http://www.sec.gov/edgar.shtml, and Adobe's adjusted stock

price (ADBE) compared to the S&P 500 Index, NASDAQ Composite Index, and the total return on Microsoft's stock (MSFT) for the time period from the first trading day of 2001 through the last trading day of 2007, using adjusted stock price data from Yahoo! Finance, http://finance.yahoo.com.

- In 2006, HP profitably reclaimed its lead in PC sales over Dell by focusing demand generation, product packaging, new product development, and distribution on leveraging HP's independent retail store network. Source: *The Wall Street Journal,* "How H-P Reclaimed Its PC Lead Over Dell," June 24, 2007. This article provides fascinating details on HP's retail marketing and sales tactics that helped them catch up and surpass Dell.

- Information about Adobe's AlterCast revenue goal, route, and budget. Source: Private communication with Adobe management.

- Adobe's marketing and sales expenses were 32% of revenue, on average, and Adobe's cost of revenue (cost of goods sold) averaged 11% of revenue, about the same as other software companies. Source: the authors' review of Adobe's SEC 10-K filings (annual financial reports) for 2001 through 2007, and 10-K filings of other public software companies, available on the US Securities and Exchange Commission EDGAR website at http://www.sec.gov/edgar.shtml.

- Everett M. Rogers, *The Diffusion of Innovations,* 5th Edition, New York: The Free Press, 2003. Everyone who wants to sell innovative ideas, products, services, etc., should read this book.

- Geoffrey A. Moore, *Crossing the Chasm: Marketing and Selling Technology Products to Mainstream Customers,* New York: HarperBusiness, 1991. *Inside the Tornado: Marketing Strategies from Silicon Valley's Cutting Edge,* New York: HarperBusiness, 1995. *Dealing with Darwin: How Great Companies Innovate at Every Phase of Their Evolution,* New York: Portfolio, 2005. The first two books have become the bible for marketing high-tech products. In the third book, Moore extends his thinking beyond the Technology Adoption Life Cycle.

- Plantronics' Bluetooth headset case study. Source: personal experience of author Jean-Claude Malraison, who was Managing Director of Plantronics EMEA (Europe, Middle East, Africa) at the time.

Chapter 2. RTM Workshop

- The story of Bob Wilson, Skyline Software, and the other characters and events in Chap. 2 is fiction. Any resemblance to persons living or dead, or to actual companies and events, is purely coincidental.

Chapter 3. Market Segmentation

- Information about Zipcar, Inc. Sources: Harvard University Gazette, Zipcar creator looks toward bigger challenges, October 21, 2004, http://www.hno.harvard.edu/gazette/2004/10.21/11-zipcar.html. *The Seattle Times,* Seattle's Flexcar merges with rival Zipcar, October 31, 2007, http://seattletimes.nwsource.com/html/businesstechnology/2003984391_flexcar31.html. Zipcar, Is it for me? How to use a Zipcar, http://www.zipcar.com/is-it/profiles.

- Information about Time Inc. Source: Time Inc. corporate website, http://www.timeinc.com/.
- IBM's market segmentation pyramid and customer quadrants. Source: personal experience of authors Jean-Claude Malraison and Antoine Leboyer, who held positions in marketing and sales with IBM during the time IBM used these segmentation models, 1971–1999.
- The Sony Walkman … had been developed to satisfy Akio Morita, the chairman of Sony, who wanted to listen to music while playing golf. Source: Paul du Gay, Stuart Hall, Linda Janes, Hugh Mackay, Keith Negus, *Doing Cultural Studies: The Story of the Sony Walkman,* London: Sage Publications Ltd, 1997. This story has been told many times in slightly different ways; each version is probably true to some extent.
- Michael Treacy and Fred Wiersema, *The Discipline of Market Leaders: Choose Your Customers, Narrow Your Focus, Dominate Your Market,* Reading, Massachusetts: Addison-Wesley Publishing Company, 1995. See page 122 for additional information after the quoted sentence, "Of course, more recently IBM has lost its way."
- Louis V. Gerstner, Jr., *Who Says Elephants Can't Dance? Inside IBM's Historic Turnaround,* New York: HarperBusiness, 2002.
- The role of RTM in IBM's turnaround. Source: all three authors participated in the development and adoption of the Routes-to-Market methodology at IBM. The work ranged from getting senior executives to buy in, to developing the core concepts, to building financial models and decision trees, and rolling out a "no expert required" workshop process to hundreds of cross-functional teams in every geography and division. Almost every decision on resources for marketing and selling IBM's products and services were run through RTM. The performance of every IBM business improved with RTM, compared to their performance before RTM.

Chapter 4. Define Whole Solutions

- The ecosystem of call centers. Source: personal experience of author Jean-Claude Malraison, who launched IBM's European call center organization in 1996 as Vice President of Distribution and General Business for IBM EMEA (in which he was the senior executive approving purchases of products and services for call centers), and, from 1999 to 2003, was Managing Director of Plantronics EMEA, which sold headsets to call centers.
- See Chap. 1 reference for Geoffrey A. Moore above.
- Clayton M. Christensen, *The Innovator's Dilemma: When New Technologies Cause Great Firms to Fail,* Boston: Harvard Business School Press, 1997. Clayton M. Christensen and Michael E. Raynor, *The Innovator's Solution: Creating and*

Sustaining Successful Growth, Boston: Harvard Business School Press, 2003. Clayton M. Christensen, Scott D. Anthony, and Erik A. Roth, *Seeing What's Next: Using the Theories of Innovation to Predict Industry Change,* Boston: Harvard Business School Press, 2004. These books provide excellent strategic and tactical guidance for developing and executing innovation strategies.

Chapter 5. RTM Life Cycle

- See Chap. 1 reference for Everett M. Rogers above.
- See Chap. 1 reference for Geoffrey A. Moore above.
- Baracoda's Bluetooth barcode scanner case study. Source: personal experience of author Antoine Leboyer, who was Senior Vice President for Baracoda at the time.
- Jim Collins, *Good to Great: Why Some Companies Make the Leap ... and Others Don't,* New York: HarperBusiness, 2001. Carefully researched, well written, inspirational to everyone who believes that figuring out what works and making that the core of one's business is the best strategy for long-term success.

Chapter 6. Constructing a Route

- In March 2008, Mullen, a marketing agency headquartered near Boston, Massachusetts, distributed a poster titled "The New Marketing Ecosystem" which identified over 850 different types of resources for generating demand in B2C markets in the USA. Source: http://mullen.com/ecosystem.
- GEICO, State Farm, Coca-Cola, and Allstate spending, revenue, and growth figures, and Warren Buffett quote. Sources: *The Wall Street Journal,* How a Gecko Shook Up Insurance Ads, January 2, 2007; *Advertising Age,* Geico's $500M Outlay Pays Off, July 13, 2007.
- Seth Godin, *Permission Marketing: Turning Strangers into Friends and Friends into Customers,* New York: Simon & Schuster, 1999. Godin has written several best-selling books since his first, *Permission Marketing,* and his blog at http://sethgodin.com/ has become the most popular blog about marketing. Highly recommended for thoughtful and entertaining content.
- November 2007 survey of 4,400 information technology (IT) decision-makers. Source: 2007 ITtoolbox/PJA IT Social Media Index: Wave II Survey Results, Sponsored by ITtoolbox and PJA Advertising + Marketing, http://research. ittoolbox.com/surveys/survey.asp?survey = purchasing_smt_survey2.
- ITtoolbox and Corporate Executive Board profiles. Sources: ITtoolbox Timeline, http://www.ittoolbox.com/Help/timeline.asp; Corporate Executive Board, http:// www.executiveboard.com/about.html.
- SAP ... has changed the way that it markets to IT managers as a result of the growing importance of customer communities such as ITtoolbox .... SAP has changed its communication style to accommodate the dynamics of the customer

community. Source: the authors' March 2008 analysis of SAP's marketing communications from 1990 through 2007, including SAP's participation in ITtoolbox discussion forums.

- You can get three times as many responses from a mailing if you put the person's name on the address, not just their title (in a B2B campaign) or "Resident" (in B2C). You are five times more likely to reach prospects on the phone if you ask for them by name instead of by department or position. Source: the authors' experience with hundreds of direct mail and telemarketing campaigns in North America and Europe since 1986.

Chapter 7. Go-to-Market Performance Assessment

- Profile and history of F5 Networks, Inc. Sources: Jeff Meisner, "Staying alive at F5," *Puget Sound Business Journal (Seattle),* December 17, 2001, http://seattle. bizjournals.com/seattle/stories/2001/12/17/story4.html; "Ingram Micro introduces new security products," *Memphis Business Journal,* January 28, 2002, http:// memphis.bizjournals.com/memphis/stories/2002/01/28/daily12.html; Jeff Meisner, "F5 sharpens 'blade' in search for profitability," *Puget Sound Business Journal (Seattle),* September 2, 2002, http://seattle.bizjournals.com/seattle/ stories/2002/09/02/story6.html; Jeff Meisner, "Growth concerns plague Seattle-based F5 Networks," *Puget Sound Business Journal (Seattle),* June 23, 2003, http://seattle.bizjournals.com/seattle/stories/2003/06/23/story6.html; Jeffrey L. Covell, *[Company History of] F5 Networks, Inc.,* Advameg, Inc., 2007, http:// www.referenceforbusiness.com/history/En-Ge/F5-Networks-Inc.html; F5 Networks, Inc.'s SEC 10-K filings (annual financial reports) for 1999 through 2007, available on the US Securities and Exchange Commission EDGAR website at http://www.sec.gov/edgar.shtml.
- Interviewed by Jeff Meisner of the *Puget Sound Business Journal* in December 2001, McAdam said, "When I came on board [in July 2000], our business model was broken. It was a real problem. Expenses were out of control. We had to take some quick action. We moved really fast." Source: Jeff Meisner, "Staying alive at F5," *Puget Sound Business Journal (Seattle),* December 17, 2001, http:// seattle.bizjournals.com/seattle/stories/2001/12/17/story4.html.
- "It's a definite turnaround for this company [F5 Networks]," said Brent Bracelin, an analyst with investment bank Pacific Crest Securities of Portland, Oregon, in December 2001. "You have to give credit to McAdam and his team. F5 went from being 80 percent reliant on dot com customers to 90 percent reliant on large enterprises." Source: Jeff Meisner, "Staying alive at F5," *Puget Sound Business Journal (Seattle),* December 17, 2001, http://seattle.bizjournals.com/seattle/ stories/2001/12/17/story4.html.
- Assessment of F5's go-to-market performance by F5's cross-functional team in 2002, and F5's experience in using RTM. Source: Private communication with F5 personnel.

- F5's revenue, profit, and stock performance. Source: the authors' spreadsheet analysis of F5's SEC 10-K filings (annual financial reports) for 1999 through 2007, available on the US Securities and Exchange Commission EDGAR website at http://www.sec.gov/edgar.shtml, and F5's adjusted stock price (FFIV) compared to the NASDAQ Composite Index for the time period from the first trading day after September 30, 2001 (which was the end of F5's 2001 fiscal year) through the first trading day after September 30, 2007 (the end of F5's 2007 fiscal year), using adjusted stock price data from Yahoo! Finance, http://finance.yahoo.com.

Chapter 8. Connecting RTM with Corporate Strategy

- Adobe's revenue and profit. Source: Adobe Systems Incorporated's SEC 10-K filings (annual financial reports) for 1999 through 2007, available on the US Securities and Exchange Commission EDGAR website at http://www.sec.gov/edgar.shtml.
- Adobe's market share, projected growth rate of Adobe's market segments, revenue mix. Source: Private communication with Adobe personnel; confidentiality period expired prior to January 1, 2005.
- Adobe's Network Publishing strategy, information about Adobe's server software products, the process and conclusions for analyzing the gaps in Adobe's go-to-market strategy and capabilities, Adobe's desktop software and server software routes, and the development of Adobe's routes for AlterCast and related financial information. Source: Private communication with Adobe personnel; confidentiality period expired prior to January 1, 2005.
- Adobe's revenue and profit, stock price gain, and comparison to indices and to total returns for Microsoft's, Oracle's, and SAP's stock. Source: the authors' spreadsheet analysis of Adobe Systems Incorporated's SEC 10-K filings (annual financial reports) for 1999 through 2007, available on the US Securities and Exchange Commission EDGAR website at http://www.sec.gov/edgar.shtml, and Adobe's adjusted stock price (ADBE) compared to the S&P 500 Index, NASDAQ Composite Index, and the total return on Microsoft (MSFT), Oracle (ORCL), and SAP (SAP) for the time period from the first trading day of 2001 through the last trading day of 2007, using adjusted stock price data from Yahoo! Finance, http://finance.yahoo.com.

Chapter 9. Implementing RTM Company-Wide

- IBM's internal call center start-up experience. Source: personal experience of Jean-Claude Malraison, who launched IBM's European call center organization in 1996 as Vice President of Distribution and General Business for IBM EMEA.

Author Biographies

Peter Raulerson Peter Raulerson is an expert in go-to-market strategies and tactics, and a Partner with The PARA Marketing Group, a management consulting firm. He has consulted extensively with executives of Adobe, Canon, Cisco, F5 Networks, HP, IBM, Microsoft, Oracle, Sun, Symantec, and other technology companies including venture-backed start-ups. He has helped them increase corporate value by bringing new products and services to market, building new value chains and distribution channels, and improving the productivity of product development, marketing, sales, and distribution. Prior to PARA Marketing, Peter was CEO of InterConnections, Inc., a privately-held developer of multivendor network software, founded in 1986 and acquired in 1990 by Emulex Corporation. From 1972 to 1986, Peter held engineering, sales, marketing, and management positions with Digital Equipment Corporation, GTE Telenet, and 3Com. Before receiving his BA in math from Harvard in 1972, he wrote the first network graphics application on the ARPANET and was a research associate in managerial economics and decision analysis at Harvard Business School. He has been a member of the board of directors of the Washington Technology Industry Association.

Jean-Claude Malraison   Jean-Claude Malraison is Vice-Chairman of the Supervisory Board of Solucom Group, a leading IT consulting firm in France, and a member of the board of Critical Eye, an executive leadership community headquartered in the United Kingdom. Prior to these roles, he was the Managing Director of Plantronics EMEA (Europe, Middle East, Africa) from 1999 to 2003, where he drove the highly successful launch of Plantronics' products into consumer electronics channels across Europe. From 1971 to 1999, Jean-Claude served in several leadership positions with IBM, most recently as a member of the Executive Committee of IBM EMEA. Jean-Claude initiated many advances that transformed IBM's marketing, sales, and distribution. As the head of the IBM PC Division in France in 1989, he launched IBM's first retail PC channel, which increased IBM's market share after a severe drop. As General Manager of the newly-created UNIX Division of IBM EMEA in 1993, he took IBM from 0% to 19% market share in 2 years by tapping new distribution channels. He initiated the development and worldwide roll-out of the Routes-to-Market methodology which restored IBM to profitable growth. After becoming Vice President of Distribution and General Business for IBM EMEA in 1996, Jean-Claude launched IBM's European call center organization and significantly expanded IBM's business with small and mid-sized enterprises. Jean-Claude is a graduate of the Institut Supérieur d'Electronique du Nord.

Antoine Leboyer   Antoine Leboyer is the President and CEO of GSX, the worldwide leader in monitoring solutions for Communication Servers. Antoine has more than 20 years of experience in IT organizations in various international positions. He started his professional career with IBM. He held positions in sales and marketing with IBM France, and then ran the distribution strategy for all of IBM Europe except PCs, where he led initiatives that achieved significant growth for IBM by leveraging European IT distributors. After 12 years with IBM, Antoine joined Candle Corporation where he started and ran the European indirect business. He was then General Manager for Hyperchannel France, a B2B marketplace for European IT distribution funded by General Electric Capital and Goldman Sachs. Subsequently, he was Senior Vice-President for Upaid Systems, a provider of software for real-time billing and mobile payment services, and Senior Vice-President for Baracoda, the leading producer of Bluetooth industrial devices, which he helped achieve record growth. Antoine holds a diploma in engineering from Ecole Superieure d'Electricité in France and an MBA from the Harvard Business School. He served on the Board of Directors of Akoura Biometrics, an emerging company in Information Security.

Index

Printed in the United States of America